CITIZEN LORD

STELLA TILLYARD

CITIZEN LORD

The Life of Edward Fitzgerald, Irish Revolutionary

Farrar, Straus and Giroux
New York

Farrar, Straus and Giroux
19 Union Square West, New York 10003

Copyright © 1997 by Stella Tillyard
All rights reserved
Printed in the United States of America
First published in 1997 by
Chatto & Windus Limited, United Kingdom
First American edition, 1998

Library of Congress Cataloging-in-Publication Data
Tillyard, S.
    Citizen lord : the life of Edward Fitzgerald, Irish revolutionary
/ Stella Tillyard.
        p.   cm.
    Includes bibliographical references (p.   ) and index.
    ISBN 0-374-12383-7 (alk. paper)
        1. Fitzgerald, Edward, Lord, 1763–1798.   2. Ireland—History—
Rebellion of 1798—Biography.   3. Revolutionaries—Ireland—
Biography.   4. Nobility—Ireland—Biography.   I. Title.
    DA948.6.F5T55   1998
    941.507'092—dc21   [B]   97-39055

For Jenny Uglow,
who helped me

Contents

Acknowledgements

I would like to thank the staff of the following libraries, record offices and archives who made my research possible: the British Library, the European University Institute, the Irish Architectural Archive, Kent County Record Office, the London Library, the National Gallery of Ireland, the National Archives of Ireland, the National Library of Ireland, the National Museum of Ireland, the National Portrait Gallery, the National Register of Archives and the Public Record Office of Northern Ireland.

Many individuals helped me as I went along. Jonathan Burnham of Chatto and Windus, my agent Gillon Aitken and Elisabeth Sifton at Farrar, Straus all allowed themselves to be convinced that I could write a book in a year while having a baby and coming and going between Britain and Italy, and then waited trustingly when I took a little longer. Patrick Masterson generously gave me space to work at the European University Institute in Fiesole, where Olwen Hufton, Luisa Passerini, Monika Mommertz and Giannis Giannakitsas all helped me forget the book when necessary. By looking after my children with calm assurance, Maria Tabilo put my mind at rest and let it do its daytime job. John Brewer is everything to me and it is useless to thank him for all that he has done.

John Styles helped me with information about fabrics, Roy Porter provided medicinal details, Brian Allen was, as ever, a wonderful repository of painting knowledge and David Bindman discussed portraits of black people with me. Nigel Smith reassured me about eighteenth-century readings of *Paradise Lost* and Clare l'Enfant pointed me towards secondary material. Mark Laird sent details of flowers and typical eighteenth-century plantings from Canada, and Michèle Cohen very kindly checked my dyslexic spelling and my French. Guy Strutt and the Duke of Leinster were, once again, enormously helpful and Sir William Seymour kindly checked military dates and details. My friends Deborah Colvin, Allen Martens, Peter Mandler, Ruth Ehrlich, Juliet Gardiner, Dorothy Porter, Rachel Watson, Rosemary Davidson, Alex and Diana Good and my dear brother, Jason Tillyard, helped me through a lonely six months. Caroline and Gerry Jury and Jane and Maurice Taylor showed me the importance and pleasure of good neighbours.

In Ireland, the historians of 1798 have been generously supportive of a gate-crasher. Sir Richard Aylmer, contacted via the Internet, showed me the relevant areas of the vast Rebellion Papers in the National Archives of Ireland. He also introduced me to Tom Bartlett, who very kindly lent me his transcripts of the letters of Francis Higgins, read my manuscript and made me feel part of a wider historical project; to Kevin Whelan, who put me on the trail of Lord Edward's uniform, which threw up a pair of bagpipes said to have belonged to Lord Edward and mysteriously dated 1768, when Lord Edward was five; and to Con Costello, who discussed the strategic importance of Kildare with me. Patrick Bowe helped with Dublin gardens, Simon Lindsay sent me recently collected photographs of Frescati, Desmond FitzGerald pointed me towards information about the Dublin Shakespeare Gallery and Daire Keogh offered suggestions and ideas. Conor Malagher let us wander round

Carton House. Ian Cornelius and Attracta Ingram put us up and drove us through the Bog of Allen to Kildare Town, where Lord Edward lived for much of the last four years of his life.

Picture
Acknowledgements

We are grateful for permission to reproduce the following pictures:

Colour:
1. Lord Edward Fitzgerald, by Hugh Douglas Hamilton, 1796: private collection.
2. Lady Pamela with her daughter by Mallary, c. 1800: reproduction courtesy of the National Gallery of Ireland.
3. The Linley Sisters, 1772, by Thomas Gainsborough: by permission of the Trustees of Dulwich Picture Gallery.
4. Tony Small, by John Roberts, mid-1780s: private collection.

Black and white:
1. The south front of Carton House: by kind permission of the Irish Georgian Society.
2. James Fitzgerald, 20th Earl of Kildare, 1st Duke of Leinster, by Allan Ramsay, 1762: private collection; photography courtesy of the Paul Mellon Centre for Studies in British Art.
3. Lord Edward aged 7: reproduced by permission of the British Library.
4. William Ogilvie, sketched by Charles Lock, c. 1795: photograph private collection.
5. The chateau at Aubigny: by kind permission of the Trustees of the Goodwood Collection.
6. Emily, Duchess of Leinster, by Sir Joshua Reynolds: private collection.

7. Omai, prince of the South Seas, by Sir Joshua Reynolds, 1776: by permission of The Castle Howard Collection; photograph copyright The Courtauld Institute of Art.
8. Elizabeth Linley, painted as St Cecilia, by Sir Joshua Reynolds, 1775: by permission of The National Trust, Waddesdon Manor; photograph copyright The Courtauld Institute of Art.
9. Tom Paine, engraving by William Sharp, 1793, after George Romney: by courtesy of the Trustees of the National Portrait Gallery.
10. Richard Brinsley Sheridan, engraved by John Hall, 1791, after Sir Joshua Reynolds: by courtesy of the Trustees of the National Portrait Gallery.
11. Charles James Fox, sketched by Henry Eldridge, 1796: private collection.
12. The Countess de Genlis, by George Romney, 1792: courtesy of Sotheby's Ltd.
13. Pamela Sims, by George Romney, 1792: courtesy of Sotheby's Ltd.
14. Louisa Conolly, by George Romney, 1776: by kind permission of the Trustees of the Goodwood Collection.
15. Frescati in 1911: photograph by kind permission of the Irish Architectural Archive.
16. Arthur O'Connor by J. D. Herbert, engraved by W. Ward the Elder, 1798: reproduction courtesy of the National Gallery of Ireland.
17. Lord Henry Fitzgerald, engraved by J. Park, 1789, after John Hoppner: copyright British Museum.
18. Leinster House, Dublin, engraved by Malton, 1792: copyright British Museum.
19. The arrest of Lord Edward, engraved by George Cruikshank the Elder, 1845: by permission of the British Library.

Preface

In this book, three narrative strands wind themselves into the story of its subject, Lord Edward Fitzgerald. Lord Edward was a soldier and radical politician who turned republican and became an active revolutionary. Like Wolfe Tone and others in the Society of United Irishmen he demanded an Irish republic independent of Britain, and as a practical soldier he argued that violence must be used, if necessary, to achieve it. But the republic he wanted was an inclusive one, based on an Enlightenment commitment to rights. It was a republic that would be tolerant, ecumenical and democratic. The story of Lord Edward's passage from Ascendancy peer to citizen and revolutionary is the first strand of the narrative.

The second strand tells the intimately connected story of Lord Edward's daily life. Lord Edward was brought up to be idealist and cosmopolitan and to allow feeling to seep through into every sphere. His politics were thus passionate and personal. By the same token, his passions were determinedly political. Every action of his private life, from his devotion to his mother to his love affairs, his travels and his enthusiasm for gardening, had political overtones and effects. His principles and his pleasures were inseparable, joined together in an adventure which for two centuries has seemed romantic, but which I hope this book shows to have been much more: logical, consistent, and tragically inexorable.

If Lord Edward's mother was his great love, his constant companion was Tony Small, the runaway slave who saved his life in North America in 1781. We have some idea what Tony looked like – at least, we have his portrait. But aside from a few comments in Lord Edward's letters we know little else about him. Yet without Tony, Lord Edward is incomplete, perhaps inexplicable; Tony embodied and brought to life his master's commitment to freedom and equality for all men. Believing that it makes a nonsense of Lord Edward's life to leave Tony out, I have every so often put him in, making the third strand of the narrative, a story of loyalty that counterpoints the multiple betrayals at the book's end.

Family Trees

THE FITZGERALD AND OGILVIE FAMILIES

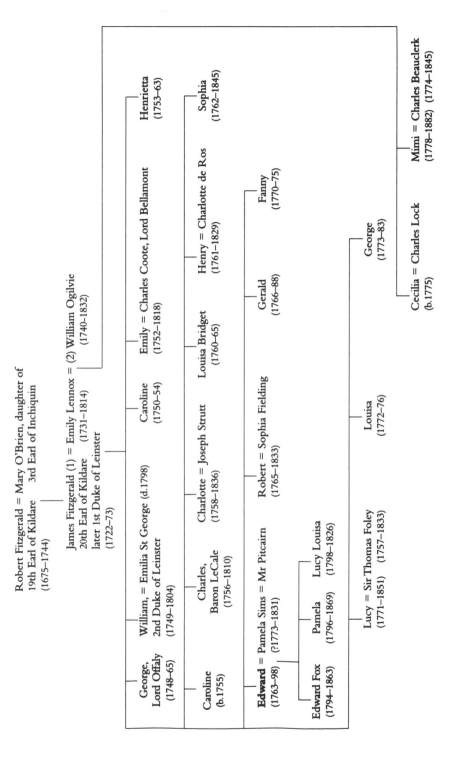

THE LENNOX FAMILY

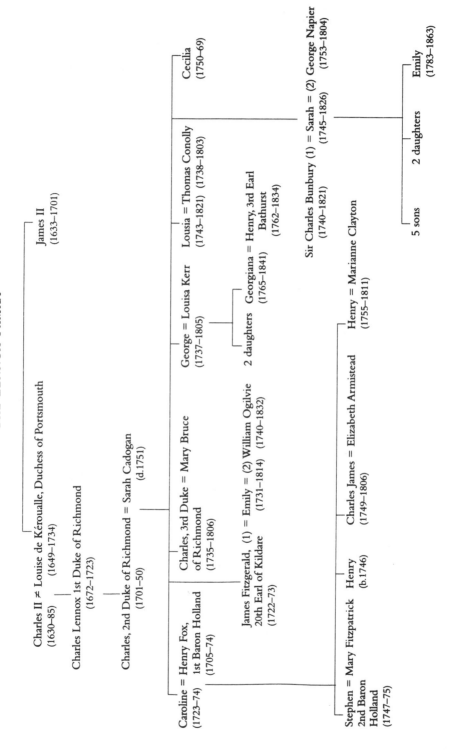

James II
(1633–1701)

Charles II ≠ Louise de Kéroualle, Duchess of Portsmouth
(1630–85)   (1649–1734)

Charles Lennox 1st Duke of Richmond
(1672–1723)

Charles, 2nd Duke of Richmond = Sarah Cadogan
(1701–50)   (d.1751)

Caroline = Henry Fox,
(1723–74) 1st Baron Holland
        (1705–74)

Charles, 3rd Duke = Mary Bruce
of Richmond
(1735–1806)

George = Louisa Kerr
(1737–1805)

Lousia = Thomas Conolly
(1743–1821) (1738–1803)

Cecilia
(1750–69)

James Fitzgerald, (1) = Emily = (2) William Ogilvie
20th Earl of Kildare (1731–1814) (1740–1832)
(1722–73)

2 daughters Georgiana = Henry, 3rd Earl
        (1765–1841) Bathurst
            (1762–1834)

Sir Charles Bunbury (1) = Sarah = (2) George Napier
(1740–1821)   (1745–1826)   (1753–1804)

Stephen = Mary Fitzpatrick Henry
2nd Baron   (b.1746)
Holland
(1747–75)

Charles James = Elizabeth Armistead
(1749–1806)

Henry = Marianne Clayton
(1755–1811)

5 sons   2 daughters

Emily
(1783–1863)

Lord Edward Fitzgerald to the Duchess of Leinster
  [undated]

Dearest Mother, I am off, but shall not be long away . . .
Bless you, dear Mamy, look at your carnations, and
remember, though I do take a frisk from you now and then,
I do dote on you, and in being with you. Good-bye. Yours,
  E.F.
Do not be angry with me for going.

CITIZEN LORD

Prologue

South Carolina, 8 September 1781

From a safe distance, sixty miles from Charleston, and thousands of miles from his African homeland, Tony Small watched a battle. The British, under the command of Colonel Stewart, stood across a hillside, their red coats and black hats limp in the sultry heat, the men exhausted from scavenging the ravaged lands around for vegetables and water. Behind them was their camp with wagons, stores, greying tents and doctors tensely waiting. In a woody thicket in front of them General Greene had concealed his American troops. At the bottom of the hill ran Eutaw Creek rising from two swampy springs and winding through what had once been a rich plantation. Everything was desolate now, the fields choked with grass and weeds, the red-brick mansion house, gutted and roofless, crumbling slowly back into the earth. When its owners had left, bundling their goods and slaves into wagons and heading for safer country, Tony Small had escaped and stayed on. For months there had been troops around him. That day he saw his world become a battlefield.

It was early afternoon when the Americans came out from the woods, blinking in the hazy sunshine and sweating in the thick southern heat. On the orders of their commander, the cavalry crashed through the undergrowth and charged down on the British right. Footsoldiers, their packs bumping about uncomfortably, rushed towards the other end of the British line, and then, with half the British force fearfully turning towards the horses, the other half firing on the infantry, the rest of the Americans ran straight at the undefended centre. Clouds of gunsmoke were floating above the mêlée, obscuring the view downhill. Squeals of frightened horses mixed with the sobs of wounded men as hundreds of Greene's troops, ragged in their blue and buff uniforms and nearly invisible in the smoke, broke through the British line and ran into the camp behind. Pushing aside the camp followers, they made for the tents and the baggage, where they found shade, plunder and a large quantity of rum. They knelt behind the huge rum puncheons, split them open with their bayonets and drank, mouth on wood, protected by the barrels from British guns.

Distracted and divided, the Americans paused and Colonel Stewart gathered up his forces. He sent scores of grenadiers into the plantation house from where they could fire directly on to the marauding Americans who were weaving between the tents and the liquor stores. Artillery men with field guns hid in the shrubbery and behind the picket fence that ran around the garden and fired volleys of heavy shot into the camp at ground level, scattering the Americans, smashing wagons and burning tents and stores. By early evening the Americans were retreating, stumbling drunkenly over ground already littered with wounded and dead men. Back in the wood they counted their losses. Six hundred men were missing, lying among the weeds in the scorched and cratered earth. Four hundred British soldiers lay with them.

General Greene wrapped the disaster in orderly prose, writing in his dispatch to the American Congress, 'We collected all our wounded, except such as were under the command of the fire of the house and retired to the ground from which we marched in the morning, there being no water near, and the troops being ready to faint with the heat and want of refreshment, the action having continued over four hours.' To the British the battle was hardly worth an official mention. For both sides it had been a pointless fight: nothing had been gained because the bigger battle was already over. Eutaw Springs was the last engagement of the American Revolution. Six weeks later Lord Cornwallis surrendered to General Washington at Yorktown and independence for the colonies was won.

When the Americans had retreated and darkness fell, Tony Small emerged on to the battlefield and began to search for plunder. Other men were out with him. Teams of doctors and orderlies hurried across the dry, bloodstained ground, turning over bodies, feeling pulses and comforting the dying with water and laudanum. While the wounded were carried away the dead were stripped. Camp followers and ordinary soldiers, raucous with rum and exhilarated by survival, emptied pockets and hastily cut the silver buttons from the corpses' coats. Letters, with the careful signatures of mothers, fathers and beloved wives, stirred in the night air and settled on the bodies of the dead, each one telling a story of lives ruined and griefs to be suffered.

Moving like a wraith from man to man, Tony came across something unusual, the blood-soaked uniform of a British officer of the 19th Regiment of Foot. The man was alive but unconscious, overlooked by the search parties of both sides. Here was a prize, booty to be bartered for money right away or for freedom when the war ended. The officer was very young, soft-skinned and slender. Blood seeped through his mud-stained white breeches from a deep thigh wound. Round his neck hung a locket with several twists of auburn hair inside. Heaving the man over his shoulder, so that his thick, dark-brown hair fell towards the ground with his dangling arms, Tony trudged back to his hut.

The man who opened his eyes to the gloom of Tony's room was Lord Edward Fitzgerald, an eager, thoughtlessly courageous lieutenant who had recently arrived from Ireland. Through a haze of pain, Lord Edward looked on trustingly as Tony washed and bandaged his thigh. His fellow soldiers might have seen Tony as a fearful apparition, a black shadow redolent of everything sinister and devilish, base and corrupt. But Lord Edward saw Tony as a man revealing the essential goodness of mankind, a goodness found in all its purity among the simple and the uncivilised, the black and the brown. A spiritual journey begun ten years before in a school-house near Dublin reached its first destination here on a humid night in the American South. Lord Edward's grey-green eyes looked on Tony Small who had saved his life and saw a noble savage and a black Samaritan.

When the soldiers of the 19th Regiment left Charleston harbour for Jamaica three months later, they took scores of Negroes along with the baggage and ordnance, black people who for years had heard their white masters demand liberty for themselves without a thought of giving it to their slaves. These men and women, squeezing into the unhealthy holds of the troop ships, believed their turn for freedom had come. A few found it, on the streets of London, Liverpool or Quebec, or as seamen working the dangerous passages between the Old World and the New. Most, though, would labour on West Indian plantations, slaves in all but name, trading years of sugar cutting for their freedom, often dying before they gained it.

Tony Small was one of the lucky ones. Lord Edward saw the matter simply. Tony had saved him; in return he offered him liberty and a new life working as his servant, receiving wages. Tony seized his chance. He abandoned his hut and embarked as a free man for the unknown. But he had no idea that he would soon be bound to his master by a force made of servitude and freedom in equal measure: the force of love itself.

FROM BOY TO SOLDIER

Carton, Ireland, January 1764

Turning the carriage on to the drive the coachman bent stiffly and slightly with the pull of the horses. Raindrops that had gathered into glistening puddles on his black leather gloves ran down his cape in rivulets and dripped on to the dove-grey footboard by his boots. The horses' hooves slapped rhythmically on the stony road as they turned in time, sharp to the left and then, like a lazy snake, back and forth between the shallow, artificial hills of the park. At intervals they passed young beech trees that in summer cascaded into deep pools of shade but now, in winter, hung down like frozen fountains towards the ground. To his right the coachman could look through a new wood to the glint of water. Behind him he sensed the progress of the cavalcade as one by one the carriages wheeled off the Dublin road.

Approaching the new bridge across the lake the horses slowed down. As the coach rolled up the slight rise the clattering and shaking echoed between the underside of the arch and the river that rippled like pewter-coloured silk beneath. Over the bridge the horses lifted their heads and made for home, where the great block of Carton House sat dour and square among its offices and stables.

The travellers, too, began to stir with anticipation. In the first carriage the Countess of Kildare pushed one plump foot beyond the hem of her velvet overcoat and pressed it to the floor as if she were stepping out of bed after a long sleep. Her blue-grey eyes opened wide, like summer flowers caught out of season, and she began to point out to her husband the park, the lake and, through the gloom, their house. As she talked with increasing animation, seeing in her mind's eye her children running out to meet her, he leaned forward from the opposite bench. He was attentive and informal, but all the time he maintained some dignity in reserve, some burden of his dynasty which he could never shed.

The Earl glanced out of the window with an impatient anticipation of annoyance, noticing the brambles revealed by the wintry bareness of his park and the slovenly attitude of his gatekeeper leaning on a long, gnarled stick. But he turned back to look at his wife with an expectation of pleasure, contemplating her auburn beauty with as much satisfaction as he had done on the day he had married her sixteen years before. Kildare had married his Countess for love and her political contacts. The second had proved of little use to him; but the first had endured. Even now, four months after she had given birth to their twelfth child, the sight of her small, exquisite hand reaching up to slide down the glass window as they turned the last corner to the front of their house filled him with pride and desire.

When the carriage stopped, bouncing on its springs, the horses shook their heads freely from side to side, releasing the tension of the metal bits and bridles. A valet, resplendent in black worsted breeches, fitted coat and cockaded hat, ran to open the door, and Stoyte, the Earl's butler, emerged from under the portico, stooping slightly as he came down the broad, shallow steps to greet his master. Grasping Stoyte's hand the Earl jumped on to the gravel drive, then leant back into the carriage and handed the Countess out. Together they walked up the steps and in the wide front door, into warmth, yellow candle-light and a crowd of children, some standing silently, others jumping impatiently from foot to foot, all delighted at the interruption of their daily routine. First to reach their mother was Lady Emily, tall enough to throw her arms around her, old enough to be restrained by her own sense of importance and her shyness. Charlotte and Louisa Bridget, five and three, came next; unhesitant, demanding, squealing with excitement. The Countess, casting propriety aside, knelt down to receive her favourite, two-year-old Henry, who came skidding into her across the marble floor shouting, 'Mama, Mama'. Holding him tightly to her she watched little Sophia, whom she had left just crawling six months before, stagger towards her, more intent on walking than on arriving at the skirts of this unfamiliar figure.

Greeting their father with an awed and respectful embrace the children ran one by one to the open door, looking for their brother Charles, who had gone to England with his parents, and their newest brother, Edward. Charles ran in, full of the self-importance of the traveller, waving airily at his admiring siblings. Little Edward was a disappointment, a pair of muddy slate-coloured eyes staring out of a woollen shawl in the arms of his nurse. He was four months old, sickly, and bound for the nursery upstairs.

Lord Edward was born to a great dynastic heritage. The Kildares were the 'premier peers' of Ireland – the family who had been, by a combination of opportunism and canny marriages, the first recognised members of an aristocracy formed and given legitimacy by the English monarch. Originally *banditti* from Florence, they were said to have served successively Norman, English and Irish kings, before fighting for Edward III and being given, as a reward, the earldom of Kildare. Settling in Ireland, the Fitzgeralds acquired huge tracts of the country's fertile central flatlands and, over the next four centuries, successfully oscillated between pragmatic gestures of loyalty to the English Crown and spectacular acts of defiance that allowed them to claim a distinct Irish identity. They became Protestants at the

Reformation and supported William of Orange against Stuart claims to the English Crown. But despite accumulating land and wealth, they maintained their links with Ireland's other old families and never deserted Dublin and the Irish parliament for more lucrative and heady pursuits in London and Westminster.

When he met his future wife, James Fitzgerald, the twentieth Earl, had lived almost all his life in Ireland. Unlike many, more recently settled Protestants, he had no English title, and was unable to pursue his political interests through a seat in the English House of Lords. In Ireland though, Fitzgerald – or Geraldine – power and prestige were immense. The twentieth Earl had estates of getting on for fifty thousand acres and an annual income of around fifteen thousand pounds. He commanded a sizeable block of MPs in the Irish House of Commons and carried on the family tradition of symbolic opposition to Westminster and the surrogates of the British Crown who ruled Ireland from Dublin Castle.

Ireland existed almost as a state within the British state in the eighteenth century. Ultimate authority for Irish legislation was vested in the British parliament in Westminster, and executive power rested with a viceroy who was nominally appointed by the British monarch. But the Irish executive – the cabinet and other office holders – was usually home-grown, and the viceroy could not govern effectively without its compliance and the support of the Irish parliament. So, while maintaining their loyalty to the British Crown and the Anglican Church, Irish parliamentarians used their considerable powers in the jealous preservation of the privileges and authority of the class they represented. The Irish opposition, to which Kildare belonged, was the group most consistently hostile to the dictates of Westminster. It constantly demanded more local control over legislation and finance without ever going so far as to compromise the Anglican grip on parliament or to claim completely independent sovereignty for Ireland.

When he married Lady Emily Lennox in 1747, Kildare had had ambitions to shine in Westminster as well as Dublin. Besides being a beauty and a minor heiress, Emily was a means to the ear of the monarch George II and to the gates of Westminster. Her parents, the second Duke and Duchess of Richmond, were prominent courtiers: the Duchess was Lady of the Bedchamber to Queen Caroline, the Duke Master of the Horse and a member of the cabinet. Equally important, her elder sister Caroline was married to one of the fastest-rising stars of the House of Commons, Henry Fox. To underline Kildare's political ambitions, his new father-in-law procured for him a British peerage which carried a seat in the House of Lords. A few days before his marriage, Kildare was created Viscount Leinster of Taplow and given the promise of a dukedom which was fulfilled in 1766 when he became Duke of Leinster.

This bright political future, however, came to nothing. Kildare prided himself on his upright truthfulness and on his outspoken honesty. But he was too punctilious to seize political advantage and too unsociable to cultivate the loyalty of potential supporters. He hated to drink to excess, disliked convivial entertaining and had no gift for bonhomie. Refusing to participate in the intrigue and spectacle of the political process on either side of the Irish Sea, he was easily sidelined by those like his brother-in-law who regarded Irish concerns as entirely peripheral to the great affairs of state. Kildare soon gave up his English political ambitions, concentrating on Dublin instead. In the opinion of Castle officials his aim was now the Lord Lieutenancy itself. Balked of that prize, he contented himself with making occasional forays into Dublin politics, socially upstaging a series of English viceroys who could never match his receptions for splendour or pomp, and cultivating his lands.

Carton's undulating park and huge estates were destined for Lord Edward's eldest brother, George. His own choices would be few. In Ireland, younger sons did not go into the

Church and make a bridge between the local population and the families that ruled it. They left for estates of their own or for the armed forces. Lord Edward's destiny was always clear. After a spell in one of the services, preferably in a largely inactive regiment based close to home, he would be offered one of his father's estates to cultivate. If the land did not suit him, and he proved of an intellectual or combative turn of mind, he might practise at the Irish bar. None the less, his purpose in life would be primarily dynastic: to be returned to the Irish parliament for one of the seats under family control and to marry an Irish heiress whose money and connections would help maintain the Kildares' position as Ireland's pre-eminent family.

Lord Edward came quietly into the world, as befitted a younger son. Throughout the later stages of her pregnancy, his mother, Emily, was consumed with anxiety for her third son, Lord Charles Fitzgerald, a lively, chatty little boy of seven. Charles had been sickening for some time, and doctors diagnosed consumption. Convinced that the damp Irish climate would kill him, the Countess of Kildare took Lord Charles to England, despite the fact that she had started another pregnancy. When they arrived at the end of May 1763, they went straight to Malvern in Worcestershire, where Charles was to have the benefit of country air and Malvern's curative mineral water. Advice poured in from all sides. Her brother-in-law Henry Fox wrote from Paris that 'sea-water, burnt sponge and diet are the only cures for Lord Charles, which a warm climate could greatly help'. His wife, Caroline, anxiously asked for news every two weeks, although she did remember the imminent arrival long enough to send from Paris a 'most comfortable bed gown and petticoat *pour vos couches*, quite smart, light and warm'. The Countess stayed at Malvern until mid-September with her sisters Louisa Conolly and Sarah Bunbury for company. When she could not delay any longer, she travelled up to

London for her confinement. But Edward's birth on 15 October was overshadowed by 'bad accounts' from Malvern and the sudden death of one of her little daughters in Ireland, nine-year-old Henrietta, four weeks earlier. Henrietta had not been a favourite with either her mother or her aunt Louisa. 'I think I rather loved her the least of the children, yet I loved her so much that I cannot, at times, help regretting her', Louisa wrote to Sarah. But her death emphasised the frailty of young children and discouraged too much love for the new arrival.

Lord Charles Fitzgerald got better, but the Countess had little time to recover from her fright about him. A year later, George, Lord Offaly, her eldest son and heir to the Kildare earldom, died suddenly in London at the age of seventeen. George had been her favourite son, and in her grief, the Countess first recoiled from life, wanting to die herself, but then, recovering, fastened her affections on Edward. The Earl of Kildare called Lord Edward a 'poor, starved little thing'; but his 'delicacy' was offset by his mass of brown, curling hair, large grey-green eyes and 'air of prettiness'. Although the Countess wrote to her sister Caroline in February 1766 that she was worried of growing fond of 'the little Neddy' in case he, too, became sick, by that summer he was established as her new favourite.

The Countess, who in 1766 became the Duchess when her husband became the Duke of Leinster, was a demonstrative woman. Her reliance on emotion was fostered by a new emphasis on feeling in the 1760s and brought to the fore by her grief over the deaths of her children. 'Moments of overflowing tenderness' are 'in my nature', she wrote in the 1770s, and she remarked towards the end of her life, 'there is no comfort in life I think, like that one feels from mutual perfect confidence with those one dearly loves, reposing all one's distresses in the heart that truly feels for one and understands one's feelings.'

The Fitzgerald children felt the full force of their mother's emotionalism. The Duchess expected her children to love her but she loved them well in return and constantly told them so. 'I do dote on you my dear girl,' she wrote reassuringly to her daughter Lucy in 1794. 'Satisfy your dear mind my love that you have never given me for one moment any cause of real uneasiness, but that you have given hours, days and years of satisfaction, content, pleasure and amusement. Your affection, your duty, your kindness have never varied. If I have been out of humour with you about trifles and that very seldom, it is no more than what occurs between the tenderest parents and the best children; human nature is such and those who expect anything beyond it will – must – be disappointed.'

Demonstrative and loving though she was, the Duchess was also imperiously demanding. To twelve-year-old Lucy, struggling to produce handwriting that was both elegant and legible, she wrote sternly in 1783, 'you know my sweet love how very anxious I am that you should do everything well and believe me, you should never on any account allow yourself to blot, scribble or scrawl at any time. A very little attention will make it just as easy and pleasant to do things well as to do them ill.' Such perfectionist intervention was not directed solely at the Fitzgerald girls. William, heir to the earldom after the death of his brother George, constantly failed to live up to his mother's expectations. But in general, Emily was less exacting with her sons. Adoration, though, she did expect, and Lord Edward's rapid ascent in her heart owed much to his evident and passionate devotion to his mother. 'Dear Angel,' she wrote when he was grown up, 'he has always loved me in an uncommon degree from childhood.'

But Lord Edward soon captivated everybody. By the time he was a toddler, he had become a general favourite with his siblings, with the household servants and particularly with his aunts, Louisa Conolly and Sarah Bunbury. 'That pretty Eddy I dote upon, and have quite given myself up to love him, which I did not intend to do,' Louisa told Sarah in December 1765 when he was just over two. By the summer of 1766 Edward's delicacy had vanished and he had become a robust, bustling little child. 'I really think now that he would not strike a stranger as an unhealthy child,' Louisa Conolly wrote, adding, 'he has got such a wholesome fresh look, has grown large, is in violent spirits, sleeps and eats and is as well as possible.' Henceforth, Lord Edward was never described as sickly. He grew into a lithe, wiry boy, with large eyes, red cheeks and limitless energy.

This transformation in Lord Edward's health was always attributed by his family to the regime at Black Rock, the family school to which he was sent in 1767 or early 1768. Some time in the mid-1760s the Duke of Leinster bought a villa at Black Rock, a fishing village five miles south of the centre of Dublin on the road to Dalkey. It was a modest house, intended as a place for the Fitzgerald children to stay while they enjoyed the marine air, the sandy beach and the swimming in Dublin Bay. But after the death of her son George in 1765, the Duchess's plans for Black Rock changed. Determined never again to send any of her children away to school, she decided that her huge brood would be educated at Black Rock. Fearful for their health and at the same time a devotee of Jean-Jacques Rousseau's *Émile*, which insisted on practical lessons from the outdoor and everyday world rather than strict book learning, she realised that Black Rock could be transformed easily to a Rousseauian establishment. Instead of being merely healthy entertainments, sea bathing and outdoor exercise might become the focus of her children's education. Always a perfectionist and no stranger to the extravagant gesture, the Duchess first asked Rousseau himself to take charge of the experiment, but the sage declined. A substitute, William Ogilvie, a Scot who had been running a school in Dublin, was recruited instead. Ogilvie was given a modest salary and instructions to bring Rousseau's *Émile* to life on the shores of Dublin Bay.

The house at Black Rock was enlarged and given a poetic-sounding name, Frescati. Hay-fields and pasture, a dairy and stables were added in the grounds, while school-rooms and servants' quarters were tacked on to the house. By the end of 1767, Lord Charles Fitzgerald, then aged eleven, was installed. One by one, as they were weaned from their wet nurses when they were about a year old, his siblings were sent after him. By 1768, Lord Edward was there, and by 1773, when Lord Charles had left for the navy, William Ogilvie had charge of almost all the younger Fitzgeralds. By then, Charlotte, oldest but least loved of the girls, was fourteen; Henry was eleven, Sophia ten. Edward, who was nine, came next, followed by Robert, Gerald and Fanny, who were eight, seven and almost three. Before long, Lucy, who was nearly two, and Louisa, about a year old, joined them.

William Ogilvie was thirty-eight when he took up his appointment. He was tall, thin and prematurely bald and seemed to the Duchess's family to behave more like a servant than a gentleman. When annoyed or perplexed he had a habit of thrusting his hands into his pockets, chewing his lips and scowling at the ground in a way that was regarded as vulgar and underbred. As Louisa Conolly put it, 'his manner' was 'against him'. So was the obscurity of his origins. A rumour ran round Dublin that he had been denied favours due to him by the Scottish Lord Findlater and such stories carried hints that he was an illegitimate son who had been educated by his father and then abandoned. Ogilvie himself kept studiously quiet on the matter of his ancestry, neither confirming nor denying the reports. It was only certain that he had eked out a living as a Dublin schoolmaster for several years before his appointment by the Duke of Leinster, that he had acquired a good education somewhere and had an excellent reputation as a teacher. An air of mystery surrounded him, which Ogilvie did nothing to dispel. He was a forceful, even a calculating man. Behind a well-maintained façade of coldness and discipline, there glittered both a hard shrewdness and a dominant and heady sexuality. Ogilvie was not a man of charm, but, as women who met him quickly realised, he was a man of power, a man whose dominance, once honed and directed, was difficult to escape.

With the Black Rock children, however, Ogilvie was always kind and gentle. Besides teaching them their school-work, he carried the toddlers in his arms, took the older children fishing in Dublin Bay, played at amateur theatricals with them and watched over their every scratch and illness with a devotion equal to that of their anxious mother. All these activities he described in notes to the Duchess. Writing at night in his book-lined study, he recorded what the children ate, what they said, what they did and how he loved them. Nothing escaped his notice or his pen: exactitude and solicitude went hand in hand. 'I am provoked at myself beyond all measure to have given your Grace any uneasiness about Lady Lucy,' he wrote in 1771, when Lucy Fitzgerald, the Duchess's ninth daughter, was a little baby and staying briefly at Black Rock because she had a cold. 'I cannot yet conceive that anything I wrote about her would have given your Grace any real foundation of being distressed about her, but as your Grace has so repeatedly commanded me to be minute and particular in my account of the least change I could not, consistent with that, omit acquainting you with her uneasiness from the little blister in her mouth, but always thought it so common a thing when a cold is break-ing, that I thought your Grace would be rather delighted to hear it. I beg now that your Grace will be perfectly easy and satisfied about her in every particular. Her mouth is vastly better and scarce gives her the least uneasiness now.'

William Ogilvie was given licence to be fond of the Fitzgerald children that was unusual for a family servant, but was sanctioned by Rousseau and encouraged by the Duchess. In the many notes and letters that he sent from Black Rock to Carton describing the children's progress for his employer, Ogilvie never hid his affection for them. 'All the dear children are just gone to bed and are all as perfectly well as could be wished and the happiest I am persuaded of earthly beings. It is impossible to tell your Grace how cheerful and pleasant they are,' he wrote in the early 1770s. As for Eddy, Ogilvie wrote in 1774, 'he certainly loves you more than ever – every day gives strength to his affection'.

Within this world of warmth and security, Ogilvie skilfully followed Rousseau's precept of 'well regulated freedom' and much of his educational programme. Discipline was taught by example rather than punishment: Ogilvie cheerfully let the Fitzgerald children test the limit of his patience and experiment with naughtiness. The Duchess, too, often chose to see her children's transgressions as the expressions of naturally strong passions rather than unacceptable behaviour. In return they acted freely with her. When Lord Edward was a toddler, for instance, he threatened to 'knock his mama down with a poker'. Although 'she put on a grave face' and said she 'positively would not allow it', Edward was not punished and his mother proudly told the story as an example of his spirit rather than his wickedness. Rousseau advocated plenty of fresh air and sea bathing. The Fitzgerald children got both, usually swimming in the sea twice a day. Like Émile, they turned their hands to gardening, ploughing and hay-making, learning a respect for the land and the moral lessons it could teach. Like him they ran races, drew from nature, went barefoot and learnt such skills as carpentry and needlework. Wherever possible, moral and theoretical principles were learned from nature rather than books, and religious instruction was, to begin with, confined to simple prayers and illustrations of God's immanence in all living things. Later the children were taught an uncomplicated and benign form of Anglicanism that stressed God's goodness rather than man's sin, and which remained with Lord Edward all his life.

Not everything was Rousseau. The Fitzgerald children mixed book learning with learning from nature from a much earlier age than the sage recommended, perhaps at the Duke of Leinster's insistence, perhaps out of a recognition that by the age of fourteen or so, younger sons had to have enough formal education to embark on training for a profession. Lord Edward did well at the 'business' of book learning that made up about six hours of the Black Rock day and was especially quick at learning poetry, prayers and geography. By the age of ten he was learning Latin, French, mathematics and grammar; he was reading widely in ancient history, travels and geography and from masters in Dublin had lessons in geometry and fencing. Lord Edward was the only Fitzgerald boy, apart from the Duchess's first son, George, who had much intellectual aptitude or application. Lady Louisa Conolly reported in 1778 that William, who became heir to the Leinster dukedom when George died, 'very good humouredly said, that as to *Latin* and *Greek* it was not a genius belonging to the family; that except Eddy, they were all very dull. I did not tell him that Mr Ogilvie had made the same observation, but, to be sure I believe it's true.'

In the evenings at Black Rock the children read plays and novels and occasionally staged theatricals, despite the resistance of their father. In the late summer of 1771, Ogilvie reported that the Black Rock children were practising Addison's *Cato* and Fielding's *Tom Thumb*, and in September they performed them at Carton House. Louisa Conolly described the performance for Sarah Bunbury. 'The Duke of Leinster, you know, does not approve of his children's acting, therefore only indulged my sister with these plays for her own amusement provided there was to be no company, therefore the audience consisted of only the servants and ourselves. Eddy did Tom Thumb and you have no notion how pretty it was to see him; his figure, his voice, his action and grace with a vast deal of spirit was really enchanting. One was ready to eat him up, he was so lovely. One's vanity tempted one to wish a better audience to see him but as my sister says, 'twas much better for him that they should not, for fear that so much admiration should spoil him and that would be the greatest pity, for in every respect he is just the child one could wish'.

By this time Lord Edward was nearly eight. He was sturdy and affectionate, devoted to his mother and adored in return. When Sarah hinted in a letter that too much attention might be spoiling him, Louisa replied fulsomely in his defence, 'Your first paragraph is about Eddy and I will allow that all you say is very natural to suppose, but the fact is, that it is such an uncommon child, I do not think it can be spoilt. He is not in the smallest degree set up by the admiration he meets with from his friends; as to that of strangers, he will ever be indifferent to, rather too much so, for I see 'tis the nature of him, not to give himself any trouble but about those he loves. He has not a spark of envy or jealousy in his composition, which is very extraordinary considering his excessive feeling. But really it is not fair to judge of any other child by him, for I do think, that 'tis an almost perfect little Being, literally having no fault but too much warmth of temper, which much oftener is against himself than against other people, because if he feels himself to blame of any-thing, there is no such thing as putting him in a good humour with himself.' 'I should be the most ungrateful mortal upon earth if I did not adore him,' she concluded, 'for his love for me is quite astonishing, not at all like a child's but that of a steady friend, and I assure you I do depend upon it as much as if he was grown up.'

Lord Edward bore up well under this torrent of feeling. Good-humoured and full of energy, he bustled about Black Rock, acting, and looking, more like a child of nature than the son of a duke. In the afternoons after schoolwork, he cheerfully grubbed up weeds, or 'ramps', as he called them, and gathered warm eggs for his supper. In the evenings, more formally dressed, he was occasionally taken with his elder brothers and sisters to the Crow Street or Smock Alley Theatres in Dublin, where, during the farce, he might delight the audience by forgetting the dignity required of his social standing and unselfconsciously 'roar out . . . with such fits of laughter that he set the house laughing with him'.

Already, Lord Edward was learning to charm his elders and beginning to put his considerable epistolary skills to the service of a desire to please and to be beloved. In the late 1760s before he could write, he sent messages to his mother by William Ogilvie. By the early 1770s he was writing himself, mixing expressions of endearment with anecdotes about things close to his mother's heart and coaxing her into ever greater love for him. 'My dearest Mama,' he wrote when he was about eight-and-a-half or nine, 'I am mighty happy at your letter, but will not cease teasing you until you come to see us, as your cold is much better; and why may you not bring Lucy with you; sure we could take very good care of her, and play with her and divert her. We'll be all out with you if you don't, for it is a monstrous long time since you were here . . . I dote on you dearest mother, but will not love you unless you come to see us.'

By the time he was ten, Lord Edward had developed the beginnings of the style that was to give his mature letters their charm and immediacy. A letter from Black Rock in early 1774 began: 'My dearest Mama, if I could go to see you, I would gallop away this very minute. I long monstrously to see you . . . Oh, do, my dearest Mama, come to see us. Indeed it would do your spirits good for we would keep you very quiet and nurse you as we used to do, and not rout you; and you need not fear to get cold, for there has been a fire constantly in your room . . . Ah, now, do, do, dearest Mama, and I'll dote on you monstrously.' Lord Edward loved to tell stories too. 'I do not know what to say about Sophia. I believe she goes on well enough with the French woman,' he told his mother. 'But the French woman does not go on very well, for she does nasty tricks and empties her pot with . . . over her window into the garden on brother Charles' side very cunningly to make Mr. O. believe that it was brother Charles. But Mr. O. knew who it was and was in a great fury, and scolded all the women and called them nasty B–s, and Mama, with all her dirt the French woman has spoiled the horse chestnuts. We have been working very hard at the fields and picking off the weeds and we made a great many bonfires of them, and all the spots that the fires were on will be the soonest green. Dear mother I was so hungry in Dublin that I ate a whole roll and two crackers.'

Freedom to express emotion and the exercise of 'natural reason' were given pride of place at Black Rock and the Fitzgerald children matured in an atmosphere of tolerance quite different from the regime that had reigned at Carton under the stern and unyielding eye of the Duke of Leinster. But this hot-house atmosphere of unrestrained emotion, in which every blister and boil was an occasion for an emotional outpouring, soon generated a world of hidden meanings and passions that was at variance with the Duchess's commitment to openness. Within a few years, the Duchess of Leinster had begun to respond to the tutor's powerful gaze and emotionally loaded communications with adoration. If the children loved Ogilvie openly, calling him 'O' and 'Ogy' and climbing on his back for piggy backs around the nursery, the Duchess began to love him illicitly and obsessively. By the early 1770s, she and Ogilvie had become lovers.

In sanctioning the love between tutor and pupil and between mother and son in *Émile*, Rousseau did not intend to loosen the patriarchal bonds between the members of the family and its head which provided the model for the monarchical order on which social stability depended. But, as his critics pointed out, *Émile* removed the authority of the father figure by removing the father altogether, leaving the boy an orphan. By the 1780s Rousseau and his followers were accused of licensing an excess of emotion and mother-love that sidelined the father figure and fostered the social climate in which national disdain for patriarchy could slide into patricide and regicide, democracy and republicanism, fatherless peoples and fatherless lands.

In the early 1770s the children at Black Rock were unaware equally of the coming political whirlwind that would reap the seeds Rousseau was accused of sowing, and of the degree to which William Ogilvie, himself fatherless and mysterious, had replaced the Duke of Leinster in their hearts. But their memories of Carton and feelings for their father were fading. The Duke of Leinster took his paternal duties seriously, feeling responsible for the children's education and worldly standing. But he disapproved of their boisterous games, frowned on their amateur theatricals and was too conscious of his dignity to take his coat off and romp round the garden. Once his children had moved to Black Rock, he rarely visited them and they began to forget the country-house life. Their father became a shadowy figure to whom they owed respect and for whom they must cut a presentable figure in the world. But soon he was not a man they loved. Lord Charles Fitzgerald, writing to his mother in 1772, when he had just taken up a commission in the navy, unwittingly encapsulated the distinction the Black Rock children had come to make between their tutor and their father. 'Write me word how dear Ogilvie's leg is, and give my love to him; give my duty to the Duke of Leinster and tell him I have wrote him an account of the affairs of Denmark.'

In the autumn of 1773 the Duke became seriously ill with fluid in his legs. He was brought from Carton to Dublin and, Louisa Conolly reported, 'is in very good spirits, the swelling in his leg is very considerable and is up as high as the knee from the feet with scarcely any pain which they look on as a bad sign. But his feeling well gives me great hopes, for I think nothing can be very bad inwardly when that is the case.' The doctors called his condition a 'dropsical gout'; but the diagnosis was uncertain and was not revealed either to the Duke himself or to the Duchess, who, Louisa told Sarah, was 'but too apt to take alarm'. It was a measure of William Ogilvie's acknowledged importance in the family that the doctors, Quinn and Smyth, told him that the Duke's 'disorder' was likely to be a 'lingering one', and that it was Ogilvie who carried the responsibility of not telling the patient. He did, however, confide in Louisa, who wrote to Sarah that 'you must not tell anybody that Mr Ogilvie told me this, for we have agreed to keep the doctors' opinion a secret.'

For his children, the most noticeable result of their father's illness was a sudden end to their mother's visits. Always an active man who enjoyed business and took a frequently overbearing interest in the running of his ruinously expensive estate, the Duke now found himself idle and a prey to callers in Dublin. The Duchess had to stay by his side and her stays at Black Rock stopped abruptly. Lord Edward wished for his father's recovery. But he wished for it so that he could see his mother again. Before the Duke was moved to Dublin, Lord Edward wrote to his mother, '[We] will be extremely glad to see you as we were very much disappointed not to see you Thursday . . . I hope Papa will be well before that time, as I know you cannot come until he is well.'

But the Duke did not improve; his body was filling up with fluid. By 7 November the swelling had reached his thighs and the Duchess was facing the prospect of widowhood. 'My poor sister is very unhappy about it and I believe has very little hopes in her own mind; whether 'tis likely to be lingering or end soon, God knows; the prospect is very bad,' Louisa Conolly wrote. By this time Louisa realised that the prospect was not just the Duke's death; it was also the unmasking of the Duchess's long-standing affair.

But not for nothing was the Duchess of Leinster a believer in the value of feeling. As she sat in the white damask drawing room of Leinster House in Dublin after her husband's death on 19 November 1773, paced its shadowy corridors and distracted herself with games of cards, she quickly decided that passion must override propriety. Six weeks after her husband's funeral the Duchess announced to her family that she and the children would be leaving as soon as possible for France and that William Ogilvie would be going with them. Far from worrying about their father's death or their mother's grief, the children were agog with excitement about the trip to France all through the winter. Writing to his mother in the spring of 1774, Lord Edward mentioned that his sister Charlotte was going to see a Flemish dancer, 'and I believe thinks herself as happy now as we shall be when we go to France, which will be soon I hope', and reminded his mother that she had promised riding lessons for all the boys when they got there. Nowhere did he write about his father's death, the family's adherence to the rigorous practices of mourning, or reveal any anxiety about leaving his homeland. Henceforth, Lord Edward never mentioned the Duke of Leinster; in his letters at least it was as if his father had never been.

The family's departure for France was delayed by the illnesses and deaths of the Duchess's sister Caroline and her husband Lord Holland. But the whole 'flock', as Louisa Conolly called it, together with the Duchess and Ogilvie, Rowley the Duchess's maid, Mrs Lynch her faithful housekeeper, several other servants and scores of boxes and trunks, finally left Dublin for Waterford and Bordeaux on 27 August 1774. Pausing only in Toulouse to go through an official marriage ceremony that ratified a secret Dublin marriage of a few weeks before, Ogilvie and the Duchess had settled the whole family in rented lodgings in Marseilles by the end of November. The children – the boys, Robert, Edward, Henry, Gerald and George; the girls, Charlotte, Fanny, Lucy and Louisa – were put under the care of nurses or tutors according to their ages. Ogilvie made his first experiment in life as a gentleman; and the Duchess, after nearly thirty years of childbearing, which had already produced nineteen children (the last of whom was probably Ogilvie's), settled into a new pregnancy. 'How pleasant it is to me to hear that you are well and in good spirits,' Louisa Conolly wrote to her sister. 'I like to hear of all your fine doings and think it charming for the boys who will have all the advantages of being abroad while their other education goes on. My love to dearest Eddy, whose very pretty letter I will soon answer.'

Lord Edward easily accepted his new life in France and settled in quickly, perfecting his French and developing a sympathy for what he called 'the true French character'. In his letters he rarely mentioned their old home. Books, family life and the transient company of boys his own age in Marseilles did duty for experience of the complicated rules of Ireland's Ascendancy. This isolation from his peers was increased when the whole family left Marseilles, which had some civic life and a local élite, and moved in April 1776 to the Château of Aubigny in the Department of Berry, half way between the towns of Orléans and Bourges. Aubigny was a mediaeval château owned by the Duchess's brother, the Duke of Richmond. With its thick walls, round towers and winking, mullioned windows, the château was old-fashioned, inconvenient and horribly cold. But it was also cheap, with gardens that could supply vegetables, fields for horses and woods for fuel. The Duke of Richmond rarely visited his French property, which he kept largely because it came with a French peerage that added a mellifluous variation to his many English titles. He was delighted that his sister should stay there well out of the way of the English press which might gossip about her unconventional life and complicate his own political career.

Aubigny and its estate were in the middle of the Solange, a district of rivers, lakes and forests, drained by the Rère and

Sauldre, tributaries of the Loire. It was far more isolated than Black Rock, a rural Arcadia excellent for hunting, but less good for teaching children the ways of the world. The family lived there until 1779, Ogilvie ferociously pursuing economy, his wife relentlessly spending money on transforming Black Rock into the sort of home she would need if she ever returned to Ireland.

Ogilvie had given up teaching the children when he and the Duchess were formally married. At Aubigny he looked after the gardens and woods, hunted, read, wrote letters and took over 'the purse' entirely, skilfully investing and spending the Duchess's annuity and the children's allowances. At his death, the first Duke of Leinster had left his hapless heir debts of one hundred and forty-eight thousand pounds. Ogilvie, by contrast, was able within twenty-five years to buy up the estates of two of the Duke's sons, and he died a wealthy man.

Now that her obsession with Ogilvie was legitimate, the Duchess lived it to the hilt. In Ireland, illicit passion had sprouted, a tropical growth among the acceptable and more decorous flowering of domestic and filial affection. At Aubigny, the passion between the Duchess and Ogilvie was openly and extravagantly expressed. Ogilvie counselled the use of reason to counter an emotionalism he regarded as excessive. The Duchess agreed, but allowed feeling the ascendant, claiming, as she might not have done two years earlier, that reason was not strong enough to control it. 'What poor uncertain creatures we are', 'how unaccountable', she told her husband after he had argued restraint, adding in self-exculpation, 'But of all creatures, those that love to excess are most so, and while love is so strong a passion as it is with us, my Angel, I fear we must, at times, be unreasonable, tho' it should be the constant aim of all our thoughts not to let it transport us too far. I say *us*, but I mean myself chiefly, for you, my Angel, are very, very seldom led away by it into anything wrong.'

The Duchess insisted that the overflow of feeling at
Aubigny should be accompanied by a greater informality
than had operated at Black Rock, where Ogilvie's position as
family servant and her own as employer had meant that a
public protocol of deportment and language had to be
observed. She now wanted these hierarchies collapsed in the
interest of intimacy. She ordered the children to call Ogilvie
'Papa' and she reacted angrily when in 1778 Ogilvie
inadvertently slipped into his old role of tutor to the aristocracy and called his stepsons 'young gentlemen'. 'How could
you call them the *young gentlemen* in your letter? It
sounded so cold and formal. I am sure you are out of
humour with them; and to lump sweet Eddy under that
appellation. Oh, indeed, I am quite angry at it; but maybe I
may forgive you.' Ogilvie was uneasy that informality might
be accompanied by a disdain for the authority which
children ought to see embodied in their parents. Without filial respect young adults could easily stray from rectitude.
'What I have wished otherwise in your conduct has been
only to suppress an over great tenderness that I have thought
injurious to them by removing the restraint of authority that
parents ought, in kindness to their children, to hold over
them – for with strong passions and high spirits, it is scarcely
possible for the best . . . understanding to guide a young person safe . . . I have maintained and I have always thought it
wrong in parents not to assist their children in this manner.'

Despite such admonitions, of which her children were
well aware and in spite of which they took her part, the
Duchess persisted in demanding displays of feeling. By the
1770s, men, too, had felt the shock waves of the fashion for
sensibility. The 'man of feeling' who loved and wept, sighed
and suffered, was a modish creation of novelists and play-
wrights. His fictive image, which reached its apotheosis in
Henry Mackenzie's *Man of Feeling* of 1771, was a manifestation of the openly expressed desire of many women for
greater domestic commitment and greater demonstrativeness

in their husbands. Ogilvie, stern and emotionally dominant, was never a thoroughgoing recruit to this new way of behaving. But Lord Edward became an apt pupil in his mother's school of love. He confided everything to her and, once in Aubigny, always included Ogilvie in the magic circle of right-feeling people. Mr Ogilvie 'understood' his 'odd' feelings, he wrote to his mother in 1780, adding, 'he is the only person besides yourself I could mention them to, so pray show this letter to nobody but him. How happy am I to have two people to whom I can thus express every sentiment of my heart!'

During the time the family spent at Aubigny, Edward's letters to his mother became ever more intimate and touching, a remarkable testimony to the intense and untrammelled affection a son felt for his mother. No detail was too small to mention; no feeling too fugitive to capture and express. When his mother was away, Edward described his own activities as still determined by her and by his love for her. In August 1779, when he was fifteen, he thus explained his garden: 'I have . . . put up two benches in the most shady parts, with boards under them on purpose to keep dear Mother's feet from feeling any damp from the ground as I hope she will sometimes come and sit there.'

By this time, Lord Edward was on the verge of manhood. He had begun to express opinions as well as feelings in his letters, and was following closely in the French press the progress of the war the American colonists were waging against their British rulers. Although at the beginning he sided with the British Crown, his national allegiances were weak. In 1776, when he was just thirteen, he wrote with subdued patriotism to his mother after hearing the news of a British victory in the battle of Brooklyn, 'I suppose you can't help being glad at our having gained so signal a victory over the Americans, though if possible, I am sure you could have wished it to have been finished in a more amicable manner.' Although Lord Edward had never lived in

England, he was cut off from Ireland. As time went on, he became more and more rootless; a young man with an Irish father, an English mother and a Scottish stepfather, remembering Ireland as home, but not understanding its customs, speaking French as easily as English and feeling just as at home in Paris as in London. He was ready to embark on life as a cosmopolitan figure, whose conduct was determined more by abstract, universal principles derived from Enlightenment philosophies than by any national traditions or patterns of behaviour.

The form of his life would be dictated by his position in the family. Like most younger sons of men of property, Lord Edward had to have a profession, preferably one that carried a hope of wealth or glory. His little estate at Kilrush would never be enough unless he could charm an heiress into marriage. With all the political patronage at his brother's command a seat in the Irish parliament would be easy to come by, and with the help of his uncle, Lord Edward might even try for an English constituency. But for his income he would have to choose between the law, the army and the navy. The Duchess of Leinster did not give him much advice; she was lazy about her sons' futures, wanting to have them around her, more ambitious that they should marry well than that they should succeed in public life. But in looking forward to his manhood, Lord Edward sided with Ogilvie's energy rather than his mother's indolence. He was unexpectedly eager to leave the school-room for what he imagined were the excitements of the world. He decided to join the army and persuaded his mother to allow him to go to Paris in the autumn of 1776 when he was just fourteen years old. There he joined his English cousin Charles Lennox, heir to the Duke of Richmond, and his cousin's tutor Mr Kempson. The two boys studied at a military academy, perfected their riding and fencing and probably began their social and sexual education. But he could not stay in Paris for long and he was too young to leave home for good. When Charles Lennox left Paris, Lord Edward returned to the country, to books, hunting, the château garden and his mother's adoration. He was bought a lieutenant's commission in the 96th Regiment of Foot in 1777, but it was not until 1779, when he was nearly sixteen, that the Duchess finally agreed that her son could leave her. Even then Lord Edward was not allowed to join his own regiment: he left France for the south coast of England, where he joined the Sussex Militia, which was in the charge and on the payroll of his uncle the Duke of Richmond.

After the end of the Seven Years' War in 1763 a huge army of ninety thousand men was rapidly shrunk to between thirty and forty thousand permanent troops. But this peacetime army was deliberately scattered; both the Crown and parliament discouraged large gatherings of idle soldiers and only in Ireland were troops regularly housed in barracks. Elsewhere, soldiers were billeted in towns and villages, regimental sizes were allowed to drop and officers lounged at home on half pay, ran their estates, gambled in clubs, scarcely ever in uniform. Complementing this standing army were the militias, set up in 1757 under the control of the Lords Lieutenant of the counties and intended as a locally based back-up to the professional force. They had never been popular, either with the men who were encouraged to enlist or with the aristocrats who were expected to pay for them. Some regiments were kept up as ornamentally spruce, showy toys for their commanders. Lord Edward's uncle Thomas Conolly, for instance, was colonel of the Derry Militia, and after its establishment in 1778 made two or three trips a year from Dublin to Derry to inspect it. He was inordinately proud of the men's specially commissioned, Irish-made, dark blue uniforms. But many commanders were happy to let their troops forget about musters and training and drills when peace came; the militias, unlike their troublesome American counterparts, mostly faded out in the 1760s and 1770s.

With the outbreak of the American war, the army expanded again, growing year by year with the gravity of the war. By the time Lord Edward joined the Sussex Militia, the combined forces of the regular army, the militias, foreign mercenaries fighting in the British army and the American militiamen loyal to the Crown, numbered about a hundred and twenty thousand men. Local militias had reluctantly reassembled and started to train and drill.

Putting the sixteen-year-old Edward under his uncle's eye was a gentle way of starting him in a rough profession. His mother and Ogilvie accompanied him to England and anxiously awaited first reports of his progress at Stoke, the Sussex house of the Duchess's younger brother, Lord George Lennox. The Duke of Richmond was laying out a new encampment for the Sussex Militia, and Lord Edward eagerly tried his hand at the precise impromptu architecture of hessian and rope, telling his mother in his first letter that the Duke 'left the pitching of his own company to me, and I was not one inch wrong. I like what I have seen as yet of my profession very much.'

But the Duke of Richmond was not a steady teacher. He was unpredictably moody, and more given to abstract speculation than to the practical niceties required of army officers. The Sussex Militia, as Lord Edward gradually realised and his mother had known all along, was hardly the place for an ambitious young officer to catch the eye of the army's high command. Besides, the Duke of Richmond had been hostile to the American war from the start, siding openly with the American colonists and sailing his private yacht through the British fleet in the Solent with the rebels' flag flying defiantly from its mast. It was easy to assume that the Duke's young nephew felt the same and to conclude that he would be half-hearted about fighting the Americans.

At the beginning of the American Revolution, the Duchess of Leinster and her sisters were less outspoken than their brother. They deplored the war and the misery it caused soldiers, their families and all those impoverished by trade embargoes. But they refused to take sides. In October 1776, three months after the American Declaration of Independence, Louisa wrote to the Duchess, 'I wish our ringleaders at home (of this horrid war) and those of America could all be jumbled together and thrown into the bottom of the sea.' But by the summer of 1777, after the French had come into the war, family attitudes had hardened. Both Sarah and Louisa now echoed their brother's view that the war was the work of a corrupt government deceiving a foolish monarch. Hearing the news of the surrender of General Burgoyne at Saratoga in October, Louisa burst out in a letter to Emily, 'surely the King's eyes will be opened at last! He cannot be deceived forever! God grant that he may see his error and give up the point before greater destruction comes upon us.' In Ireland, opposition groups, especially Presbyterians in the north who had familial connections with the American rebels and many people suffering because of interruptions in commerce, sided openly with the colonists. 'The Irish here have no reason to love the English,' Louisa Conolly wrote in 1779, noting and fearing rumours of a French, Spanish or even American landing in Ireland. 'They have many friends among the Americans and are courted by them. I trust in God that England will consider all of this before it is too late.' By this time she had come round to her brother's view that the government's justification of the war was a self-serving sham 'to screen a Tyrannical set of people', both in Westminster and in Dublin. She praised her brother, who she found was 'the first political toast all throughout the Northern parts of this kingdom'.

As the years of conflict passed, the war crept remorselessly closer to the Fitzgerald family. By the middle of 1779 two of the Duchess's sons had already seen American service. Lord Charles Fitzgerald, a lieutenant on the frigate *Arethusa*, had been involved in sea skirmishes. Lord Henry, a lieutenant in the 66th Foot, was back from stints in New York and with General Howe on the Delaware river, but might have to re-join his regiment at any time. Lord Edward, moreover, was determined to gain more experience of war than pitching the camp of the Sussex Militia on the close-cropped grass of the South Downs.

At the end of his life, Lord Edward commented sadly that he had fought in America '*against* the cause of Liberty'. But at the age of sixteen, he was far more interested in the excitement of soldiering than in the legitimacy of this particular war. After a year in Sussex, he was begging to be allowed to move into a regiment whose fighting was more than a desultory exercise against an imaginary foe.

Junior officers' commissions, in theory in the King's gift, were in practice up for sale. Once inside the army, officers could move up the hierarchy either by purchase, as was usual in peacetime, or by promotion, as death made possible in war. If they found their place uncongenial, too far from home, too near to the battlefield, they might swap their positions for the equivalent rank in another regiment.

What Lord Edward wanted was purchase into a regiment on active service in America; not a costly request, since most young officers were trying desperately to stay on the other side of the world. Ogilvie and his mother moved half way towards his desire, agreeing to let him go to his regular army regiment but refusing to sanction his departure for danger. By December 1780 Lord Edward had finally taken up his commission in the 96th Regiment of Foot and was living in lodgings close to the barracks of Youghal, 'a nasty fish town' as Ogilvie derisively called it, overlooking St George's Channel about thirty miles east of Cork. His mother and Ogilvie travelled to Ireland with him, moved into a house in Kildare Street, Dublin, and nervously waited to see how soon he would be bored and how well they would be received in Ascendancy society.

The 96th Regiment was technically mobilised for war, and

likely to be as near full strength as its colonel and recruiting officer could make it. Regiments totalled about four hundred and eighty men, and were subdivided into companies of several dozen men and up to six non-commissioned officers. As a lieutenant who had to learn the disciplines of a junior officer, Lord Edward came under the beady eye of the Major, 'a very strict disciplinarian', who oversaw his military education.

In the barracks, the day's routine was unvarying, carried out to the calls of bugles or trumpets. While Lord Edward was probably still in bed, recovering from over-spending and over-drinking the night before, soldiers were summoned by the 'reveille' and struggled into their waistcoats, breeches, gaiters and long red topcoats. After breakfast they prepared their arms and equipment for roll-call and inspection, over which Lord Edward and his fellow officers, wearing uniforms or civilian clothes according to the whim of the senior officers, presided. Guards were posted round the camp boundaries at about nine or ten o'clock each day, the troops were inspected and paraded and then put to work practising the recently adopted techniques of drilling and other battle manoeuvres, perfecting (usually without ammunition) the use of bayonets and muskets. In the afternoons Lord Edward and his fellow novices learned their craft, studying fortifications, ballistics, mechanics and battle routines. By early evening many of the men had drifted to the brothels and alehouses, where they would spend whatever was left after subsistence money had been deducted from their daily sixpence. Despite his constant assurances to his mother and Ogilvie that he was fond of his business and 'ambitious' of being 'a good officer', Lord Edward had plenty of time for both genteel visits to local gentry families and less genteel carousing with his fellow officers. 'Some of our young men are grown very idle since they came here,' he admitted, 'and have been in a great many scrapes, and although I have kept them company, I never have been in one.' But he did confess to extravagance, running through the first instalment of his four hundred pounds' annual allowance by the beginning of March, which left him with the prospect of a month's abstinence before the next payment arrived. In his defence, he could cite a host of calls on his income – besides his uniform and camp equipment, he bought and stabled a horse, and kept a man, Walsh, 'the best, quietest and most attached servant in the world'.

Lord Edward hoped that the Youghal station was temporary and expected to set off for the war within a few weeks. But regiments in Ireland could not be transferred abroad without the permission of the Lord Lieutenant and now that invasion was possible from either France or Spain, the Dublin authorities may have been unwilling to let professional troops leave the country. The weeks of Lord Edward's apprenticeship stretched out into months and the routines of army life slackened towards those of civilians.

By February of 1781 he was 'quite tired' of Youghal and the 96th Regiment. Unwilling to wait any longer for active service, he had exchanged his commission for one in the 19th Regiment of Foot which was ready to sail out of Cork for America. Just before he set off for the transport ship he wrote delightedly to his mother, 'You may guess how happy I am . . . I believe I am at this moment the happiest creature in the universe; except a little thought which comes in the midst of my joy and tells me I leave my dearest Mother behind. I received dear, dear Mr O's letter this morning, at the same time I heard of the orders for marching. It made me think how happy I shall be at my return.' A day later he wrote, 'Dear Mr O, the General has just beat, and we march immediately and embark at nine o'clock. The wind is also fair for sailing, so that we shall be off immediately . . . Adieu. Believe me for ever your affectionate son, E.F.'

In America the British army was grinding through the dog days of the war, demoralised by innumerable small reverses in the field and by considerable opposition to the war at

home. The force Lord Edward was sailing to join had captured Charleston, the principal port in South Carolina, after
a well-conducted siege. It was now striking out across the
country, but had abandoned the city's suburbs and hinter-
lands, leaving outlying forts in American hands and devas-
tated estates to those local people who had not fled months
before.

Lord Edward gave no hint that he had any idea of this
chaos. He had set off with eager anticipation of improving
his professional reputation and of the tumultuous excitement
of the battlefield. His desire, he said, was above all to distin-
guish himself 'as an officer', giving the men under his command an example of courage and leadership. Although he
carried miniatures of his mother and Ogilvie in his luggage –
criticising the latter as 'a little plump and blooming' – he did
not dwell on times of misery and danger, when they might
comfort him. Until he was wounded at Eutaw Springs, he
relished the war with the thoughtlessness of his youth and
sought out skirmishes and dangerous patrols on which to
flaunt his reckless courage.

When he had recovered from his wounds, Lord Edward
was given the task of escorting American prisoners into
Charleston. One of them, a Colonel Washington, said of
him then, 'I never knew so lovable a person, and every man
in the army, from the general to the drummer, would cheer
the expression. His frank and open manner, his universal
benevolence, his *gaîté de coeur*, his valour almost chivalrous,
and above all, his unassuming tone, made him the idol of all
who served with him. He had great animal spirits, which
bore him up against all fatigue; but his courage was entirely
independent of those spirits.' In 1781 Lord Edward was still
the Black Rock child, confident in his charm, cheerfully
accepting the devotion all around him and with his belief in
human goodness confirmed by Tony's act of seemingly
benevolent altruism.

At Black Rock, his mother and family anxiously thumbed

the newspapers and army gazettes, longing for news, yet
fearful of seeing any Fitzgerald names among the dour
printed lists of the dead and wounded. The Duchess had no
interest in stoicism; she was not patriotic and felt none of the
glow of glory by association that could be claimed by the
relatives of those who died or distinguished themselves in
military action. She saw wars in general as monuments to
human folly and this war in particular as a consequence of
monarchical obstinacy. When her son was reported missing
at Eutaw Springs, she worried as a mother, and when in
February 1782, she finally heard that he was safe, she
rejoiced as one too. 'Her nerves have not recovered the agitation of the fright,' Louisa Conolly reported to Sarah on 18
February. 'But she is so happy at his escape, that I hope they
will soon throw off the effect of the alarm we all had about
the dear boy, whom I do most sincerely wish out of that
horrid place. I have quite a superstitious dread of America's
being the grave of most of our young people: good God!
will that hardened wretch the King never give up the point
until he has sacrificed all our subjects?'

Louisa Conolly did not have long to wait. Four days later,
General Conway brought a motion in the House of
Commons to end the war. Its defeat by a single vote effectively ended Lord North's reign as Prime Minister. On 20
March the government fell, destroyed by years of relentless
opposition at home and by prolonged failure abroad. Lord
Shelburne speedily took up office but peace came much
more slowly, with the French and British fighting over the
rich islands of the Caribbean right up until the moment of
formal ceasefire. But Lord Edward was, at any rate, out of
the war, promoted to major on the staff of General O'Hara
in St Lucia. Although England was in theory still at war with
France, the contact between the two sides was purely pacific.
Lord Edward was useful as an interpreter, and took a party
of prisoners over to the neighbouring island of Martinique
under a flag of truce. 'I am not like my brother Charles in

hating everything French,' he told his mother. He admired the capital of Martinique, St Pierre, and he enjoyed its women, who, he wrote, 'are pretty, dance and dress very well, and are, the French officers say – to use dear Robert's words – vastly good natured.'

The soldiers knew that peace was on the way, and Lord Edward wrote at the beginning of March, 'What would I not give to be with you . . . dearest mother! But I hope the peace will soon bring the long-wished-for time. Till then, my dearest mother will not expect it. My profession is that of a military man, and I should reproach myself hereafter if I thought I lost any opportunity of improving myself in it, or did not at all times do as much as lay in my power to merit the promotion I am entitled to expect.' What he did immediately was to buy himself a majority in a new regiment, the 90th, in the hope that he might thus advance more quickly than he had in the 19th.

Many regiments were recalled and disbanded when the peace was finally ratified. As his prospects for active service shrank, Lord Edward cast his eyes ever farther afield, scanning the world map for sites of imperial struggle in which death or glory might guarantee a stripe. 'I might get the rank of Lieutenant Colonel by going to the East Indies, which, as it seems to promise to be an active scene, I should like extremely,' he said. Before he could set out, however, his new regiment was ordered home. Lord Edward and Tony, one in the cramped officers' quarters of the creaking troopship, the other among the swinging hammocks of soldiers and servants, were on the way back to Britain. Although he did not know it, Lord Edward's battle days under the British flag were over.

Tony could not know what his master thought of him. But as the troopship wallowed its way between St Lucia and Liverpool, and as he attended Lord Edward in the officers' quarters and then retired to the noisy squalor of the hold, he must have wondered. He was the rescuer, he knew, and this freedom – this half freedom – was his reward. So was this journey, already made by hundreds of others of his colour. But he was still a servant, practising for his master the habits of deference learned so well on the plantation. Although he had his own wages and on British soil would be free to go wherever he wanted, he knew little of the country to which he was travelling and his ignorance was another form of dependence.

In the weeks at sea Tony studied Lord Edward, seeing how he liked to lounge about in the morning reading and talking to the officers and men. Probably unable to read, and certainly unable to write, Tony had become a good watcher. He noticed Lord Edward's boisterous and boyish high spirits, his love of high-jinks and fun. But he also noticed a thoughtfulness in him. Lord Edward's long-lashed eyes followed Tony and seemed to offer him a trust beyond that usually given to a servant or to a slave.

Yet the two men had every imaginable form of difference; one was white, rich, eagerly awaited by a doting family and looking forward to a life replete with exciting choices and pleasing rewards; the other was black, penniless, alone and dependent for his future on others. What held them together was Lord Edward's belief that they were both, at bottom, members of the same human family with the same emotions and rights. In the benevolent light cast by his optimistic humanism, a singular companionship was formed.

In the cities and towns of England, Tony saw others who had taken some of the risks that he had. Around the docks in Liverpool lived several hundred black families, already mingling with sailors who had left ships from Portugal, Spain, India and beyond, and producing children in many shades of brown. Beyond the cities, black people were fewer. But many regiments returning from the American wars had come with a few freed slaves. Some stayed on in England as soldiers. Others, if they got to England, became servants, street sellers, coachmen or beggars. In London there were as many as ten or fifteen thousand black people. As their post coach rumbled through the northern suburbs down to the Duchess of Leinster's new house in Harley Street, Tony saw black servants, many of them very young, accompanying the rich as page boys, footmen or coachmen. In the teeming streets men who had left their employers, and the children of unions between black and white, mingled with the crowd. They were feared by some, shunned by many, already a people apart, living in the east by the river, or in the slums of St Giles', coming to the West End to offer their skills for sale and their bodies for labour or pleasure. Very few were prosperous, fewer still accepted. But Tony, walking behind Lord Edward as he ran up the steps to his mother's door, trusted that his new master would reward his service with a loyalty that would prevent his having to join them.

In St Lucia, Lord Edward had looked forward gloomily to his peacetime life. The Duke of Richmond, though Master of the Ordnance, had refused to advance his nephew's claim to a lieutenant-colonelcy. But Lord Edward arrived home to find his prospects transformed and his family revelling in an intimate connection with a new government. Shelburne's government, defeated on a resolution that the concessions made to the French in the peace treaty were too liberal, had resigned. The Duke of Richmond was out of office and Lord Edward's cousin, Charles James Fox, was in. The new administration was run by Lord North and Fox, old and bitter enemies who had been reconciled by the lure of power. Far from having to wait deferentially upon his uncle and beg for a promotion, Lord Edward was now on easy terms with his cousin the Secretary of State, and could reasonably expect a swift and easy advance up the army hierarchy.

In 1783 Charles Fox was thirty-four, nearly fifteen years older than Lord Edward. Described by his father as beautiful when a boy, Fox had lost his youthful good looks. His stockiness had run to fat and his thick, curly, dark hair was thinning to sticky wisps that flew disorderedly out from his head. Once a dandy, he was now slovenly about his appearance, usually dressing in the buff and blue of the rebel American army but often missing at least one button. Despite a life in the public eye, he was selfconscious in the presence of other people, frequently clearing his throat and spitting noisily on the carpet. When he was bemused he dug and turned his fat fists energetically in his eyes. In private, though, this habitual shyness gave way. For he was, he himself noted, 'a very painstaking man', and when this quality of attentiveness was turned on friends and acquaintances they felt at the centre of his world and inscribed themselves without hesitation into his circle of devotees. This sense of private intimacy was increased by Fox's informality; he often received the most august visitors in his bedroom, unkempt, unshaven and in dirty night clothes.

When Edward Fitzgerald first felt the force of Fox's charm, his cousin had been in parliament for a dozen years, astonishing MPs with brilliant speeches, his grasp of arcane subjects like taxation, and his impromptu oratory. 'Fox began his sentences', said one, 'and God finished them.' The long American war fixed for ever Fox's public persona. By the end of it he had come to exemplify and embody a set of attitudes and a way of life. To be Foxite – which Lord Edward swiftly became – was to embrace reform as a general outlook, to be hostile to Crown power and to welcome religious emancipation, a reformed constitution and a powerful House of Commons. Fox waged a life-long, often personal, campaign against the power of the Crown and was rewarded with the titles of 'Champion of the People' and 'the Voice of the People'. 'Fox' was joined with 'Liberty' because Fox lived his life through the belief that all sorts, conditions and colours of men were entitled to the same freedoms. But 'Fox and Liberty' was a personal as well as a political slogan. Fox's demeanour and behaviour were continual challenges to the prevailing hierarchies of money and status. He was open and warm, he was convivial – and frequently drunk – he was an unabashed libertine and he placed no store by titles or wealth. He gambled away a huge fortune, was outrageous in his demands for loans from impecunious friends, but was placidly unconcerned when faced with bankruptcy. When pressed, during his final illness, to accept a peerage, he replied, 'I will not close my life in that foolish way, as so many have done before me.' He seemed hungry for power, but when he lost it he retired quite happily to the company of books, friends and the flowers of his Thames-side garden.

Like his father before him, Fox was an over-hasty politician. He was convinced that almost any political expedient was justified to win power and wrest control of the House of Commons from the King and his friends. By the time Lord Edward swung into Fox's orbit in the summer of 1783, the political cost of this miscalculation was not yet clear. But Fox's coalition with his erstwhile enemy Lord North was hated by the King and regarded as unjustified by many voters.

Lord Edward, loving Fox as his cousin and sharing with him both a belief in rights and a rebellious turn of mind, was only a minor star in the Foxite firmament. In the coalition, Lord John Townshend went to the Board of Admiralty, Lord John Cavendish was Chancellor of the Exchequer, Edmund Burke was Paymaster of the Forces, the playwright Richard Brinsley Sheridan, elected to parliament three years earlier, was Secretary to the Treasury. Richard Fitzpatrick, a wit, a dandy, and Fox's old friend as well as a relative by marriage, was Secretary at War, while the scholarly and serious Frederick, Earl of Carlisle became Lord Privy Seal. Outside the Cabinet, but still in the inner circle, was the young Robert Adair, who was joined to Fox by blood and like him was the child of a runaway and scandalous marriage. Unmissable, if sometimes unwelcome, was George, the dissolute Prince of Wales. The Prince of Wales was bound to

Fox by a common hatred of his father the King and a mutual love of gambling, drunken conviviality and women.

Like Foxite attitudes, the Foxite alliance was temperamental and social as well as political. Fox and Burke may have had little in common – though they sometimes walked arm-in-arm through St James's to the House of Commons – but many of the others frequently met outside parliament. During the day in the racing season they often met at Newmarket. In the evening they congregated in the green-rooms and boxes of the Haymarket or Drury Lane and as the night wore on, they fleeced one another across the baize tables of Brooks's club in St James's Street. As drunken night gave way to bleary morning, conversation and cards continued in the town houses of Fox's followers – at Carlton House, where the Prince of Wales was already indulging in the taste for interior magnificence that would reach its apogee in the brilliantly eccentric pavilion in Brighton; at the Treasury; at Devonshire House and Cavendish Square, where Georgiana, Duchess of Devonshire, and her sister Harriet, Lady Duncannon were both hostesses and members of the coterie. In these grand drawing rooms the Foxites were joined by a host of hangers-on and entertained by sympathetic actresses and wits. Cards, phrases, sexual and political favours were all traded in an atmosphere that was frenzied and often self-regarding.

Despite its air of louche and drunken modishness, the group was seriously committed to the practice and appreciation of the arts. At the Treasury, the diminutive Lord John Cavendish specialised in recitation of verse. Fitzpatrick was a famous hand at light satire, and his 'Dorinda, a Town Eclogue' was widely circulated as a flawless example of the genre. Lord Carlisle amassed a fine picture collection and wrote tragedies and poems, the Duchess of Devonshire produced music and verses. Fox himself said poetry was 'the best thing after all' and read widely in French, Italian, Greek and Latin. But his reverence for literature obstructed his own efforts; his *History of the Early Part of the Reign of James II, with an Introductory Chapter* was as turgid as its title. Lengthily researched and frequently rewritten, it was sadly acknowledged to be a literary failure.

Lord Edward arrived home to find his brother Henry already a Foxite devotee, living, as their aunt put it, 'vastly at Devonshire House and at the Treasury'. Henry was soon accompanied by Lord Edward, who shadowed Fox at assemblies and happily mingled among the drawing-room crowd when his new idol came to supper at Harley Street. But although Lord Edward became, as his aunt put it a year later, 'a thorough Foxite', he was temperamentally out of sympathy with the mixture of seriousness and expediency that necessarily characterised the world of professional politics. As a young man Lord Edward was not a sophisticated politician. He did not consider that political standpoints were debatable and he thought of ideas not as autonomous constructions with their own realm and rules but as instigators and forerunners of action. Moreover, the brilliant sallies and showy speeches of the Foxites, in which matter and wit were effortlessly played off against one another, were beyond him. He listened and admired, but was unable to reproduce their characteristic mix of substance and satire. His approach to politics was direct and simple. He said of being in command of men, 'No person of feeling and justice can require from others what he won't do himself'; fatally, his attitude to politics was the same.

Lord Edward's understanding of literature was similarly straightforward and emotional. Neither a game nor an object of study, literature was for him, as it had been for his mother, a key to the human heart and a vehicle for understanding behaviour. Political pamphlets, the poetry and prose of Milton, the tracts and novels of Rousseau and Voltaire: for him they were not models of style but clarion calls for action, just as parliament should be not a theatre for wit but a site of change.

Impressed though he was by the glittering Foxite world, Lord Edward could see his future only in the practical business of soldiering. In the time left over from the family and fast living, he tried to use his government contacts to get himself a better commission. Now that Fox was in power he had high hopes of success. But while he often agreed to use his office to procure sinecures for his family and followers, Fox had no interest in the distribution of patronage. Lord Edward's aunt Sarah, who in his absence had married an impecunious and unsuccessful soldier, George Napier, complained that Fox would 'never serve his *friends effectually*, as he has not the *faculty of obtaining favours*, and is vastly *too* complaisant to other Ministers'. She was right: Fox did nothing for Lord Edward's military prospects. But in the summer of 1783, and in the next few years, he did give his cousin a political education and a set of political beliefs. From the time he was nineteen, Lord Edward became consistently interested in questions of political reform.

Before the impact of the American war was fully felt, and before the French Revolution, hopes of reform were pinned on improvements to the constitution, that vague agglomeration of rights and duties supposed to have been laid down in the Magna Carta, but more pertinently, in the Bill of Rights that accompanied the Glorious Revolution of 1688. Very few people in the 1780s believed that the constitution should be dismantled. The question was rather how quickly it could be revived and improved. When William Ogilvie suggested that reform could be gradual and cumulative, Lord Edward responded impatiently: 'I do not think we have (as you say) been improving in our Constitution. On the contrary, I think we have been losing; or, at least, the falling off is greater than the improvement. I think our Constitution may be compared to a young person, who though improved in his outward appearance, is grown worse in his heart; and in fact, has only learnt the art of hiding his corruption.' In 1783 Lord Edward looked to parliament, in both London and

Dublin, to make the improvements that many outside parliament were demanding. Believing that man was essentially good and that institutions and laws that had corrupted that goodness should be reformed, Lord Edward wanted to mend the heart of the constitution so that it could mirror the goodness of man and allow it to flourish. He passionately wished, at this stage, to renovate the constitution and had no thoughts of dismembering or killing it off.

Instead of staying at Fox's feet slowly learning the craft of British politics and looking forward to a political career in England as he might have done, Lord Edward turned his thoughts to Ireland. Although when he wrote about 'our constitution' he referred to the one in operation at Westminster, he was beginning to think more and more of the curiously symbiotic relationship it enjoyed with the supposedly independent constitution of Ireland. Perhaps encouraged by the Foxites, who had for some time enjoyed good relations with the Irish opposition and who would welcome close friends there now that they were in government, Lord Edward decided to begin his life as a politician in Ireland and allowed or asked his brother to put him up as a candidate for the borough of Athy in the forthcoming election. Besides, now that he was on half pay, he needed money. When he was twenty-one he would come into possession of his estate in County Kildare, whose rents would bring him eight hundred pounds a year. The Duke of Leinster was urging him to sell the estate, but Lord Edward was uncharacteristically cautious, knowing that he was extravagant, telling Ogilvie, 'if I were to have so much a year for it, I think I should get on more prudently'. Now that he was receiving so little from the army and was immersed in London pleasures he also needed to decide the fate of his Kilrush estate.

A few weeks before the election Lord Edward returned to Ireland and to Carton, to the places and people of his earliest childhood. In the years that he had been away some of the laws that had most hindered Catholics and Dissenters from owning land and advancing in the professions had been repealed. Lord Edward, brimming with confidence after his American adventures, came with high hopes that Foxite liberty could quickly be spread throughout the country. But coming home to Dublin, to Carton and to Ascendancy life was an unexpected and unpleasant shock. It confirmed to him in an immediate and practical way that Ireland was indeed in need of radical reform.

Lord Edward was patriotic about his homeland, but linked it primarily with family happiness. Ireland meant first Frescati and his childhood, his mother and her flowers, and second a land, its people and its soil. When he expressed a love for Ireland, he meant the whole country, an imagined land that existed in the mind and on the page rather than anything he found when he got back to Dublin drawing rooms. For the fervent Ascendancy patriots demanding freedoms for Ireland did not include the Catholic population in their definition of the Irish nation. Their patriotism, like their sense of permanence and their hold on wealth, was inherently unstable and liable to challenge, because it excluded so many. Ascendancy braggadocio and political power coexisted with insecurity.

Protestant anxiety had thrown up, as its visible manifestation, the great country house; bricks and mortar against the green beyond. The expense of building these symbols of permanence was often ruinous. Familial destruction and the spoliation of family finances often came not from outside the walls but from the walls themselves. As if in acknowledgement of this absurdity, life in the great house was often almost surrealistically grand, a kind of self-parody in which extravagance energetically signalled to the bankruptcy just round the corner.

When Lord Edward arrived at Carton House in the summer of 1783, he found himself at the epicentre of this rickety splendour. The Duke of Leinster's sense of Irishness and his claim to his land were much more secure than those of most of his fellow Protestants, but his behaviour was no different. Indeed, as Ireland's 'Premier Peer', he had almost a duty to display to the hilt the most flagrant grandeur of which the Ascendancy was capable. The first Duke of Leinster had spent a small fortune on improvements to Carton and its park and left his son vast debts to show for them. But he had not left William Carton itself, which was handed over to the Duchess for her lifetime. The new Duke had to have the ruinous pile – it represented him. So he paid his mother a huge sum for her life interest and his indebtedness grew with his grandeur.

In this way William Fitzgerald started his ducal life massively in debt. Even he, once derisively dismissed by his parents as 'without parts', realised that finding a wealthy wife was imperative. In Paris, in June 1775, he met Emilia St George, who was short, poorly educated, prone to nervous upset but undeniably rich. 'I like her manner much,' the Duke told his mother, adding, 'and by what I hear she has a charming temper. She is very quiet and don't seem riotously disposed. In short, if her fortune is what they say, I think it is very likely to take place.' The Duke had little experience of courtship (although plenty of experience of courtesans), and found this pavane between the Leinster title and the St George money excruciating, writing to his mother, 'you know I told you I should be the most awkward of lovers, and [as] she is rather shy, it makes it more distressing', and adding, 'two colder lovers never was seen'. By the end of the year though, they were married and a few years later he was able to dispose of her property and reduce his debt by sixty-five thousand pounds.

Relatives struggled to find merits in the Duchess. Louisa Conolly wrote, 'I am sure there is a great deal in her character which time will discover, which her extreme diffidence hides,' while Sarah Napier added hopefully five years into the marriage, 'I hear the little Duchess of Leinster improves every day'. But the Duke made up for their deficiency of praise, telling his mother with typically unselfconscious egocentricity, 'she seems very inclined to like the country, but I must say her chief study is to be pleased with everything I like . . . I shall be brief in saying when I proposed for her, I thought I was doing a prudent thing in point of *circumstance*, and that I should be very happy, but did not know her good qualities, which have surpassed my imagination.'

Conscious of being 'très médiocre', as his mother said, and fearful of those more able than himself, the second Duke became both pompous and extravagant, dull and magnificent. Life at Carton became grander and more silly. 'Everything seems to go on in great state here,' a visitor to Carton noted a couple of years after the Duke's marriage. 'The Duchess appeared in a sack and hoop and diamonds in the afternoon; . . . quantities of plate, etc . . . and there are servants without end . . . The ladies sit and work and the gentlemen lollop about and go to sleep – at least the Duke does, for he snored so loud the other night that we all got into a great fit of laughing and waked him.' Another guest mentioned 'French horns playing at breakfast and dinner', adding 'the house is crowded, a thousand comes and goes. We breakfast between ten and eleven . . . We have an immense table – chocolate, honey, hot bread, cold bread, brown bread, white bread, green bread and all coloured breads and cakes.'

Stuffed and sleepy, guests were released from this boredom to cavort round the park. Louisa Conolly described with astonishment a party in the summer of 1784 when Lord Edward, his brother Henry and the famously bibulous Lord Lieutenant, Lord Rutland, were among the two dozen guests. 'The Duke of Leinster gave . . . a cold dinner at the cottage, and they were to drive about Carton first . . . Charlotte [Fitzgerald] says, that to be sure they might have it *to say*, they drove about Carton Park but the deuce a bit did any one of them look at the place, and the whole employment of the Ladies was playing the Gentlemen tricks, pulling their pocket handkerchiefs out of their pockets, pushing them off their Seats and in short romping like so many school Masters and Misses.' The day ended with 'a riot in the dining room, where the Gentlemen had revenged their own quarrels and the Duke among others had thrown a glass of wine in the Dss's face, which it was also reported made her Grace very cross. But then it began to rain, and the fun was to go in a boat, in the dark with the Gentlemen. About ten o'clock they all came in dripping wet and dried themselves as well as they could, the Gentlemen taking off their shoes and socks, the Ladies their cravats, and drying their petticoats all in the same room. This operation over, they all got up and danced and stayed till three o'clock in the morning with all the Gentlemen . . . completely drunk.'

A year earlier Lord Edward found Carton empty of guests. Life revolved around the family, country pursuits and the rituals of sociability which demanded attendance at meals and an acceptance of uncongenial company. Lord Edward derisively compared the endless alternation between food and sport to the domesticity and fox hunting that delighted 'Mr B', the hero of Samuel Richardson's novel *Pamela*, complaining in a letter to his mother, 'I have made fifty attempts to write to you, but have as often failed for want of subject. Really a man must be a clever fellow who, after being a week at Carton, and seeing nobody but Mr and Mrs B, can write a letter. If you insist on letters, I must write you an account of my American campaigns over again, as that is the only thing I can remember. I am just now interrupted by the horrid parson; and he can find nothing to do but sit by my elbow.' He missed the excitement of war, complained that he found all 'home life very insipid' and pleaded with her to banish his ennui. 'I wish you would come over for literally Ireland without you is very disagreeable. I never felt it more so than today, which is the day two years ago I was wounded, and when I compare the two days,

I literally think I was much happier then than I am now, for I did not feel that vacancy in my mind.'

Lord Edward tried and failed to enjoy his brother's company. His charm and restlessness were a world away from William's anxious pomposity. Fourteen years divided them; years in which Lord Edward had had all the advantage of his mother's happiness at Black Rock and Aubigny, while William had had to live with his parents' grief at the death of his elder brother and shock at finding himself heir to huge debts and family responsibilities. The Duke was conscious of being a disappointment, Lord Edward only of being a general favourite. Neither had been able to cross the gulf between them. William had tried, by offering to act as guardian for Lord Edward's estate when he went to America. Although Lord Edward had agreed, he did so reluctantly, complaining to William Ogilvie that the Duke had 'no turn for business' and saying, 'I cannot be upon the same open footing with him as I am with you, although my brother'.

As soon as he decently could, Edward left the stultifying magnificence of Carton, with its echoes of his father, for Dublin and his initiation into politics. Before his election on 26 August, he tried half-heartedly to revive his knowledge of the legal framework of government by dipping in and out of Sir William Blackstone's *Commentaries on the Laws of England* which for twenty years had been the standard, forbidding textbook of aspirant politicians and student lawyers. But try as he might he could not resist the lure of saucier reading. Blackstone's learning was no match for Rousseau's spellbinding and newly published *Confessions*. 'I [have] *relevé* Blackstone's *Commentaries* with *Les Confessions de Rousseau*,' he wrote to his mother from Merrion Street in Dublin, where he was lodging with his brother Charles. 'I began them this morning; they are charming and I like Rousseau at Lambercier's full as well as in any other parts of his works. I have not as yet gone further in the *Confessions*.

I hope it goes on as well as it begins. I assure you, dearest Mother, nothing but a letter to you could make me leave it; I am afraid Blackstone will not go on the better for it. I know Mr O. will abuse me.'

When he read the *Confessions*, Lord Edward passed over the fact of Rousseau's fatherlessness, which seemed to him unremarkable. Instead he dwelt on his motherlessness. Even now that he was nearly twenty, Lord Edward never stopped assuring his mother of his love, telling her everything, and insisting that she was the most important person in his life. The remarkably candid *Confessions* brought out his most intense filial devotion. 'Dearest Mother,' he burst out after starting them, 'what would I give that Jean-Jacques had had a mother such as you are to me! What a happiness it would have been to him to have [had] such a heart to open himself to! By a few *peeps* into the second volume, I see he wants such a person; for *entre nous*, your best *male* friend will not do. One is afraid to open all one's weakness to a man. Let him be ever so closely united to you, one is afraid of his sense or of his advice, and I own I do not perfectly under-stand friendship with a woman without *un petit brin d'amour*, or *jealousy*, which I often think is one of the pas-sions attending love, and very often the first to discover it.'

Although Lord Edward was now regarded as a man and was well versed in the rules of polite courtship, the ways of courtesans and the customs of brothels from Cork to Charleston, the Duchess of Leinster kept her unique place in his heart, and he happily allowed her to keep it. To some extent this was true of all her younger sons. Robert, Henry and Edward, she told her daughter Lucy in 1794, 'have shown me on all occasions how much they prefer being with me than anything else'. But Edward was special; he loved her best and she loved him best. 'I do not pretend to say that Dearest angel Edward is not the first object,' she explained needlessly to Lucy, adding, 'you have all been used to allow me that indulgence of partiality to Him, and none of you, I believe, blame me for it, or see my excessive attachment to that Dear Angel with a jealous eye.' The Duchess demanded primacy without a scruple; Lord Edward ceded it without a qualm. Nothing clouded his devotion except the thought of her eventual death. 'You are the person I commit my most secret thoughts to,' he told her in the loneliness of his return to Ireland in 1783. 'I am not half so merry as I should be if you were here,' he confirmed four years later. 'I get tired of everything and want to have you to go and talk to. You are, after all, what I love best in the world. I always return to you and find it is the only love I do not deceive myself in. I love you much more than I think I do – but I will not give way to such thoughts, for it always makes me grave. I really made myself miserable for two days since I left you, by this sort of reflection; and in thinking over with myself what misfortunes I *could* bear, I found there was one I *could not*!'

The bibulous formality of his election over, Lord Edward went down to Frescati, where the spirit of his mother reigned supreme. In the decade since the family's departure for France, the house had lost its school-room look. Lord Edward's aunts Louisa and Sarah had overseen the building of a new block of kitchens, a scullery, beer cellar, coal-holes and a dairy. The house had been transformed inside, with new servants' quarters in the basement, a grand drawing room twenty-four feet square and a book room that looked out on to the garden, a showy round room, a dining room and two large loosely connected suites of bedrooms and dressing rooms. The simplicity of the school-room decoration had been replaced by marble and stucco, carving and gilt. Italian fireplaces and acres of French damask and silk completed the furnishing.

The garden, though, was much the same as the family had left it, thickened by years of growth but with its planting intact. The flower garden, started nearly fifteen years earlier, was now densely packed with shrubs, borders and trees. In the spring, the white and purple of lilacs mixed with the pink and yellow of early roses. Beneath them the white bells of lily of the valley nestled among its dark shiny foliage. There were creamy primroses with soft furry leaves, and common polyanthus added splashes of scarlet and yellow. All through summer, carnations and roses bloomed, their bright flowers set against banks of Portuguese laurels that flourished well in the damp acidic soils. Beyond the flower beds and shrubbery were clumps of trees, the orchard, a braided, rippling stream and the hay-meadow where the Fitzgerald children had worked through summer evenings in their smocks. At the end of vistas, over the inconvenience of the Bray road, the lapping sea glittered, and away across the bay loomed the dark lump of Howth Rock.

Whenever he went to Frescati, Lord Edward renewed his love for his mother. All its happy associations centred on her and they became intertwined in his memories and his thoughts. 'It is time for me to go to Frescati,' he told her in 1787. 'Why are you not there, dearest of mothers? But it feels a little like seeing you too, to go there.' When she was not there the garden at Frescati stood in for her and he could paint a delicate picture of her in its sun-lit spaces. 'You cannot think how I feel to want you here. I dined and slept at Frescati the other night, Ogilvie and I tête-à-tête. We talked a great deal of you. Though the place makes me melancholy, yet it gives one pleasant feels. To be sure, the going to bed without wishing you good night, the coming down in the morning, and not seeing you, the sauntering about in the fine sunshine, looking at your flowers and shrubs without you to lean upon one, was all very bad indeed.'

With thoughts of his mother came memories of childhood and innocence; Frescati was not only a paradise, it seemed like Paradise itself. The Duchess of Leinster had first made explicit this connection, comparing Frescati to Eden and Ogilvie and herself to Adam and Eve. Writing from Aubigny to Ogilvie when he was at Frescati in 1777, she had declared, 'it is a dear place and I follow you my love thro' every part of it but more particularly my love through those parts where we have spent many hours in *conversation sweet*, as Milton says.' Lord Edward's feelings for Frescati already echoed his mother's, but his temperamental rebelliousness also picked up the republican overtones of Milton's garden, where Adam and Eve, the originals of every man and woman, had no need for any authority to mediate between themselves and God. Frescati already stood in his mind for his mother and Ogilvie as surely as Carton did for his father, and represented feeling and freedom, the exuberance of novelty and change against a mausoleum of tradition and decay.

As always with Lord Edward's feelings, the intensely personal and the political were merged. It was impossible for him to separate his feelings for his childhood home from his wishes for the whole world. Frescati, his private Eden, would very soon stand for the world he wanted to create. Moreover, because ideas and actions were fused in his mind, he would become a gardener himself. So the very idea of the garden, as well as the practical activity of gardening, became for him both a way of summoning his mother's spirit in lonely times and a political act, an attempt to create with soil, seeds and labour a miniature Eden and a place of innocence and purity. Every time Lord Edward dug a garden – and he was to dig gardens in the most dangerous and inhospitable circumstances and places – he was at once re-creating Frescati and creating anew man's first, uncorrupted home.

But in the autumn of 1783, Lord Edward could only rejuvenate himself at Frescati for a few days. The parliamentary session opened in October, and he had to move back to Dublin to attend it. Lord Edward made the short walk from Merrion Street to the splendid Parliament House on College Green full of hopes for a thorough reform of the Irish constitution and universal religious emancipation. Coming from the Foxite drawing rooms of London, Lord Edward believed that his enthusiasm for emancipation and constitutional overhaul would be widely shared by discontented politicans in Dublin.

At first sight his optimism looked justified. If few Irish politicians placed much store by Rousseau, many had imbibed the language of the radical pamphleteer Tom Paine. Paine's *Common Sense*, the brilliant and inflammatory tract published in 1776, which provided much of the intellectual justification for American independence, had been widely circulated in Ireland, reprinted in the influential opposition newspaper *The Freeman's Journal*, and seized on by politicians who demanded complete legislative independence from Westminster.

Common Sense began with a scurrilous attack not only on the Hanoverian Crown, but on the institution of monarchy itself, which Paine claimed was inherently despotic, practically absurd, and unnecessary for the orderly functioning of civil society. Citizens themselves, Paine asserted, had every right to establish a state and elect representatives to an institution which could express their will and govern on their behalf. There was nothing in law or custom to prevent the declaration of a sovereign, independent America.

Parts of this argument fell on receptive ears in Ireland, whose 'Patriot' politicians were eager to seize on any precedent that would shore up their demands for legislative freedom. When Paine ridiculed American dependence on British law, which led to 'three millions of people flocking to the American shore every time a vessel arrives from England, to know what portion of liberty they shall enjoy', the Irish 'Patriots' were happy to endorse him.

But Lord Edward was mistaken if he thought that Irish politicians would endorse the whole of Paine's argument, or indeed those of Christopher Wyvill, another fashionable radical who had been touring the country. Wyvill had been airing his reform plans in the Irish press, and Lord Edward had been impressed by his strategy of using local associations of voters to press for constitutional reform. But within the confines of Ascendancy politics anything beyond legislative independence for Ireland, even anything as moderate as Wyvill's plan for the abolition of boroughs in the gift of local aristocrats, was likely to run to grief in the quicksands of religious differences and the insecurities of a colonial class dependent on Westminster for its power and part of its identity. Patriot politicians in Dublin, seeking legislative independence, had no particular interest in reforming the electoral system and even less in separating the Irish government from that in Westminster. That would mean repatriating a Lord Lieutenant, who, ensconced in Dublin Castle with his hands on the purse-strings of hundreds of lucrative offices, was the prime symbol and practical core of Ascendancy power. Even outside the political class demands for reforms were not necessarily universalist. Dissenters, especially those in the northern counties, may have demanded religious emancipation as a right, but they did not all want religious freedom and freedom to hold office extended to the majority Catholic population.

Although he did not immediately realise it, by the time Lord Edward joined the Irish parliament much of its zeal for reform had been sated. For several years before his election, groups of Volunteers – local independent militias whose great conventions were political jamborees, with fluttering banners, piping bands and addresses by orators – had been demanding reform and setting the pace for change. Especially hated were Poynings' Law, the fifteenth-century Act which stipulated that Irish parliamentary business had to be approved by the English government, and the Declaratory Act of 1720. In an important symbolic victory for the Irish opposition, both were repealed in 1782. After this the fire of reform burned low. Debates centred on vexed questions of trade and tariffs rather than on Catholic emancipation and reform of the franchise, as Lord Edward had hoped. The contrast was stark. While Irish opposition politicians were taken up with local questions of trade and patronage, Lord Edward, steeped in the universalist language of Rousseau and Paine, always interpreted events in terms of rights. Political intrigue did not interest him and he had neither the canny patience nor the political savvy to want to manipulate local grievances for larger ends. 'I own . . . I like *not* to be Lord Edward Fitzgerald, "the County of Kildare member, etc, etc" – to be bored with "this one is your brother's friend" – "that man voted against him", etc,' he told his mother. Very soon his hopes for a thorough reform of the constitution and universal religious emancipation began to fade, and his nascent political career was stunted by a refusal to abandon idealism and radicalism for the whisperings, caballing and rhetorical struggles of Dublin's political class.

In the summer of 1784, discouraged by the backslidings of his former idols in the Irish parliament, Lord Edward turned again to Charles James Fox in England, still seeing in him a beacon of liberty and tolerance. But in England, too, political reform was about to come to a disastrous end. Fox had had a calamitous time in government, which culminated at the end of 1783 in the failure of his Bill to overhaul the East India Company. With the Bill's defeat, the King took the opportunity to dismiss the Fox-North coalition and bring in Fox's rival, the twenty-four-year-old William Pitt. Although Fox and his supporters still had a majority in the Commons, Pitt was determined to consolidate his power by calling a General Election that could at once act as a referendum on his unpopular predecessors and put most of them out of parliament. By the beginning of March scores of Fox's allies had defected to Pitt, leaving the opposition with a majority of only seven and on 24 March Pitt managed to force the dissolution of parliament.

In the ensuing General Election 'Fox's Martyrs', as his followers came to be called, were decimated. Lord John Cavendish, the former Chancellor, was beaten at York. Thomas Coke, who prominently displayed a bust of Fox in his mansion in Norfolk, and Sir Charles Bunbury, Sarah Napier's first husband, were both thrown out by their constituents. The greatest contest – perhaps the most famous election of the eighteenth century – was Fox's own in the London Borough of Westminster. Westminster returned two MPs; it had a large electoral roll of almost twenty thousand and a wide franchise which included almost all the local freeholders, including the small tradesmen. Votes could be bought but the results were open and electors had to be canvassed and cosseted. Voting took place over forty days, which turned the election into a carnival and allowed the voters to hold out for more money and drinks, more speeches and favours.

Fox himself was the star of this jamboree. Despite his weight he was still nimble and athletic; stomach before him and friends beside him, he led his supporters in a daily procession through the borough. Banners proclaimed 'Fox for ever' or 'Fox and Liberty'. The Duchess of Devonshire, her sister Lady Duncannon, Fox's childhood acquaintance Mrs Crew, his mistress the courtesan Elizabeth Armistead and several famous actresses of the day delighted the press and print-makers by canvassing for him, making overt the influence women had always exercised in politics. Even the Prince of Wales joined the throng, wearing a cockade in his hat of a fox-tail entwined with senatorial laurel leaves. The atmosphere was burlesque and heated; crowds assembled each night in the piazza of Covent Garden to hear speeches. There were mock funerals (of opponents), mock elections (of friends), several riots and the death of an officer of the peace. Fox was eventually declared elected, second behind Admiral Hood, whose status as a national hero ensured that he topped the poll.

Among Fox's supporters who came to watch the spectacle and to canvass for him were Lord Edward Fitzgerald and Elizabeth Sheridan. The former was inconspicuous in his cousin's entourage. The latter was noticed by the press, dubbed 'the chairwoman of a petticoat-committee', but exempted from the ribaldry and satire that were directed at the Duchess of Devonshire and her sister. Mrs Sheridan escaped censure partly because she was more self-contained and retiring than her fellow female politicians, and partly because before her marriage to the playwright Richard Brinsley Sheridan she had been Miss Linley, the most famous female singer in the country, a celebrity who could earn hundreds of pounds a performance. Elizabeth Sheridan was thirty years old, her face and her voice beautiful. But she had not sung in public for many years. After their runaway marriage in 1772, Sheridan had refused to allow his young wife to sing again for money, insisting that his writing would keep them and that she should live as a gentlewoman.

Unlike almost all Fox's friends and acquaintances, Elizabeth seemed to be incorruptible, a woman who enjoyed her talismanic status and accepted compliments but not lovers. Although she was to play an important role in Lord Edward's life, it is unlikely that Elizabeth noticed him much when they first met in 1784. He was only twenty-one. He was good looking, but not nearly as handsome as his brother Henry, whose beauty helped to secure him a very rich wife. He was amusing, had a talent for 'fun' and a way with words, but made no impression in a circle where verbosity and wit ran amok. He was thoughtful and constantly kept those he loved in mind, but his kindness paled before Fox's mesmerising geniality. In 1784 Fitzgerald was happy to be a minor supplicant before the Foxite throne, and Elizabeth Sheridan, even if she noticed his thick hair and his luminous eyes, did not pick him out of the crowd.

When all the Westminster victory celebrations were over, when the bunting had come down in Carlton House and the flood of prints and satirical verse had dried up, Pitt astonished Fox and his supporters by calling a recount of the votes. Fox's winning margin over an erstwhile follower, Sir Cecil Wray, was only thirty-six votes. None the less, the election had not broken the elastic rules of the day, and Pitt's reaction was regarded even within his own House of Commons as a personal vendetta. Henceforth, the differences between the Foxites and Pittites were regarded and played out as a struggle in which political attitudes were tied ever more closely to ways of living, behaving and appearing. Set against Fox's openness and libertarian tolerance – symbolised in cartoons by an undone waistcoat and arms flung wide – were Pitt's secretiveness and paranoia. Contrasted with Fox's financial and sexual profligacy were Pitt's primness and reputation for probity, despite the fact that Fox preferred virtual bankruptcy to a place on the government payroll, while Pitt shrank his debts by granting himself the office of Warden of the Cinque Ports, which guaranteed him a steady ten thousand pounds a year. Where Fox openly drank huge quantities of champagne and burgundy and grew fat with gormandising, Pitt was lean and spare, drinking himself to an early grave, in secret and alone. Fox promised much hope to the cause of reform; he squandered most of it in opposition and was careless of his public reputation. Pitt was careful and skilful with his public image and although in twenty-two years of power he brought forward few measures of genuine reform, he managed to convince his supporters and successors that he had served the cause with zeal and honour.

Despite winning the Westminster recount, Fox knew that Pitt had beaten him in 1784 and he foresaw that his exile on the opposition benches would be a long one. Lord Edward's aunt Sarah wrote on 8 September, 'he gives up all hopes of a change in Ministry and comforts himself with Mrs Armistead, and all he seems to lament is the want of £2,000 to buy the house at St Anne's Hill which he longs for.' Twenty years later, Fox was still not in power, although he had for some time been married to Mrs Armistead and the happy owner of St Anne's Hill. Temperamentally, he seemed to be suited to opposition; the squandering of wealth and talent, the disdain for titles, his marriage to a courtesan: all these were rejections of the status quo. 'I love a rebel,' he declared and his life would look like one long rebellion. But had he been a more careful and more patient politician, he could have brought all these qualities and the Foxite way of life to government, moulding Britain to the round curves of liberty rather than the straitjacket of Pittite austerity.

The election of 1784 bound Lord Edward anew to his feckless cousin's camp, but he did not stay long in England. Soon he was back in Ireland with his mother and Ogilvie, his siblings Gerald, Lucy and Sophia and his half sisters Cecilia and Mimi Ogilvie, and for the next two years he drifted with them between London, Dublin and continental spas. Most of the time they stayed at Frescati, and much later William Ogilvie recalled that in 1784 and 1785 Lord Edward 'was with us, indeed, wherever we went, and those were the happiest years of any of our lives.' Remembering it afterwards, Lord Edward wrote to his mother, 'I would give a great deal for a lounge at Frescati this morning,' adding that 'getting up between eleven and twelve, breakfasting in one's jacket *sans souci, se fichant du monde*, and totally careless and thoughtless of everything but the people one loves, is a very pleasant life, *il faut le dire.*'

They were happy years too for Tony Small. When Lord Edward went to Dublin in August 1783, he had left Tony in his mother's house in London. But after only a few weeks, Lord Edward summoned him to Dublin. 'I must have my black again, as I shall want him to take care of my horses,' he told his mother in September. From this time onwards Tony accompanied his master everywhere. In Dublin, where black people were much rarer than in London, he quickly became a signpost to his master's whereabouts. When people saw Tony walking through the wide streets or leading Lord Edward's horse Prudente, they knew his master could not be far away.

Black people came loaded with negative associations to

the shores of Europe and the houses of the nobility whom they served. But Lord Edward had no interest in hostile views of different peoples, preferring to see mankind as indivisible. He understood Tony in the framework offered by writers on innocently primitive peoples. Rousseau, Black Rock's presiding genius, showed him the way. Rousseau's *Discours sur l'origine et les fondements de l'inégalité*, published in 1754, offered the first developed model of a simpler and purer world than the one in which the writer and his reader lived. In it Rousseau suggested that modern men had much to learn from primitive man's natural piety and physical well-being. In *La nouvelle Héloïse*, Rousseau showed his modern hero learning that lesson. Saint-Preux travels to the South Seas to recover the innocence he loses when he falls disastrously in love with Julie, his pupil. British writers quickly followed Rousseau. The *Gentleman's Magazine* and the *Edinburgh Magazine* liked to stress the benevolence of primitive man and Laurence Sterne's *Sermons of Mr Yorick* (another Black Rock staple) emphasised that man is naturally good and compassionate.

In 1767 art came to life. Five years after the publication of *La nouvelle Héloïse*, Captain Wallis discovered Tahiti. Four years after that the French explorer de Bougainville published a romantic account of the Tahitian islanders. Supplemented by enthusiastic newspaper reports and a series of Diderot's imaginary 'dialogues' between de Bougainville and an islander, this fantasy established Tahitian society as a model of purity. The island itself became both Eden and Utopia, the lost world and the world hoped for. De Bougainville's account, which extolled the untouched purity of Tahitian life and at the same time assimilated it into France and French ways of thinking, was read to the Black Rock children as soon as it appeared in 1771. The story made a strong impression on the eight-year-old Edward, as Louisa Conolly told her sister Sarah. 'I must tell you that Eddy is so diverted with the idea of the women painting their posteriors black in this new discovered island, that he wants to paint his sisters, and means to catch them in their sleep.'

On his return to France de Bougainville brought a Tahitian called Aouteouvou along with his geological and botanical specimens. Aouteouvou was the first of several South Sea islanders to do the rounds of Europe's drawing rooms. Sailing in soon after him came Omai, collected by Captain Cook from Tahiti. Pacific islanders were by no means the first exotic or primitive visitors to European capitals. Eskimos were shipped to the court of Henry VII; Pocahontas curtsied at the throne of James II; so many North American Indians had put on their feathers and war paint in the parlours of Paris and London that they had gone out of fashion.

When Omai arrived in London in 1774 he was extravagantly praised for his grace and his natural reason, even as his simplicity was fast absorbed into the modern, commercial world. A selection of his phrases enriched a bookseller, he inspired a successful pantomime at Covent Garden, he accepted an allowance from the monarch and he was interviewed by James Boswell. Before he left to go home in 1776, Omai was painted by Joshua Reynolds.

As if to emphasise Omai's prelapsarian purity Reynolds painted him barefooted in the verdant landscape of an imagined Tahiti. Behind his right shoulder feathery palm fronds wave, and in the distance is the blue cone of a volcano. Omai himself, facing the viewers but gazing to one side of them, is dressed in a belted cream robe, loose cloak and turban. This costume gives him an exotic magisterial dignity, while his solitariness in a wild landscape, without fellows or the personal possessions that portrait sitters usually stood among, or held, makes him seem representative rather than individual, a noble primitive indeed.

Lord Edward knew that Tony was not Omai. Omai was a prince from the South Seas, Tony a freed Negro slave from

America, and Africa before that. Omai had conversed with the King and graced the drawing rooms of St James's; Tony brushed Lord Edward's horses' dusty coats and slept in the straw beside them. But still, Lord Edward resolutely saw Tony as a personification of virtue, and sometime in the lazy years of the 1780s, he decided to have Tony painted, to create a visual version of him that would show to the world his natural grandeur as well as his figure and face.

Following his sense of Tony as a natural man Lord Edward did not choose a portrait painter to paint his picture. He selected an Irish landscape artist, Thomas Roberts. Roberts's brother had painted four landscapes for the second Duke of Leinster and his new bride between 1775 and 1777, so Lord Edward probably chose a painter whom he knew and liked. Roberts had a difficult brief. He had somehow to reconcile his subject's humdrum role with his exalted image. The portrait that came out of his studio was a curious hybrid, part heroic, part humble; it had a strained and almost amateurish air. Yet at the same time it was unique; there was no other painting of a black man like it.

Tony stands in the middle of his picture with his weight on one long leg, leaning slightly towards a nervous-looking pony that he holds by the bridle. At his left one of the poodles that ran around Carton and Castletown crouches playfully, balancing the pony and making the picture seem at first sight a portrait of three of Lord Edward's favourite playthings.

But Tony is not painted like a servant. There is nothing humble or servile about him. He seems huge, towering above the horse and suggesting that his name, Small, was a humorous soubriquet. Lord Edward was five feet seven inches tall, a man of middle height. If this portrait is more than whimsy, Tony must have stood head and shoulders above him, conspicuous by height as well as colour on Dublin's streets, protector as well as Samaritan. His expression and demeanour are similarly lofty. A large, elegant hand loosely holds the pony's bridle while he gazes out of the picture beyond us. With his heavily hooded eyes and serious air, Tony radiates a melancholy dignity, an image of withdrawn sobriety rather than the playful innocence that was thought to be characteristic of man in his natural state.

Tony's clothes, though, are exotic and fanciful. He wears loose pantaloons, a jacket bordered with ermine and tied with a sash. A cloak falls from his shoulders, a ring encircles one ear and his feet rest in golden slippers. Although the whole outfit gestures to the long-outmoded fashion for all things Turkish, it is an entirely imaginary costume that conjures up associations of Renaissance magi, of the exotic East rather than the fetid slave plantations of the American South.

Tony stands in this costume outside the gates of a grand house – not Carton, which did not have a wall rusticated in this way, but any grand house. Behind and beyond him is the Irish countryside, more gates, woodland and a blue mountain escarpment in the distance. Walls and gates would be easily recognised by the painting's viewers. They stood for power and possession and the boundary between rich and poor. In Ireland they also hinted at the whole country-house world, the Ascendancy culture that Lord Edward had already begun to reject. Tony is outside all that, in nature.

Yet Tony is a mysterious as well as recognisable type. His costume is exotic and Eastern, his manner grand and melancholy, his features sculpted towards an ideal with very little of the African in it. His hair is almost straight and his skin a rich umber tinged with olive, suggesting that he may have been a mulatto, in whose blood ran traces of his white owner. If this is Tony as he appeared to the world he was no ordinary Negro slave. If this was Tony as Lord Edward saw him he was indeed a lesson, a beautiful giant, dignified and remote, a picture of mankind as it ought to be.

Lord Edward did not yet need Tony for comfort or company. He spent the years from 1784 to 1787 moving restlessly between London and Black Rock, following his mother's whims, his desire for political excitement and the turns of his heart. He claimed he had a 'system' for the progress of romance; 'that of yielding to my inclinations where I am the only person that can feel the bad effects', but this system led to one-sided love affairs. In the autumn of 1783 he was briefly infatuated with a Miss Mathews, whom he described to his mother as 'the most beautiful creature you ever saw, a beautiful, *douce* and sensible countenance, and at the same time comical – two things I never could resist'.

But in the spring of 1786 he fell in love much more seriously with Lady Catherine Meade, an heiress and daughter of the first Earl of Clanwilliam. 'Sweetest Kate', 'pretty Kate', he called her, as if he were Shakespeare's victorious King Henry V rather than a younger son with only eight hundred pounds a year and few prospects of advancement in a peacetime army. Lord Edward sent Kate anonymous presents, persuading her brother to act as go-between. But he knew that without war to make him a hero or land to make him rich, his chances were slender. Only a defiant passion on her side could overcome these disadvantages. 'Her loving me is the only chance I have,' he wrote disconsolately to his mother in July 1786.

Kate's parents saw Lord Edward as anyone but an all-conquering warrior. When he went to her mother to ask if he could put his proposals he was briskly dismissed. Lady Clanwilliam suggested that he should leave the country for two years and renew his proposals when he returned, hoping perhaps that he would then have more stripes on his shoulder and more money in his pocket. Lord Edward agreed to go, as anxious as she was that he rise up the army hierarchy and, as he put it, lay 'a foundation for taking away the obstacles that now oppose me'.

Aiming both to obey Lady Clanwilliam and to re-enter active service with the army, Lord Edward travelled to

London that summer and tried to dissolve his disappointment in gambling and champagne. But he was still only twenty-three and had optimism enough to revel in his melancholia and to enjoy describing it to his mother. 'I get up in the morning hating everything – go out with an intention of calling on somebody – and then with the first person I meet go anywhere, and stay any time, without thinking the least what I am about or enjoying the least pressure. By this means, I have been constantly late for dinner wherever I have dined . . . From dinner somebody or other (quite indifferent to me who) carries me to wherever I am asked and there I stay till morning and come home to bed hating everything as much as when I got up and went out.'

His spirits improved a little when he went down to study gunpowder manufacture in the government munitions laboratory at Woolwich. Woolwich was in the charge of his uncle the Duke of Richmond who, with the demise of the Fox–North coalition, had resumed his old office of Master of the Ordnance and had responsibility for the supply of all military equipment. Lord Edward worked hard there, he told Ogilvie, but as he pulverised saltpetre or studied the workings of cannon, he reflected gloomily on his future and only found the present tolerable as a trial that would bring him Kate's hand when he had successfully endured it. 'I am sure you will feel for me when I tell you I really have not one happy moment or one pleasant thought or prospect that I do not find it immediately dampened. It is so different from what I used to feel when I enjoyed almost every moment in the day. I never have had, since I left Ireland, a moment when I could say *je suis heureux* or *je suis content*.'

In affairs of the heart, Lord Edward knew that Ogilvie, counselling reason, would not be on his side, especially if a disparity of fortune made his case hopeless. 'I hope, my dear Ogilvie,' he wrote with a show of sternness, 'you will not be ill-natured and hinder my Mother writing me everything about Kate . . . It is the only satisfaction I have, and you must allow I deserve it.' He begged the Duchess to keep his delicious misery alive. 'Pray do not let Ogilvie spoil you,' he demanded at the beginning of July. 'I am sure he will try, crying, "Nonsense fool! fool! all imagination! – by heavens! you will be the ruin of that boy". My dear Mother, if you mind him, and do not write me pleasant letters and say something of pretty Kate, I will not answer your letters, nor indeed write *any* to you.'

This rhetorical petulance was in vain. Lord Edward hated being apart from his family and used writing to transport himself to Ireland. His letters were crowded with questions about his siblings; their names brought them to mind and, he hoped, would elicit news of them that he could inhabit in his imagination, making a home of his barren Woolwich lodgings. 'Have you been to Carton since you returned?' he asked William Ogilvie at the end of June. 'How is William? I hope he got the long letter I wrote him. I am glad to hear dear Charles is so much better . . . What delightful weather you have had for Frescati! How my dearest Mother will have enjoyed it! . . . I do so long to see her. I feel constantly angry with myself for not feeling my absence from her more than anything else. At the same time, I know I love her more than anything in the world. I hope all her flowers and shrubs go on well.' It was not long before Lord Edward came to see partings and separations as results of a corrupted aristocratic way of life that forced all but the eldest son to part from those they loved best. Younger sons had to leave the family and follow professions, daughters were bargained away in marriage settlements, all to serve 'custom', as Lord Edward called it, rather than the happiness for which man was intended.

In his loneliness at Woolwich, where he kept company with soldiers and local prostitutes, Lord Edward turned to Tony for companionship. Tony had begun to be a mainstay in difficult times, offering Lord Edward the comfort that came with constancy. Tony's job, though, was changing; as well as looking after Lord Edward's horses he became his personal servant. He brought meals, attended Lord Edward in the house and accompanied him if he rode out. His devotion grew and the epithet 'faithful' stuck to him like part of his name. No longer 'my black', he was 'the faithful Tony' or simply 'Tony'.

At the end of June, Lord Edward and Tony left Woolwich and travelled down to Goodwood in Sussex to accompany the Duke of Richmond on a tour of Channel Island fortifications. Dreaming of Kate did not stop Lord Edward collecting a dose of venereal disease in London on the way. 'I am so ashamed of myself, I do not know what to do or what to say to you,' he confessed to Ogilvie from Portsmouth. 'I came here today and find I must return to London immediately. There is no mincing the matter, I must tell you I am very ill and must go and see my friend Mr Mann again. I only stayed two days in London. Was there ever so unlucky a dog?'

The inspection of the Channel Islands complete, Lord Edward stayed on at Goodwood to study mechanics. Three miles away, at Stoke, lived his second uncle, Lord George Lennox, and in the afternoon Lord Edward rode there to dine and enjoy what he called 'amusements and *Stoke idleness*'. As soon as he became an habitué of Stoke, Lord Edward's spirits rose and he cheerfully compared himself to le Huron, the guileless hero of Voltaire's novel *L'Ingénu*, brought up in a state of natural goodness by North American Indians. Returning to his world-weary native country, he is hopelessly distracted from his mathematical studies by a pretty young girl. Le Huron loves Mademoiselle de Saint-Yves; Lord Edward was captivated by Lord George Lennox's three daughters, particularly the youngest, twenty-one-year-old Georgiana.

Lord George Lennox was not intimate with his brother or sisters, who mistrusted his moodiness and believed that he was cruel to his wife. A career soldier who eventually

reached the rank of general, he was dissatisfied with his position of younger brother to the Duke of Richmond. By the
1780s, however, Lord George had something to plan for.
The Duke of Richmond, married for nearly thirty years, had
no heir, and Lord George's son Charles was in line for the
Richmond title, the family's estates and its grand houses in
Sussex and London. That in turn meant that Lord George's
three daughters would one day be no longer the children of
a younger son but the sisters of a Duke. The Lennox girls'
marriage prospects were transformed by this future.
Younger sons like Lord Edward, chatting the evenings away
at Stoke, were welcomed as impecunious relatives but
quickly shown the door if they hinted at any closer relationship. Edward's brother Charles had already been dismissed;
his own turn would soon come. For the moment though,
Georgiana took his mind off 'sweet Kate' so effectively that
she began to supplant her in letters home. 'I am glad sweetest Kate is grown fat,' he told his mother on 2 September, 'I
love her more than anything yet, though I have seen a great
deal of Georgiana. I own I am not in such bad spirits as I
was, particularly when I am with Georgiana, whom I certainly love better than any of her sisters. However, I can
safely say, I have not been *infidèle* to Kate – whenever I
thought of her, which I do very often, though not so constantly as usual. This entirely between you and me.'

Lord Edward did not stay in Sussex long, preferring to
move around and accumulate new sights and thoughts with
which to soothe his aching heart. First, in the autumn of
1786, he went with the whole family to Nice. Then, when
the parliamentary session opened in Dublin, he travelled
home with William Ogilvie. Buoyed up by the winter in
France, where he was always cheerful and where he had
found a mistress, Madame de Lévis, Lord Edward 'came
over so sanguine from England,' as he put it, that the failure
of his expectations of reform in Ireland hit him especially
hard. His uncle, Thomas Conolly, had 'behaved shabbily',

he told his mother, voting for a Riot Bill which would restrict rather than increase the liberty of Irish citizens. 'I have been greatly disappointed about politics,' he concluded. He was disappointed in love too; not only had Kate forgotten him, he was no longer much interested in her. While he tried to 'put on a good face', the cumulative reversals of the last year had sobered him and revealed a febrile, melancholy side to his nature that was the obverse of his usual good spirits, but just as all-consuming. 'Though I have been doing nothing but the common jog-trot things, yet I have been thinking of a great many others, both serious and trivial,' he told his mother in February 1787.

Dissatisfaction made him restless; as soon as the parliamentary session was over he left Ireland with William Ogilvie and was scarcely able to conceal his pleasure from his aunt Sarah Napier. 'Edward was consulting us how he should do to be sorry to part for he could not compose his face to proper sorrow towards brothers, sisters, aunts, cousins, loves, fancies and engagements of another nature, from which, if the truth be known he was glad to run away, *car*, my Lord *s'ennuie à la mort*,' she told the Duchess of Leinster.

After spending a few weeks with his mother and sisters in Nice, Lord Edward caught a boat across the northern Mediterranean and along the Iberian coast to Gibraltar. Gibraltar had come to Britain at the end of the wars against Louis XIV, and General O'Hara, under whom Lord Edward had served briefly on St Lucia, was in charge of the garrison there. Lord Edward made an immediate friend of General O'Hara, although he distinguished between O'Hara's private and public personae, characteristically searching for sincerity buried under rank. 'O'Hara and I walk the whole day, from five in the morning till eight or nine at night; he is pleasanter than ever, and enters into all one's ideas, fanciful as well as comical. We divert ourselves amazingly with all the people here; but this is when he is not "all over General", as he calls it.' But Lord Edward's 'serious' thoughts, his attempt to put himself in a new relationship towards the world, ran on. Standing at the summit of the Rock of Gibraltar, he felt fleetingly proud to be a British soldier, but humbled as a man by the proximity of fathomless oceans and an almost unknown continent stretching south beyond the Straits. 'The feeling of pride is then gone, and the little-ness of your own work in comparison with those of nature, makes you feel yourself as nothing.'

Lord Edward found in Gibraltar some of the elements of the Eden for which he was restlessly searching. What he noticed there were the things he always noticed, the officers' vegetable patches, where peas, string-beans, and French beans shot up in the rich soil and warm Mediterranean sun, and the local flower gardens surrounded with high hedges of gera-niums and planted with orange and cedar trees, roses, honey-suckles and Spanish broom. Scents of verbena, oleander and myrtle rose on the warm sea breeze and made him feel that Gibraltar 'will in time be a little paradise'. Inevitably, he dreamed of transporting his family there and setting them to work among the legumes. But in the end, he contented him-self with pocketing some seeds for his mother and in the heat of summer proceeding with Tony to Portugal.

Lord Edward and Tony travelled in a great arc through Portugal and Spain, beginning at Lisbon, going on to Cadiz, Granada and Madrid and then heading up towards the French border. They travelled simply with a muleteer to carry luggage. Tony continued to look after the horses, but was as much companion as servant now. In Lord Edward's letters Tony began to speak (although he could not write), becoming his master's voice of conscience and putting up arguments against extravagant thinking and spending. When they arrived in Madrid, Lord Edward was overcome with loneliness. Madrid had good connections to the north and he decided impulsively to take the post coach to the French border and then ride on to Barèges, the Pyrenean spa where his mother and family were idling away the winter. It was

Tony, he said, who persuaded him to take his own horse and go more slowly. 'I have been but three hours in Madrid,' he told his mother. 'I wanted to set off to you by post and should have been with you, in that case, in seven days. It was to cost me £40; but Tony remonstrated and insisted that it was very foolish when I might go for five guineas, and – in short, he prevailed.'

Travelling economically and slowly, Lord Edward and Tony met the Duchess's party at Barèges in the late summer and travelled with them to England, pausing only in Aubigny on the way and taking a detour to Paris with Lord Henry Fitzgerald to sample the fleshy delights of the Palais Royal. By the autumn they were all in Sussex, and Lord Edward stayed on there when the rest of the family left for Ireland, ostensibly working at mathematics but more often allowing the charms of his cousin Georgiana Lennox to overcome the lure of his studies. His first love, for Kate, had now faded away. At Stoke, with Georgiana Lennox, he allowed his second to flourish quickly in a heart already softened. Still the man of feeling and happy to let the romance run on, he was, by the spring of 1788, deeply in love, thinking of Georgiana as his future wife and able to describe her only in superlatives. 'I never can, I think, love anybody as I do her, for with her I can find no fault; I may admire and love other women, but none can come in competition with her. Dearest Mother, after yourself, I think she is the most perfect creature on earth.' Surrendering completely to his feelings, he declared them beyond control. 'There she is in my heart and there she must stay – *C'est plus fort que moi.*'

Convinced that he had found a perfection which almost rivalled his mother's, Lord Edward impulsively proposed to Georgiana in the spring of 1788, without warning and without asking permission as form dictated. Probably primed by her ambitious parents, and led to expect a glittering alliance with a wealthy man rather than a love match with a disor-

73

ganised romantic, Georgiana turned him down. She seemed little worried by the incident, as her sister reported to Sophia Fitzgerald: 'Georgiana is quite composed now, and only was miserable at the fear of all this having put a stop to the pleasant footing we had been on together, as, if it had been anybody we liked less, she would have treated it quite otherwise, and now she feels vex'd at its making any difference from the great regard she, as well as the rest of us have for dear Lord Edward.' But Lord Edward was predictably distraught, compounding the error of his forwardness by rushing out of the house without saying goodbye to his uncle and aunt.

Lord George Lennox followed up his daughter's refusal with a pompous note that managed to stay just the right side of politeness while making it plain that Lord Edward's direct approach to Georgiana was imprudent and his subsequent flight impolite. He began by saying he was sorry not to have said goodbye to his nephew, but went on, 'However, all things considered, we maybe have neither of us any reason to regret it, as it has saved an awkward adieu after the result of your conversation with my daughter, to whom I have on this occasion, as I always have with her sisters, left every matter of that sort to be determined by themselves. With respect, therefore, to the manner of your proposal, it was not so material to me from the perfect serenity I always feel in every part of my daughters' conduct and as to the propriety of *yours*, which you are so good as to say you hope I approve of, it is now needless to enter into, since you did not think it necessary to consult me on it before. But nevertheless, my dear Lord, what has passed shall not make any alteration in those sentiments I already have for you. I am with great truth, my Dear Lord, Your Sincerely affectionate Uncle, Geo. Hen. Lennox.'

Lord Edward refused to heed his uncle's warning. He kept going back to Stoke and tried to get Georgiana to change her mind. Her parents were alarmed and after a few weeks they closed the doors of the house to their nephew.

Lord George Lennox, paying lip-service to the cult of feeling that had shaken even the rock of aristocratic marriage, insisted that Georgiana had been free to choose her own husband. Prudence rather than property had prompted her decision, he implied. But Lord Edward was convinced otherwise. He believed – and nourished his belief through a cold Canadian winter and a scorching American summer – that Georgiana had given him some hope. As long as she remained single, he allowed himself to dream that she might flout her parents' wishes and marry him for love. He reserved all the blame for Lord George Lennox. He loaded on to Lord George all his gathering disenchantment with aristocratic life and afterwards talked of him with a bitterness that seemed, to relatives, the source of all his subsequent political opinions and actions.

Just as he had when he left Ireland for Gibraltar, Lord Edward decided to salve his wounded heart with activity and change. 'When I am not happy, I must either be soldiering or preparing to be a soldier – for to stay quiet, I believe, I cannot,' he said to his mother, adding, 'why did you give me either such a head or such a heart?' Acting with decision, he swapped his majority in the 90th Regiment for one in the 54th, which for over a decade had been stationed in the northernmost garrisons in Britain's empire. As soon as they could, he and Tony set out to join it.

Lord Edward travelled with few possessions but a heavy heart. At twenty-four he had been twice rejected as a suitor to women he loved and had come to the conclusion that he was too poor to marry within his own circle. Peace had destroyed his hopes of a quick increase either in fortune or status, and four years on the opposition benches in Dublin had done nothing to bring him the wealth that could come with political success. He was disillusioned by politics and disappointed in love, and as if that was not enough, added to the burden of a hopeless passion was the weight of his mother's displeasure.

The Duchess believed that her favourite son should repay her grandiloquent love with his presence. Lord Edward tried to take the edge off his mother's anger by writing, 'If I had stayed . . . I should always have been miserable about Georgiana. I could not have enjoyed anything. I am always disagreeable when I am in love and perhaps you would have all grown to *think* me disagreeable.' But she was implacable, insisting that the journey was unnecessary. So it was with more misery than excitement that after a very brisk Atlantic crossing of twenty-eight days, he and Tony watched a line on the western horizon thicken into a jigsaw of bays and headlands, where heavy rollers crashed against granite promontories and submerged rocks, and mists from the waves drifted towards the shore on the easterly breeze. A fringe of forest clung to the barren soil beyond the shoreline, parted now and then by farm clearings and by inlets and river mouths where tiny villages were precariously established and fishermen moored their cod boats safe from the Atlantic gales. As they approached the coast and saw the town of Halifax, with its five batteries of guns mounted on hillocks looking out to sea and its dozen wharfs at right angles to the shore, a pilot boat came out to guide them to a mooring. With lowered sails, the troopship glided to the dockside and Lord Edward Fitzgerald and Tony Small touched American soil once more.

CHAPTER
TWO

—— ◆ ——

FROM ADVENTURER TO
LOVER

Halifax, Nova Scotia, 21 June 1788

After seven years, Tony Small was back on the continent of his birth, a freeman this time and a thousand miles to the north. He had swapped the dust and blanketing humidity of the southern summer, with its sweltering black nights when moths banged into his lantern, for the thin, clear light of the north. Here in Halifax the smell of sea offal and pine smoke blew with a stiff salt breeze and in the evenings clouds of mosquitoes rose and fell in the sheltered places, visible in firelight, tormentingly felt everywhere else.

But as he walked along the rocky promenade of Halifax, from the distillery and dockyard at the top of the town, past Barriet's wharf, Brown's wharf, Hardwell's wharf, Gerrishe's wharf; past the five-gun battery where the cannons scanned the harbour approach and the nine-gun battery whose barrels pointed seawards and to the east; past Crowley's wharf and Collier's wharf, all the way to the lime kiln at the bottom of the town, he saw much that was familiar from his Charleston days. Halifax, like most colonial towns, was laid down on a grid; the city blocks dense and small in the centre, large and elongated to the north, south and west. The warehouses, like those at Charleston harbour, were stacked with local produce – mostly fish and firewood. Dockhands, some of them freed slaves and black like himself, unloaded finished goods and

food, tools, guns, nails from Britain, sugar, tobacco, rum
from the West Indies, and flour and grain from New York,
and filled up departing ships with wood ballast and cod car-
goes. Just inland rose the familiar clapboard spires of
churches – two Anglican churches and St Mather's
Dissenters' Church for Presbyterians who had recently
arrived from Scotland or the northern Irish counties. Solid
official buildings sat firmly amid whitewashed wooden
façades, the local granite twinkling in the summer sunshine:
the courthouse, prison and two hospitals catered to the casualties of time, poverty and the hardship of colonial life. The
new assembly house was a testimony to its brief pleasures.

The streets of Halifax, just like the streets of Charleston,
were thronged with red-coated soldiers and sailors from
troopships and merchant vessels. From Halifax's two barracks, soldiers in regiments and battalions embarked for garrisons in St John or Fredericton, or for the city of Quebec,
hundreds of miles to the west. If they were particularly
adventurous or unlucky they found themselves bound for
tiny outposts on the great lakes and rivers: Fort Niagara,
Fort Pitt, Michilimackinack.

In the confusion of sound along the waterfront and in the
wide streets, accents that Tony had never expected to hear
again stood out: guttural German, like that spoken by mercenaries in the British army, here in the mouths of townsmen
and farmers, and many kinds of American, spoken by loyal-
ists who had come to Nova Scotia at the end of the American
war. Although most of the Americans were from New York,
some came from the South. Probably for the last time in his
life, the voices of South Carolina reached Tony's ears, bringing with them memories of the place – its colours, sounds and
smells – he had once known as home. And all around him
were the Irish who had reversed his own journey, swapping
familiar misery for the unknown hardship of the New World.

Prompted by Tony, Lord Edward dutifully reported his

arrival in Nova Scotia to his family. 'There has not passed a day yet without his telling me I had best write now or I should go out and forget it,' he confessed to his mother. At the end of June 1788, four days after their arrival, he and Tony set out across the Nova Scotia peninsula around the marshy Bay of Fundy to join his regiment in its barracks near the town of St John, in New Brunswick. The journey, trekking from settlement to settlement across the land, took over three weeks. For Lord Edward it was a revelation. He arrived at St John exhausted but exhilarated; he believed that he had found a society that, in its simple self-sufficiency, its reliance on family and its lack of a developed social hierarchy, avoided the divisive and heartless elements of the life he had left behind.

The Nova Scotia farms that Lord Edward saw on his travels were long narrow lots originally granted to settlers by the French and then by the British. They stretched back from the rivers that were still the colony's major thoroughfares. Settlers sometimes came with indentured servants who helped them clear the forests and start their farms while saving their wages for land of their own. Wheat, vegetables, wool, timber, furs, meat, butter and eggs were produced for family consumption. Anything over was bartered for tools, kitchenware and clothing or used to pay the tax collector, the parish priest or the village apothecary. Apart from large freeholders, who collected ground rents from small farmers and sometimes lived on their own farms, most farmers had about the same amount of land and there were, as Lord Edward enthusiastically noted, few really wealthy people and few very poor. Farmers' cabins – built of logs and thatched and whitewashed – dotted the riverbanks, overshadowed now and then by a church, a sawmill or a manor house. Members of large, extended families, often farming contiguous lots, came and went. It took a lifetime of hard labour to establish a farm, but it was a longer and healthier life than that they had left behind in France or in Ireland.

On their way to St John, Lord Edward, Tony and their guide stayed a night with two old settlers who had retired from running their farm and rented out spare rooms in their cabins to travellers, 'more for the sake of the company . . . than for gain'. When he got to St John, he described their farm to his mother. 'Conceive, dearest Mother, arriving about twelve o'clock in a hot day at a little cabin upon the side of a rapid river, the banks all covered with woods, not a house in sight, and there finding a little old, clean, tidy woman spinning, with an old man of the same appearance weeding salad. We had come for ten miles up the river without seeing anything but woods. The old pair, on our arrival, got as active as if only five-and-twenty, the gentleman getting wood and water, the lady frying bacon and eggs . . . and when either's back was turned, remarking how old the other had grown; at the same time all kindness, cheerfulness, and love to each other.'

The old people were not, Lord Edward knew quite well, a gentleman and lady, but humble émigrés who had arrived thirty years before with one cow, three children and an indentured servant, and had bought a concession in a virgin tract of forest sixty miles from the nearest settlement. 'The first year, they lived mostly on milk and marsh leaves; the second year they contrived to purchase a bull by the produce of their moose skins and fish. From this time, they got on very well and there are now five sons and a daughter all settled in different farms along the river for the space of twenty miles and all living comfortably and at ease. The old pair live alone in the little log cabin they first settled in, two miles from any of their children; their little spot of ground is cultivated by these children and they are supplied with so much butter, grain, meat, etc, from each child, according to the share he got of the land, so that the old folks have nothing to do but mind their house.'

In the evening, Lord Edward sat in a line with the old couple, Tony and his guide on a log in front of the cabin,

watching smoke drift over the river and the clouds of mosquitoes grey against the forest green shuddering up and
down like the veils of curious duennas. Looking at the 'contented thoughtfulness' of the settlers' faces he was swept up
by an ecstatic happiness and wanted to stay there for ever,
tossing away his old life in which he could only look forward to being 'at their age, discontented, disappointed and
miserable'. In the days that followed, he imagined himself as
a settler with Georgiana Lennox by his side. While she, back
in England, was fast forgetting him, he had visions of her as
a Canadian Eve gracing this simple New World paradise. 'I
own I often think how happy I could be with Georgiana in
some of the spots I see; and envied every young farmer I
met, whom I saw sitting down with a young wife, whom he
was going to work to maintain.'

Nova Scotia's governing class was away in England and
Lord Edward was happy to leave it there. For the first time
he thought he saw a society that was self-sufficient, self-
governing in day-to-day matters and uncorrupted by wealth
and social stratification. 'The equality of everybody and of
their manner of life I like very much,' he told his mother.
'There are no gentlemen, everybody is on a footing, provided he works, and wants nothing. Every man is exactly
what he can make himself, or *has* made himself by industry.'

Still hoping against hope that Georgiana Lennox would
abandon wealth and station for love, Lord Edward had com-
pelling personal reasons to applaud the absence of an aristocracy. But, at the other end of the scale, he also noticed
that in Europe poverty sullied happiness, making children a
burden and an anxiety rather than an unalloyed joy.
Thinking of the Irish peasantry and perhaps of those he
called his 'poor tenants' at Kilrush, he recorded with admiration: 'I came through a whole tract of country peopled by
Irish, who came out not worth a shilling, and have all now
farms worth (according to the value of money in this
country) from £1,000 to £3,000 . . . The more children a man

has, the better; his wife being brought to bed is as joyful news as his cow calving. The father has no unease about providing for them as this is done by the profit of their work. By the time they are fit to settle, he can always afford them two oxen, a cow, a gun and an axe, and in a few years, if they work, they will thrive.' Here in the New World was a lesson for the old: that with 'equality of life' could come happiness and prosperity for all.

Three thousand miles away at Black Rock, his mother was still anxious to keep her own standing in the Ascendancy world. Although by marrying William Ogilvie she had comprehensively flouted aristocratic convention and had subsequently come to espouse a hierarchy of merit rather than class, she still aimed for a summit: a summit of achievement, of wealth and if possible of title. She urged William Ogilvie to seek aggrandisement by political success – or by office holding, if it could be done – and she herself refused to cede a title to which she no longer had any right.

The Duchess – or Lady Emily Ogilvie as she should by rights have called herself – believed in Foxite liberty, in emancipation and in extension of the franchise. She was also in favour of overhauling the patronage system, having come to believe that men like her son William and her brother-in-law Thomas Conolly commanded far more influence than their talents deserved. When she got Lord Edward's paean to equality from Nova Scotia at the end of 1788, the Duchess was in the act of urging William Ogilvie to leap over her son and her kinsman and to consolidate his own political power in a bid for a title, an office, and a political empire.

Ogilvie poured scorn on Lord Edward's romance of labour and simplicity, and had already teased him about his yearning for an untrammelled primitive existence. But he himself was an unsuccessful politician. After a half-hearted attempt to fulfil his wife's ambition, he retreated from active involvement in the Irish House of Commons and contented himself with providing the money to indulge her extrava-

The south front of Carton House. Life there was formal and magnificent under the first Duke of Leinster, magnificent and dull when his son took over.

James Fitzgerald, 20th Earl of Kildare, 1st Duke of Leinster, and Lord Edward's father, by Allan Ramsay, 1762; his children felt awe but little love for him.

Lord Edward aged 7; his sweet nature, charm and long lashes had already made him a general favourite.

Above left: William Ogilvie in his fifties sketched by his son-in-law, Charles Lock in 1795. Feared by many but much loved by most of his pupils at Black Rock.

Above right: The château at Aubigny, Lord Edward's home from 1775 to 1780, where he learned to appreciate 'the true French character'.

Right: Emily, Duchess of Leinster, painted by Sir Joshua Reynolds about the time of her second marriage. Obsessional and emotionally demanding, she hung on to her sons' devotion and was more than a match for their wives.

Left: Omai, prince of the South Seas, in 1776. Painted by Reynolds in a costume that is half exotic, half senatorial and wholly invented.

Below: Halifax, Nova Scotia, from George's Island, by G. I. Parkhymes, 1801; a strategic port, and Lord Edward's gateway to the uncharted North American interior.

Elizabeth Linley painted as St Cecilia by Reynolds in 1775. By the time she met Lord Edward in 1791, Elizabeth's misery made her ready to compromise her saintly image.

Tom Paine, painted by George Romney, engraved by William Sharp, 1793; Lord Edward was determined to find him as simple and honest as Paine declared his prose to be.

Richard Brinsley Sheridan by Reynolds, engraved by John Hall, 1791. Despite trying to think the best of him, Lord Edward doubted his capacities as a parent.

Lord Edward's cousin Charles James Fox, sketched by Henry Edridge in 1796; briefly Lord Edward was 'a thorough Foxite'.

Left: Stéphanie-Felicité, Countess de Genlis, painted by Romney during her visit to England in 1792, and looking a little younger than her 45 years.

Below: Pamela, painted by Romney at the same time, when she was about 18 and already famous for her beauty and her theatrical 'attitudes'.

Right: Lord Edward's aunt, Louisa Conolly, by George Romney, 1776. She was regarded as the epitome of goodness by her family, the more so since her husband was universally mocked and called by Wolfe Tone 'a strange, rambling fool'.

Below: Frescati, in 1911, betraying its seaside villa origins despite the thousands spent by the Duchess of Leinster to transform it into a grand country house.

Arthur O'Connor, mezzotint by W. Ward the Elder after J. D. Herbert, 1798. Reckoned to be very handsome, he was vain about his hair even though it was already receding by the time this picture was done.

Right: Lord Henry Fitzgerald in theatrical costume, engraved by J. Park in 1789, after the painting by John Hoppner. A typical Foxite, radical in his politics and rakish in his habits. He never forgave Dublin Castle for the manner of Lord Edward's death.

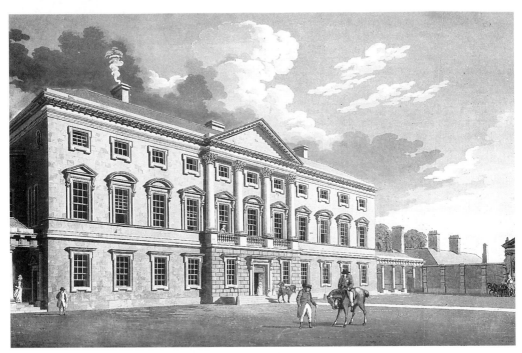

Above top: Leinster House, Dublin, engraved by Malton in 1792.
'What a gloomy house it is', Lord Edward exclaimed.

Above: The arrest of Lord Edward, engraved by George Cruikshank the Elder for W. H.
Maxwell's *History of the Irish Rebellion in 1798*, 1845, showing Stirr in the act of shooting his
captive. 'I would rather be Fitzgerald, as he is now, wounded in his dungeon, than Pitt at the
head of the British Empire', wrote Wolfe Tone when he heard of it.

gance. Along with investing the large annuities paid under the terms of the first Duke of Leinster's will, Ogilvie was also looking after the estates of his absent stepson. While Edward's letters were sailing one way, Ogilvie's were coming the other, giving news of Lord Edward's treeless domain and asking businesslike questions which were immediately forgotten. 'I have mislaid your letter, but remember you did say something about a road,' Lord Edward wrote from his snowbound winter quarters in February 1789, secure in the knowledge that Ogilvie's management was better than his memory and adding, 'I am glad to hear that, upon the whole, the little spot gets on. I believe that you will make something of it at last.'

Lord Edward did not need Ogilvie's prompting to bring Ireland to mind. He looked at the wall of forest stretching away beyond the villages and farms and wished its canopy could cover Kilrush; he looked at the vast lands around him and felt insignificant and far from home. He looked into his heart, especially when he was alone in the evenings, found his family there and remembered their happy journey from Barèges to Aubigny the autumn before. 'I contrive to be with you a good deal,' he wrote to his mother from the raw new settlement of Fredericton, near his winter quarters. 'I take fine long walks and think of last year. I think of all our conversations – our jokes – my passions when you were troublesome and fidgety . . . In short, dearest, I have you with me always – I talk to you – I look at your meek face when you submitted to all my little tyranny. The feel of the air even very often reminds me of you. We had just such a day a few days ago as that when we came to Aubigny . . . Dearest mother, when shall we have such another walk? But I won't think of it any more.'

In the first few weeks of his northern American sojourn, when everyone in his regiment was a stranger and when the climate, the sounds and the sights of the northern colonies, from the clapboard and granite of Halifax, to the big bright leaves of the maples and the rustle of animals nosing through the regimental camps at night were alien to him, Lord Edward was almost overwhelmed by his isolation. Once again he turned to Tony, admitting 'his black face is the only thing that I yet feel attached to'. And Tony, who came from Africa, from America, but certainly not from Europe or Ireland, now reminded Lord Edward of home. As Lord Edward dressed, and while Tony built up the fire and boiled stream water for shaving and for breakfast, they reminisced about Frescati and the long journey of the year before. 'The faithful Tony talks of you a good deal: he and I have long conversations about you all every morning.' In the shifting world of military stations and appointments, Tony was more than ever a fixity, a companion, a mirror and a foil for Lord Edward's thoughts and feelings. And when a letter from Dublin arrived, Tony expressed delight, even if he might reflect that he had never got a letter in his life and that if he were to receive one, he could not answer even if he could read it. 'The faithful Tony inquires after you all and seems as glad when I get a letter as if it was to him; – he always puts me in mind to write.' With this delight had come dependence. Tony had come to see his master's world as his world, to want what he wanted and to hate what he hated. He had come to love his master: that was his joy and it was to be his tragedy.

When Lord Edward's spirits sagged and talk of home was not enough to raise them, he plunged into regimental business, finding an opiate for his melancholy in its exhausting routines and his own responsibilities. After three weeks in St John, he moved to St Anne's, a hundred miles upriver, in the depth of the woods with Indian settlements all around. Many soldiers were fearful of the noisy solitude of the forest, where the moose moved through the thorny undergrowth and Indians stealthily pursued them. Drum-rolls frightening the birds, reverberating down the valley and fading into the dense forests could summon no one; the thud of boots on the

earthen floor of the parade ground served as much to invigo-
rate the soldiers as to keep them prepared for war.

Lord Edward was delighted to have charge of the garrison, and compared himself to Laurence Sterne's benign
Uncle Toby, whose love of soldiering extended in his retire-
ment to the construction of a fort in his garden and constant
expression of patriotic joy at the sound of pipes and drums.
Like Uncle Toby, Lord Edward was a kindly and conscien-
tious officer. Knowing that the brutal Canadian winter was
closing in, he exerted himself to ensure that the men would
have huts rather than only tents to ward off the searing
winds, and that when the spring finally came, they would
have fresh food as well as warm sunshine. 'I have got a garden here for the soldiers, which employs me a great deal,' he
told his mother soon after he arrived at St Anne's. 'I flatter
myself [that] next year it will furnish the men with quantities
of vegetables, which will be of great service to them.'
Meanwhile he plunged himself into running the camp,
dreaming as he did so of some happy resolution to his luck-
less love. 'I get up at five o'clock, go out and exercise the
men from six till eight, come home and breakfast; from that
till three I read, write and settle all the different business of
the regiment; at four we dine; at half after six we go out,
parade and drill till sundown; from that till nine I walk by
myself, build castles in the air, think of you all, reflect on the
pleasant time past as much as possible and on the disagreeable as *little* as possible; think of all the pleasant things that
may yet happen and none of the unpleasant ones; when I am
tired of myself, at nine o'clock, come home to bed, and then
sleep till the faithful Tony wakes me in the morning.'

Lord Edward was popular with his men. Determined to
see the noble in the men, and without any inhibiting fear of
the different lives, beliefs and aspirations of the soldiers, he
treated them seriously. While many people subscribed to the
fashionable belief in the uniformity and essential goodness
of human nature, few wished to cast aside their own sense of

superiority and difference to put it to the test. This, perhaps selfconsciously, but without fear, Lord Edward was determined to do. On his travels, he was as much an explorer of the nooks and crannies of human behaviour as of rocks and forests, rivers and seas. When asked by Spanish peasants to go into their houses, he had taken up the invitation. He now sat side by side with Canadian settlers on their log-benches and he joined in Indian dances. When his sergeant major, William Cobbett, confessed his hatred of the army and his wish to leave it and marry, Lord Edward worked hard to secure his discharge. Cobbett later became a famously cantankerous man and one so obsessed with corruption in the army that he attempted to bring a private prosecution against it. But he never forgot his commanding officer's 'great kindness' and declared him to be 'the only *really honest* officer he ever knew in the army'.

Skating on the frozen stream when winter set in, musing by the fire at night, wrapped in a coat which he had made from a thick flannel blanket, Lord Edward developed a private cult of service to his men. 'I like the service for its own sake,' he explained to his mother, who had been urging him to use family influence to obtain a lieutenant-colonelcy. 'Whether major, or lieutenant-colonel or general, it is the same to me . . . If I am found fit for command, I shall get it. If I am not, God knows I am better without it. The sole ambition I have is to be deserving: to deserve a reward is to me far better than to obtain it. I am afraid you will say I am foolish about this; but as it is a folly that hurts nobody, it may have its fling.'

It was in this spirit of cheerful open-mindedness that Lord Edward, accompanied by Tony, canoed upriver in the autumn afternoons and encountered the Iroquois Indians who hunted the forest and fished the streams. 'There is a great convenience in the canoes, they are so light, two men can carry them easily on their shoulders; so that you go from river to river without any trouble: it is the only method of travelling in this country. A canoe here is like a post-chaise at home and the rivers and lakes your post-horses. You would laugh to see the faithful Tony and I carrying one.' Indians often came into military outposts to barter meat and skin for firearms, powder and shot. Lord Edward went to their summer fishing camps, established away from their villages, where they grew maize, beans, squash and wheat, and where cattle, sheep and hogs grazed in forest clearings on the shores of lakes and rivers.

Arriving home from one expedition, Lord Edward sat down to describe half-humorously, half-seriously the advantages of savage over civilised life, distilling into his chronicle all his romantic disappointments and all his egalitarian dreams. 'I know Ogilvie says I ought to have been a savage, and if it were not that the people I love and wish to live with are civilised people, and like houses, etc, etc, I really would join the savages, and, leaving all our fictitious and ridiculous wants, be what nature intended we should be. Savages have all the real happiness of life, without any of those inconveniences or ridiculous obstacles to it which custom has introduced among us. They enjoy the love and company of their wives, relations and friends without any interference of interests or ambitions to separate them. To bring things home to oneself, if *we* had been Indians, instead of its being my duty to be separated from all of you, it would, on the contrary be my duty to be with you, to make you comfortable, and to hunt and fish for you. Instead of Lord George's being violent against my marrying Georgiana, he might be glad to give her to me, that I might maintain and feed her. There would be then no cases of looking forward to the fortune for children, of thinking how you are to live; no separations in families, one in Ireland, one in England; no devilish politics; no fashions, customs, duties or appearances to the world to interfere with one's happiness. Instead of being served and supported by servants, everything here is done by one's relations, by the people one loves; and the mutual obligations you must be under increase your love for each other. To be sure, the poor ladies are obliged to cut a little wood and bring a little water. Now the dear Ciss and Mimi . . . would be carrying wood and fetching water, while the ladies Lucy and Sophia were cooking or drying fish. As for you, dear mother, you would be smoking your pipe. Ogilvie and us boys, after having brought in our game, would be lying about the fire, while our squaws were helping the ladies to cook, or taking care of our papooses. All this in a fine wood, beside some beautiful lake, which when you were tired of, you would in ten minutes, without any baggage, get into your canoes and off with you elsewhere.'

Lord Edward's cult of Indian life, which emphasised what he saw as a familial system of interdependence rather than hierarchy, and simple substance rather than corrupt ambition, luxury and place-seeking, marked a high point in his rejection of country-house and aristocratic life. Here, by the fish-filled lakes, under the northern stars, he believed he had discovered a society in which there were no rich and no poor, no masters and no servants. Families could not afford to quarrel and had no need to divide. Politics need not spoil their affections. To his eager, romantic eye, Iroquois life seemed to combine the 'equality of life' of the white settlers in Canada with the political equalities that were the hallmark of the American republic to the south.

For two hundred years the Iroquois tribes or nations – who lived in the vast territory from the St Lawrence river in the north east to the upper reaches of the Mississippi in the west, from the Great Lakes in the north to the Carolinas in the south – had existed peacefully in a federation, named after and constructed in the same way as their characteristic dwelling, the longhouse. In the Indian villages each extended family inhabited one longhouse, a rectangular structure with walls of logs and coverings of elm bark that was partitioned and extended as families required. The Iroquois nations lived in peace, in their own territories, but under one roof; the Mohawk tribe guarded the eastern door, the Senecas the west, and grand councils of the confederacy were held at Onondaga, the 'hearth' in the geographical centre of the federation. It was at these councils that chiefs from each tribe met to repair holes in the structure of the longhouse, to make it strong and confirm peace between the nations, and to discuss policy towards the white settlers, whose increasing numbers threatened their territories and ways of life and whose wars threatened to bring the whole longhouse tumbling to the ground.

When Lord Edward encountered the Iroquois on their summer fishing expeditions, and translated their world into his own, he observed that they lacked many of the social structures that he had come to disdain. They had no system of patrilineal inheritance, whereby the eldest son received everything and younger sons and daughters had to find their way by marriage or by a profession. They had, indeed, no property rights vested in individuals or families. They had no political parties, no standing army, no monarch. As he recognised, Iroquois society was matriarchal. At the still centre of his picture of busy activity sat the Duchess of Leinster regally smoking her pipe, surveying the men bringing in the venison and fish or helping care for the children, and the women cutting wood and cooking food.

But although Lord Edward was sensitive to the power that Indian women wielded, discerning a parallel with the dynamics of his immediate family, he thought that men must necessarily be the arbiters in such matters as marriage, and that when Indian women married they would, like their European counterparts, be 'given' to men. In fact Iroquois women wielded authority and influence on a scale that few of their European counterparts had ever dreamed of. On marriage, a man came to live in the house of his wife's family. She had sole authority over their children, and they remained with her if he died. Clans as well as families were matriarchal. When a chief died the female head of the clan – of which there were several in each tribe or nation – selected another, usually but not always a close relative. A chief's authority did not derive from a usually male monarch, as did that of European aristocrats like Lord Edward, but, invariably, from a matriarch. The chief performed his political duties as the matriarch's choice, knowing that when he died his successor would be chosen not by abstract principle but by the woman to whom he answered.

Lord Edward may not have understood the degree of influence that Iroquois women held, but he did notice that Iroquois attitudes towards property and land were quite different from those of Europeans. Before the encroachment of European settlers forced them to lay claim to the lands on which they lived and hunted, the Iroquois had little sense of personal title to territory. Land was held by each Iroquois nation and used in common by all its tribes. There were no grazing, hunting or fishing rights of the sort Lord Edward had seen so rigidly enforced on his father's Irish estates. The Iroquois were semi-nomadic, moving their longhouses and villages every few years when they had exhausted the soil about them by cultivation, logging and grazing. When the first settlers arrived, the Indians welcomed them, believing that they too would cultivate and move on, tilling the land and then leaving it to regenerate. The Scottish and Irish immigrants, impoverished by lack of land at home, had other ideas. Land, fixed and bounded, was to be their security; they wanted leases and title, and, believing the Iroquois to be savages, had little compunction in lobbying their governments to acquire Indian land by any means. By the time Lord Edward met them, the Iroquois understood the need to claim ownership of the land. But they had also been encouraged to sell it, to develop a taste for European goods and liquor and to desert the movable longhouse for the fixed log cabin. By the 1780s, the Iroquois were a people under pressure, ravaged by alcohol and Western diseases and deprived of their lands and holy grounds by a greed more sophisticated than their own. Although Lord Edward did not see it, the longhouse was tottering and the Iroquois, who had for two centuries sheltered under its eaves, were out in the cold. In the backwoods of New Brunswick he thought he came close to finding his Eden, not knowing that he was meeting Adam and his Eve as they left it, defenceless and alone.

Yet what he thought he observed, he was determined to practise. With other officers and with Tony, he launched himself into the sparkling rivers to catch fish. He tracked across the forest to hunt deer or to map the virgin land for future settlement. In the middle of November, before the first of the great winter snows but after the streams had frozen over and the russet fingers of the maple leaves had curled and faded to brown on the forest floor, he embarked on one of these expeditions. 'Three of the coldest nights we have had yet I slept in the woods with only one blanket and was just as comfortable as in a room. It was in a party with General Carleton. We went about twenty miles from [here] to look at a fine tract of land that had been passed over in winter. You may guess how I enjoyed this expedition, being aware, in all probability, there had never been but one person before. I cannot describe all the feelings one has in these excursions, when one wakens, perhaps in the middle of the night in a fine open forest, all your companions snoring about you, the moon shining through the trees, the burning of the fire. Dearest, dearest mother, how I thought of you at those times, and of all at dear Frescati! And after being tired of thinking, lying down like a dog, and falling asleep till day-break; then getting up, no dressing or clothing or trouble, but just giving oneself a shake and away to the spring to wash one's face.'

This eulogy to the brisk outdoors was unlikely to convert the Duchess of Leinster, who was interested only in the ways in which nature could serve artifice. Schooled in the conventions of rococo rather than the picturesque, she liked plants and trees best in parks and gardens and only rarely attempted descriptions of the countryside in her letters. She was unlikely to be enthusiastic about open fires and spruce beds, preferring warmth all year round, insisting on importing for Frescati grand marble fireplaces to set off her blazing coals. Lord Edward was undeterred, looking forward to winter bivouacs and teasing his mother with his rejection of indoor life by writing, 'I believe I shall never again be prevailed on to live in a house. I long to teach you all to make a good spruce bed.' Simple procedures, he explained, could make the forest floors more comfortable than the most sophisticated brick and mortar constructions. 'The idea of being out-of-doors, notwithstanding the inclemency of the weather, and of overcoming all the difficulties of nature by the ingenuity of man delights me. Everybody who has tried this says it is much the warmest way of living in the winter; for, by being in the woods, you are sheltered from the winds and at night by clearing away the snow, banking it up round, and in the middle of the space, making a large fire, you are much warmer than in the best house.'

Georgiana Lennox was still in Lord Edward's thoughts. In September 1788, four months after his arrival in Canada, he was still optimistic about her, writing, 'I cannot help having hopes that Lord George will at last consent, and as long as there is the smallest hope of being happy with Georgiana, it is not possible to be happy with anyone else.' A month later, he admitted that 'the uncertainty . . . is dreadful . . . I am at times on the point of packing off and think that seeing her – looking at her dear face – would be enough.' All through the winter he imagined Georgiana by his side, sometimes seeing her as an Indian squaw, living a life without grandeur, status or possessions; but he went on hoping that one day she would marry him for love. When the spring came round and he turned his thoughts to home again, he was still writing to his mother, 'if Georgiana should love me, when I go home, I shall be the happiest fellow in the world'.

Lord Edward wrote this tribute to his constancy in the headquarters of Lord Dorchester, Governor of Quebec. At the same moment, four thousand miles away, the final preparations for Georgiana's wedding were taking place at Stoke, in Sussex. Georgiana was making a brilliant marriage; her husband to be, Henry Bathurst, Lord Apsley, was only a year older than Lord Edward, but he was already a man of substance and success. MP for Cirencester, the centre of large family estates, he was a personal friend of William Pitt, had been lord of the admiralty since 1783 and would soon become lord of the treasury. At twenty-seven, his political prospects were dazzling, and when he inherited the Bathurst earldom he would have wealth and property to match them. Married to Lord Edward Fitzgerald, Georgiana would have looked forward to an indebted life on his few Kildare acres or the discomforts of successive regimental postings. Married to Henry Bathurst she could anticipate a busy life as mistress of a large estate and hostess of a well-upholstered aristocratic drawing room. Her family were delighted and the wedding was celebrated in April.

Lord Edward's family were well aware of the contrast between his footloose wildness and Lord Apsley's rooted prosperity. 'While he is living in wild woods to pass the time till my brother George and Ly Louisa [Lennox] may be brought to consent to his marrying Georgiana, whom he adores, they have cruelly married her to Lord Apsley and the ungrateful girl has consented,' his aunt Sarah wrote. Nervously they posted him the news, but he was unreachable, deep in the Canadian interior with Georgiana still in his heart.

Although Georgiana's marriage was unknown to him, Lord Edward did receive, in letters and newspapers, Irish political news. At the end of October, he learned that his brother the Duke of Leinster had abandoned his time-honoured role as totemic leader of the Irish opposition and agreed to vote with the government of the bibulously convivial Lord Buckingham. The Duke's decision brought Lord Edward, elected as one of his brother's Members of Parliament, into the government orbit and into the sight of an instant promotion in the army. Attributing his brother's volte-face to 'weakness and folly', Lord Edward refused the bait of a lieutenant-colonelcy, telling his mother, 'however I might be flattered about getting on, it would never pay me for a blush for my actions. The feeling of shame is what I never could bear. The *mens conscia recti* . . . is the only thing that makes life supportable . . . I know dear Ogilvie, in his affection and eagerness for me, will be provoked; but then he must consider that feeling this way, I am right. Pray represent it strongly to him, and make him remember how obstinate I am when once I take a resolution.' Not for the first time he was glad of his voluntary exile and concluded, 'I am certainly better here. Leinster's conduct is too foolish and too shabby – I hate thinking of it.'

With the Duke of Leinster's defection to the government, the Fitzgerald brothers became pawns in wider conflicts: those between Pittites and Foxites at Westminster and those between the Duke of Richmond and Charles James Fox himself. Richmond was a loyal Pittite and still held the office of Master of the Ordnance. Fox was in opposition with no prospect of a return to power. But despite being in office Richmond harboured a deep jealousy towards his flamboyant nephew. He increasingly disliked Fox's politics, he was envious of his charisma and resented his hold on the affections of his sisters and the Fitzgerald children. Richmond had already made two converts to the Pittite cause, Lord Edward's brothers Robert, a half-pay officer seconded to the diplomatic service, and Charles, Ogilvie's first pupil at Black Rock, a fast-living rake who wanted a sinecure to defray his large debts. Lord Edward did not want to condemn his brothers' allegiances. Instead he put his disgust into Tony's mouth, telling his mother, 'Tony says, if Lord Robert goes on the way he is doing, he will soon be a major.' The Duke of Richmond hoped to poach a few more Fitzgeralds from the Foxite camp. Giving up on Lord Henry, who had recently been canvassing for the opposition in the new Westminster election, he concentrated on Lord Edward, appealing to him as a man of principle who, as one of his brother's MPs, should give him his vote in all circumstances. Lord Edward was incapable of and uninterested in unravelling political intrigues. Responding to the letter rather than the spirit of Richmond's appeal, he agreed to come over to the government side, although he had enough discretion to insist that he would not accept any promotion that might look like a reward for his vote.

Lord Edward's defection was luckily never tested. By the time he wrote back to his uncle in November, political turmoil in Westminster and Dublin had made his naive acquiescence obsolete. The King, who had been veering between sanity and lunacy for some time, finally became incapable of governing; sleepless, raving and violent, he was confined by his horrified doctors, first at Windsor, then at Kew. Without a titular head to sign parliamentary Bills, the process of government broke down, making a Regency constitutionally necessary. Unwilling to hand government over to the Prince of Wales and his Foxite friends, Pitt played for time, taking months to introduce a Regency Bill at Westminster. In London, the Prince of Wales could not take power without parliamentary assent. But in Ireland, which was ruled by a Lord Lieutenant with vice-regal status, power came directly from the Crown and could thus, the opposition argued, be assumed by royal fiat.

The unforeseen prospect of Irish rule quickly went to the heads of Fox and his party in London. While the Regency Bill was crawling its way through Westminster and over as many obstacles as Pitt could lay in its path, Fox was anticipating office, scattering everywhere promises of sinecures or

promotions that he himself would have scorned and probably been too lazy to secure. 'My dear Henry,' he wrote to
Lord Henry Fitzgerald from Bath, on 1 February 1789,
'with respect to you and Edward, I must be ungrateful
indeed if I did not consider the opportunity of showing my
friendship to you two as one of the pleasantest circumstances attending power. One of the first acts of the Regency
will be to make Edward Lieut.-Colonel of the Royal Irish
. . . As I shall probably return to my old office of Foreign
Affairs, I should be glad to know whether you or Edward
have any inclination to foreign employment that I may have
a view to your wishes in future arrangements.'

Before this golden dream could come to life, King George
unexpectedly recovered, seized back the reins of power and
consigned the opposition to the back benches once more.
Fox went back to his poets and his lumbering games of
cricket at St Anne's Hill; the Duke of Leinster, chastened by
the opprobrium he had gathered in his brief period of voting
with the government, stayed with the Irish opposition, surrendered his appointment, and never again ventured into the
government ranks.

Snowed-in in New Brunswick from early December until
spring, Lord Edward was plotting not his own future, but
the route between St Anne's and the town of Quebec. The
day after Charles Fox sat by his Bath fireside and wrote to
Henry Fitzgerald of the fantastic glories to come with the
Regency, Lord Edward announced to William Ogilvie, 'I am
to set out in two days for Canada; it is a journey of one hundred and seventy-five miles and I go straight through the
woods. There is an officer of the regiment goes with me. We
make altogether a party of five – Tony, two woodsmen, the
officer and myself. We take all our provision with us on
toboggans. It will appear strange to you, or any people in
England, to think of starting in February with four feet [of]
snow on the ground . . . but it is nothing. You may guess we

have not much baggage.'

The forest was still deep in the vegetable sleep of winter when the small party set off from St Anne's on 4 February. They wore blanket coats, fur hats and snow shoes like great webbed feet. Four feet of soft snow covered the forest floor, whipped cream with a sparkling, icy crust punctured by the leafless tops of saplings and criss-crossed by animal tracks and the trails of solitary moose. The forest sounds were muffled by snow; the wind shaking the pine tops and whipping the branches of the ash and elms sounded like a distant thunder storm, and the loudest noises were the creaking of the toboggan ropes, the swish of snowshoes and the men's grunts and laughter.

They got up each morning two hours before daylight, boiled water on the embers of the night fire, loaded up the toboggans and, as soon as it was light enough to see the compass's trembling needle, set off. Each man pulled his own possessions; Lord Edward and Mr Brisbane shared one toboggan between them and took turns navigating, using the sun and horizons as sailors did. Ploughing straight across the land mass, over streams, along rock-strewn and barren glacial valleys and thickly forested hills, they were completely alone, meeting no one. Each day they stopped well before sunset in a flat clearing and immediately set to work to prepare the night's camp. Two men chopped wood for the fire while others shovelled snow, banking it up to form a wall round the encampment to keep the heat in and the wind and moose out. When a fire was blazing, they cooked meat on it, eating it off the bone and washing it down with bread, water and spirits and varying it with the salt pork they had brought with them.

As soon as supper was over, they fell asleep, wrapped in their blanket coats, warmed by the fire. Anyone who woke in the night would put some wood on the embers, watch them crackle into life, eat some meat and go back to sleep. Lord Edward, too tired to worry about love or politics, rarely woke up and slept till dawn, snug in his fur-lined boots, more tousled and blue-jawed every day. He was exhilarated by the journey, enjoying the sense of danger overcome and the glow of well-being after a hard day's walk. 'I really do think there is no luxury equal to that of lying before a good fire on a good spruce bed, after a good supper,' he told his mother.

As they trudged, the party kept a look-out for food that did not hibernate: deer which survived the winter by nibbling at the lichens and bark of the forest plants, trout which sank deep down into the warmer water of the river pools. Like the Indians who occasionally tracked through this expanse of forest, they listened for the bellows and crashes of the giant moose. The moose wandered alone through the wintry landscape. Magnificent creatures that towered above men, they had antlers like fuzzy candelabra and eyes that were soulful and wary at the same time. They were difficult to catch if the snow was soft; using their broad chests as snow ploughs, they could thrust ahead of their pursuers and splash across streams for three or four days before exhaustion forced them to stand and fight. If the snow was hard and crusty, however, the moose cut their legs as they drove forward and pain and fatigue forced them to turn, heads lowered, to confront their hunters.

Lord Edward's party unexpectedly flushed a bull moose out of cover in the middle of their cross-country journey. Leaving Tony and the woodsmen with the baggage, grabbing three days' worth of bread, two days' worth of pork, their tinderboxes and their guns, he and Brisbane set off hurriedly in pursuit. The snow was deep and soft and the moose forged away out of sight of the two men who were labouring across the drifts in their snowshoes and taking it in turns to go first and make a path. They saw the creature at sundown, but he easily eluded them, and, as the light failed, they were forced to stop for the night.

As soon as the sun rose, they set off again. After about an

hour they saw the unsuspecting creature in the distance and began the cruel race again. Soon they noticed that the moose's footprints were closer together in the snow, a sign that the great animal was tiring. Then they began to see circles in the snow where he had stopped momentarily to face his pursuers, then turned again to escape. 'Accordingly,' Lord Edward explained to his mother, they sensed victory, 'and pursued faster and at last, for three quarters of an hour, in a fine open wood, pursued him all the way in sight and came within shot. He stopped, but in vain, poor animal.'

A few years later, Lord Edward himself was hunted with similar remorselessness. Unluckily for him, his pursuers would feel none of the compassion that he now felt for the cornered animal. Once the moose was at his mercy, Lord Edward was overcome with sadness. 'I cannot help being sorry now for the poor creature – and was then. At first it was charming, but as soon as we had him in our power, it was melancholy . . . If it was not for this last part, it would be a delightful amusement. I am sorry to say, though, that in a few hours the good passion wore off and the animal one predominated. I enjoyed most heartily the eating him and cooking him. In short, I forgot the animal and only thought of my hunger and fatigue. We are beasts, dearest mother. I am sorry to say it.'

After this detour, the group, ever more bedraggled, unwashed, unshaven and with their trousers, coats and blankets dirty and tattered, trudged on. Officers and woodsmen, masters and servants began to look alike and Tony was a black version of the others. Because they had to help one another with the journey's repetitive chores – wood chopping, cooking, setting and striking camp – the differences between them were temporarily erased; as one of the Duke of Richmond's correspondents wrote from Quebec when the dishevelled party stumbled in, 'in such expeditions, Lord and servants are alike'.

In Lord Edward's own imagination he was not a woodsman but an Indian, sleeping under the stars as the Indians did and hunting moose in their relentless way. When, after twenty-six days in the forest, they struck the St Lawrence river and met a band of Indians, he was delighted that they seemed to accept his romantic estimation of himself. 'They were very kind to us and said we are all one brother,' all 'one Indian,' he reported to his mother. Lord Edward's party accompanied the Indians along the river bank to Quebec and he himself cheerfully traded labour for food, giving Brisbane sole charge of their toboggan. 'You would have laughed to have seen me carrying an old squaw's pack, which was so heavy I could hardly waddle under it. However, I was well paid whenever we stopped for she always gave me the best bits and most soup, and took as much care of me as if I had been her own son . . . We were quite sorry to part: the old lady and gentleman both kissed me very heartily.'

The dénouement to this sylvan dream of fraternity came abruptly in Quebec, which the party reached after thirty days on the march. Disgusted by the men's appearance, three respectable householders refused point blank Lord Edward's request for lodgings. When they were turned away from the fourth house, Lord Edward cast aside his fantasy of equality and appealed nakedly to the owner's deference, as he explained self-deprecatingly to his mother, '*elle me prit la mesure du pied jusqu'à la tête*, and told me there was one room, without a stove or bed, next [to] a billiard room which I might have if I pleased; and when I told her we were gentlemen she very quietly said, "I dare say you are", and off she went. However at last we got lodgings at an ale-house.'

Lord Edward was buoyed up by the success of the journey and by the sense of danger and hardship overcome. 'One ought really to take these fillips now and then,' he concluded, adding, 'they make one enjoy life a great deal more.' When a long-awaited announcement of leave came through a few weeks later, he decided to travel home by way of the Mississippi river, picking up a ship at its mouth in New

Orleans. He underestimated both the length and the difficulty of the expedition.

Writing home it took only a few lines; from Montreal he would accompany a relief of soldiers down Lake Ontario, past the Niagara Falls, across Lake Erie to Detroit and up to the fort of Michilimackinack at the southern entrance to Lake Superior. He estimated that it would take three weeks and concluded that the trek would 'soon be over, for from that I shall soon reach the Mississippi, and down it to New Orleans, and then to my dearest mother [in] Frescati, to relate all my journey in the little book-room.' In fact, just getting to the Mississippi took more than three months, and getting home took more than a year. The length and difficulty of the journey, the remoteness and wildness of the country transformed his earlier trek through the Canadian forests into a gentle practice run. From Michilimackinack along the southern shores of Lake Superior and across land to the upper reaches of the Mississippi, Lord Edward was out beyond the tentacular reaches of imperial communication lines; he and Tony were alone with the Indians, the Canadian woodsmen and the forest fauna. On 14 July 1789, while the Parisian crowd was jostling and pushing at the gates of the dark fortress of the Bastille, Lord Edward was slowly gliding westwards along the wooded shore of Lake Superior, fulfilling his own Enlightenment dream of liberty and fraternity, in the forests and with the Iroquois.

The first legs of the journey, from Quebec to Montreal and from Montreal to Fort Niagara, were more easily accomplished than describing the beauty of the Niagara Falls themselves. Just as at Gibraltar he compared his own puniness to the unexplored expanse of the continent beyond the Straits, so here he marvelled at 'the greenness and tranquillity of everything about, the quiet of the immense forests around, compared with the violence of all that is close to the Falls', 'the immense height and noise . . . the spray that rises to the clouds.'

It was characteristic of Lord Edward – and perhaps characteristic of his generation – to see in this way, understanding and defining by opposites or extremes. This habit of mind, innocuous when applied to natural sublimities like the Niagara Falls, had more serious consequences when it guided Lord Edward's political outlook and conduct. It inclined him not only to pit good against bad – rather than better against worse – but also to opt for the extreme rather than the compromise. Although he started his political life as a reformer, he was not temperamentally sympathetic to the compromises and inevitable half-steps that reform entailed. Unlike his mother and aunts, who used reason as a pilot to steer a path of compromise between any seeming contradictions, Lord Edward saw the world as a chequerboard of opposites, and was thus inclined to opt for the extreme solution. This cast of mind might have seemed unforgiving. But Lord Edward's belief in the goodness and essential unity of mankind stopped him not only from stressing the bad as opposed to the good, but also from defining white against black, or English against French, as some of his contemporaries were beginning to do. His solutions would be extreme, but they would also be optimistic; he would strive for the good rather than lament the bad.

At Fort Erie – below Niagara but on the British side of the new border with the United States – Lord Edward met an Indian chief well known in the British army and to the British government; abandoning his plan to travel to Detroit by boat, he decided to go with the Iroquois instead, telling his mother, 'I set out to-morrow for Detroit: I go with one of the Indian chiefs, Joseph Brant, he that was in England. We have taken very much to one another. I shall entertain you much with his remarks on England and the English . . . Instead of crossing Lake Erie in a ship, I go in canoes up and down rivers . . . – besides, my friend Joseph always travels with company and we shall go through a number of Indian villages.'

Travelling with Brant, Lord Edward shared his bed with a young Indian woman and his thoughts with the man who, more than any other, had striven to hold together the Iroquois nations in the Revolutionary War and its catastrophic aftermath. Brant was a man of two worlds, at once an Indian chief, with his band of followers, broadcloth blanket, red painted face, shaven head and scalp lock, and a western merchant who had a large clapboard house, credit in four towns, a pension from the British Crown and a cupboard full of breeches, frock coats and stockings. Sometimes he slept on a spruce bed under the birch-bark rooves of the Iroquois longhouses, after a meal of corn, and then Indian dancing; at other times he drank wine and spirits, danced Scottish reels and lay between sheets and blankets.

When Lord Edward met him, Joseph Brant was forty-six. Described by a young girl as being of 'severe and frightful' expression, he was painted by George Romney in 1776, dressed in his broadcloth blanket with feathers in his scalp lock, gazing sorrowfully past the viewer into the distance, every inch the noble chief. But Brant had mingled with Europeans long before he travelled across the Atlantic. As a young Mohawk Indian of dubious rank but obvious talents, he was sent to school in Connecticut by Sir William Johnson, the agent responsible for liaising between the Indian nations and the British government in the northern territories. In Connecticut Brant was tutored both in English and in loyalism and given an English name. He came away literate and an Anglican. Afterwards he used his relationship with the British and his mastery of several Indian languages to rise up the Mohawk hierarchy and to become Johnson's Indian counterpart, the man trusted by the Indian nations to liaise with the colonial power. By the start of the American Revolution, Brant was a man of property and influence, serving the British as an interpreter and his own people as delegate and protector.

The government in Westminster knew the value of

Iroquois loyalty; their lands were a bulwark against American expansion; their villages sheltered British soldiers and spies, and their people, armed with muskets and rifles, could terrify and harass any rebel army. In 1776, just before the American Declaration of Independence, Brant was brought to London. Once news of American insubordination reached London, Brant was assiduously cultivated, presented to George III, given a pension and a boatload of gifts to distribute at home. But when war broke out Brant and most of his fellow Iroquois declared for the British side on political rather than material grounds. The British had never encouraged westward expansion in North America, preferring to leave the Iroquois in the centre of the continent as a buffer between themselves and the Spanish who controlled the Mississippi corridor, and eager too to keep all their colonised land on military supply lines and within striking distance of the Atlantic seaboard, where the navy held sway. What they wanted from the land, moreover, the Indians could help supply: beaver, mink and bearskin to warm British skins through damp winters, and mature forest timber to build ships that could take British sailors to the four corners of the earth.

The rebel colonists had other ideas. To them the Iroquois were the savage sovereigns of lands they coveted; they wanted Iroquois forests to cut and burn, Iroquois fields to cultivate and the animals of the forest for food. Even before the war started, settlers were encroaching, often illegally, on Indian territories; if the rebels won, Brant knew that these pressures would increase. He counted on the British to defend the Indians; as he explained sadly in 1804, 'every man of us thought that by fighting for the King, we should ensure to ourselves and children a good inheritance.'

As the war progressed, Brant proved himself a far more successful fighter than most of the British forces. When it ended he was horrified that Britain betrayed him and its Indian allies. Under the Preliminary Articles of Peace signed at the end of 1782, all Indian lands to the Mississippi were handed over to the new American government; the Iroquois were left to defend their own interests while the British withdrew to Canada.

For the rest of his life Brant fought desperately to preserve the alliance of the longhouse and the borders of Iroquois land. In 1786 he journeyed to London again, seeking compensation for Mohawk losses in the war, half-pay for himself as a captain in the British army and a general commitment of support for Iroquois claims. This time he did not make the mistake of believing that Europeans and Indians were essentially alike and could live in harmony. Taxed with the strangeness and barbarity of Indian customs he replied tetchily, playing the European game of defining by opposites: 'why, the Indians have heard that it is a practice in England for men who are born chiefs to sell the virtue of their squaws for place, and for money to buy their venison.' Henceforth Brant's comparisons between Indian and English life invariably took this form, and always in favour of the former. 'We have no law but that written on the heart of every rational creature by the immediate finger of the great Spirit of the universe himself,' he declared in 1789, appealing to *philosophes* with his trust in reason, and deists with his belief in the immanence of God, and continuing, 'we have no prisons – we have no pompous parade of court . . . we have among us no splendid villains above the control of [the] law . . . daring wickedness is never suffered to triumph over helpless innocence . . . The palaces and prisons among you form a most dreadful contrast. Go to the former places and you will see, perhaps, a deformed piece of earth swelled with pride, and assuming airs that become none but the Spirit above. Go to your prisons – *here* description utterly fails!' Brant was particularly horrified at imprisonment for debt, which put property on a level with life and liberty. 'Cease to call other nations savage when you are tenfold more the children of cruelty than they,' he concluded, with the sort of reversal guaranteed to find an echo in Lord Edward's heart.

Despairing of succour from Pitt's government, Brant turned to the opposition. On his visit in 1786 he was careful to go to Carlton House as often as to court. The Prince of Wales befriended him; Lord Francis Rawdon, soon to join the opposition ranks, gave him his portrait, and Charles James Fox presented him with a snuff box. So when, three years later, a man who was not only Fox's cousin but Rawdon's former aide-de-camp turned up quite unexpectedly on the shores of Lake Erie, Brant was eager to reciprocate this hospitality, especially as news of the Regency crisis had just reached America.

Things had only worsened for the Iroquois since the end of the American war. Time after time American representatives had persuaded drunk or cupidinous Iroquois chiefs to sell vast tracts of Indian lands for a couple of thousand dollars and a few canoe-loads of chattels. Much of the land south of the Great Lakes was under threat; the way to the west was open and Brant himself had retreated to Canada, where he lived the life of a gentleman, with his family, his portraits and furniture and – Tony and Lord Edward would have noticed with wonder and disbelief – a retinue of Negro servants and slaves.

In 1789 Brant wrote despairingly to a friend, the British officer Major Matthews, 'Dear friend it is critical times for us here I mean we the Indians. I felt very unhappy oftentimes of late. The most difficult part for me is of having a many children which concerns me about them very much. Particularly when our Indian affairs and situation stand so unsettled the civilised cruelties mean the Yankys are taking advantage all the while and our friends the English seems of getting tired of us.'

Lord Edward, dishevelled in his greying shirts, covered in bear grease to protect himself against mosquitoes, and determined to travel a long way further into the Americas before he turned homewards, must have seemed to Brant only a fragile lifeline. But if the opposition came to power in London, he might prove an invaluable and impassioned spokesman for the Iroquois. With most Europeans he met, Brant had to prove himself 'civilised' before he could advance the claims of the 'savages' he represented. Lord Edward was already a convert to Brant's Indian side (and indeed preferred not to dwell upon Brant's obvious hybridisation). The more 'savage' the Indians, the more he valued them.

Brant warmed to Lord Edward's enthusiasm for Iroquois life and as they travelled west and south towards Detroit, he plied him with stories about his own journeys in the opposite direction. Best of all, discerning Lord Edward's unease with his title and the way of life it represented, he arranged for him to be given a new name. At Detroit, under the auspices of another Europeanised chief, David Hill, Lord Edward was made a chieftain of the Seneca, one of the six Iroquois nations. It was a rare but not unprecedented honour for a European. 'I have been adopted by one of the Nations, and am now a thorough Indian,' he told his mother, and carefully preserved in his travelling trunk a paper to prove it, on which was written,

Waghgongh Sen non Pryer
Ne nen Seghyrage ni i
Ye Sayats Eghnidal
Ethonayyere   David Hill
                         Karonghyontye
                         Igogh Saghnontyon
                         21 June 1789

I, David Hill, Chief of the Six Nations, give the name of *Eghnidal* to my friend Lord Edward Fitzgerald, for which I hope he will remember *me* as long as he lives.

The Name belongs to the Bear Tribe.

*

Lord Edward knew that Brant and Hill were men of two worlds. He accepted their favours cheerfully, but he was still searching for unsullied purity. Saying goodbye to them, he and Tony prepared to head into the unknown. 'I long to be set a-going again,' he wrote to his mother from Michili-mackinack, at the southern entrance to Lake Superior. 'I set out tomorrow. I have got a canoe, with five men – everything is laid in. I am obliged to have one to myself to carry a few presents for the Indian villages I pass through. Except for Indian corn and grease we depend entirely on chance for everything else. You cannot conceive how pleasant this way of travelling is; it is a hunting or shooting party the whole way. I find I can live very well on Indian corn and grease; it sounds bad, but it is not so. I eat nothing else for four days coming here. Few people know how little is necessary to live. What is called and thought *hardship* is nothing; *one* unhappy feeling is worse than a thousand years of it . . . This next part of the journey will be I think, the most interesting and agreeable I have had yet, as the people I go among live more in their own way and have less connection with Europeans.' He posted his letter, and moved out of reach of British supply lines and disappeared into Indian country.

While Lord Edward and Tony were paddling to paradise down the headwaters of the Mississippi, his brother Robert was witnessing the grandest and most cataclysmic effervescence of the Enlightenment search for purity and fraternity, in Paris. Lord Robert Fitzgerald was minister plenipotentiary and secretary of the embassy in Paris, second-in-command to the French ambassador, the Duke of Dorset. He was a cautious observer whose surveillance of the extraordinary scene beyond the windows of the British Embassy in the rue du Faubourg St Honoré only partly distracted him from anxiety about unpaid bills and anger about arrears of his salary. Writing to William Ogilvie on 3 July 1789, Lord Robert thanked him for offering to clear his debts, wrote a long summary of his financial affairs and tetchily blamed them on insufficient pay: 'government pays excessively ill and . . . I have not received to this day, now deep in the third quarter, one farthing, and do not know when I may expect one.'

Looking up from his ledgers, Lord Robert cast a dispassionate eye on all the inhabitants of Paris. He condemned the clergy as opportunists who cunningly sided with neither the 'haughty and proud' aristocracy nor the representatives of the Third Estate. Although he called the Third Estate 'a body much the most enlightened of the three', he added disapprovingly, 'The people are much inflamed; *toutes les têtes sont montées* and all seem ripe for rebellion. A great scarcity of bread increases their discontents and an ill-judged but natural impatience for immediate relief from their many wrongs and hunger . . . renders them really outrageous. They are all flaming politicians; the coffee-houses and the Palais Royal, in particular, are crowded with people of all denominations; some mounted on tables and chairs haranguing the rest, abusing the Ministers by name and in the vilest terms; others reading inflammatory papers and encouraging each other to stand and fall for the Tiers État.' Lord Robert concluded, 'if the *Tiers* are wise and prudent, for they now direct all, they may form a good and stable government; but if they carry their usurpatious and unconstitutional measures much further, this country will inevitably be deluged in blood and its fate will be decided by the fate of arms.'

Three weeks later Lord Robert was reaching for more theatrical and sensational language to describe the drama of the popular rising. The day before the storming of the Bastille, 'all the shops and every house were shut, and nothing was seen in the streets but armed men; muskets, drawn swords, pistols, hatchets, long knives and spikes fastened to the end of poles and other horrid weapons filled every hand. Every arm was stretched and every tongue voiced vengeance against the enemies of liberty.' He noted the destruction of the Bastille, but regarded as more significant the King's journey to Paris on 17 July, when he pledged his affection to his people and thereby sanctioned the bourgeois takeover of the city. Fitzgerald was convinced that Paris and France were irrevocably changed by the King's capitulation and the simultaneous flight of the nobility, telling William Ogilvie on 23 July, 'since Friday, the memorable 17th of July '89, matters have gone on quietly enough, and travellers etc are allowed [to] pass in and out of the town; alas! many many pass out and I much fear that Paris has seen its day. The nobility, through fear or indignation, retire to their provinces or to foreign countries, and strangers leave us in disgust and horror of [the] place. The government of the town is democratical; the King's officers, held in detestation by the people, have for the most part fled and a *comité permanent* at the Hôtel de Ville directs every thing.'

The British ambassador soon joined the general exodus, and from early August until the arrival of his replacement nine months later, Lord Robert Fitzgerald was in charge at the embassy. He remained detached and cynical, seeing that things would degenerate into conflict and subterfuge. As early as the spring of 1790 he wrote to the Secretary of State, the Duke of Leeds, with details of a disaffected royalist who had offered to spy for Britain, and a year later he concluded in a note to his mother, 'There is nothing new or interesting here. *L'Assemblée va toujours son train et la nation au diable*. Paris is gay, however. There are some balls and a good many suppers, so that one is seldom at a loss for amusements.'

Lord Robert's dyspeptic assessment was rare in the summer and autumn of 1789, when enthusiasm for the revolution was widespread throughout Europe. Charles James Fox caught the mood of euphoria among reformers, exclaiming to his friend Fitzpatrick on 30 July, 'How much the greatest event it is that ever happened in the world! And how much the best.' Even the ambassador in Paris was impressed, writing in his official dispatch to the Secretary of State in

London, 'Nothing could exceed the regularity and good order with which all this extraordinary business has been conducted. Of this I have myself been a witness upon several occasions during the last three days as I have passed through the streets . . . Thus, my Lord, the greatest revolution that we know anything of has been effected with . . . the loss of very few lives. From this moment we may consider France as a free country, the king a very limited monarch, and the nobility as reduced to a level with the rest of the nation.' France, in other words, was becoming more like England.

In its early days the French Revolution offered proof to those less cynical than Lord Robert Fitzgerald that mankind, freed from the shackles of corrupt government, would revert to the purity of its original state. Lord Edward, arriving in New Orleans in late December and reading the news in the *Courier de l'Europe*, would certainly have corroborated this view with the results of his own researches in the Spanish-held lands of the great valley of the Mississippi. 'I have seen human nature under almost all its forms. Everywhere it is the same, but the wilder it is the more virtuous,' he told Lord Robert, adding that the long descent to the Gulf of Mexico had done him 'a great deal of good'.

As soon as he arrived in New Orleans, Lord Edward was given proof of his belief that so-called civilisation was really barbarous. Anxious in case letters should go astray, several different members of the family had written the previous spring to announce the marriage of Georgiana Lennox. In a letter to his brother Henry, Lord Edward dismissed the news with a passable veneer of cynicism: 'I bore all the account[s] of Georgiana very tolerably well. I must say with Cardenio, "That which her beauty has built up, her actions have destroyed." By the first I understood her to be an angel; by the last I know her to be a woman.' But he could not keep up this misanthropic bravado for long, and quickly switched to fantasies of escape, admitting to Lord Robert Fitzgerald, before he embarked for London, 'if it was not for dearest mother, I believe I should not return to England for some time.'

Lord Edward and Tony finally arrived at his mother's house in London in the same manner that they had travelled in the last two years: unshaven, informally and together. It was two years since he had seen his family, and Lord Edward was in no mood to delay another minute. Not stopping to have his presence announced and failing to notice hats, gloves and topcoats in the entrance hall, he ran shouting with joy towards the dining room, from where he could hear the muffled hubbub of voices and the clinking of glass and cutlery. Before he could reach the door his cousin Henry Fox squeezed plumply out, closed it carefully and explained that behind it were not only his mother, Ogilvie and many of his brothers and sisters, but also Georgiana and her husband Lord Apsley. Lord Edward had been half way round the world, had paddled across Lake Superior and down the Mississippi, but the rules of politeness still had to be observed. One by one his family could come out to him as he waited, but he could not go in to them.

None the less, Lady Louisa Conolly reported to her sister Sarah that the Duchess of Leinster's happiness at Lord Edward's return 'is not to be described' and that she was 'almost distracted with joy'. Edward, she wrote, was 'in very tolerable spirits' although he was 'a good deal affected at meeting [Georgiana] in the street'. She noticed a seriousness and maturity in him too. 'He is grown such a philosopher as diverts us (attach'd to the idea of *little Eddy*). Seriously, though, the scenes he has seen have really made him one and I think he will have all the advantage that a feeling heart and good sense can have in viewing human nature as he has done in all its forms. I am pleased to find he has a good opinion of human nature in its primitive state. Their faults he accounts for naturally and do not arise from bad principles and very light in the scale against their good qualities.' Lord Edward strove to forget his embarrassments. He turned his back on Georgiana, took his place again as a member of the Foxite opposition in London and read everything he could about the French Revolution, pouring out all his new-found eagerness over the dining table at Harley Street, as Lady Lucy Fitzgerald explained. 'Eddy dines with us every day, and is *quite* among us in his old way, and what is best of all in charming spirits. He has moments, one sees, but he struggles with it, and it is soon over. He is *mad* about the French affairs – the levelling principle – and, indeed, seems entirely engrossed by these subjects, upon which he converses in a charming, pleasant way, though I fear he has made out a system to himself too *perfect* for this world, and which to bring about would be the cause of much disorder, and much blood would be spilt. *This* he denies; but I fear it will too soon show itself, for it gains by his account great grounds – one must not say the *mob* before him, but *the people.*'

Lord Edward's enthusiasm for the Revolution, although not his idealistic 'levelling' schemes – named after the Levellers, some of the most radical reformers active during England's Civil War and brief republic one hundred and fifty years before – was widely shared by his Foxite friends. Despite its setback over the Regency crisis, the opposition was in buoyant mood, seeing in the French Revolution the dawn of a reform whose light would gradually spread all over Europe. For two years after the fall of the Bastille few people found much cause for alarm in French events. Edmund Burke's *Reflections on the Revolution in France*, published in November 1790, did little to dent the prevailing mood, even if it ended his friendship with Fox. Burke's rhetorical extravagance, his sanguinary obsessions and his indiscriminate attribution of every imaginable horror to the malign forces of revolution led some, not unjustifiably, to doubt his sanity, and many to dismiss his analysis.

Much closer to the temper of the times was Thomas Paine's reply to Burke, the *Rights of Man*, published in

March 1791. Paine's book not only poured scorn and humour on Burke, it also proposed, with the utmost simplicity, a new social and political order. Paine asked the question, 'What are the rights of man, and how came man by them originally?', and found his answer in the Garden of Eden, where man was created in God's image and the Creator made no mention of distinction in rank. Everyone, Paine argued, stood in the same relation to God as Adam did, 'and consequently . . . all men are born equal, and with equal natural rights.' Everything else in Paine's system followed from this premise. With equal natural rights came equal political rights; with these came the right of taxpayers to elect an assembly to write a constitution and then to govern by it. The House of Lords, the Established Church, the Monarchy; all these were old-fashioned, unnecessary and expensive. 'I see in America', he announced, 'a Government extending over a country ten times as large as England, and conducted with regularity, for a fortieth part of the expense which government costs in England. If I ask a man in America if he wants a King, he retorts, and asks me if I take him for an idiot.'

Paine declared the French and American Revolutions to be 'a renovation of the natural order of things' and a restoration of 'the natural dignity of man'. The *Rights of Man* implicitly urged Englishmen to follow suit. 'It is an age of Revolutions, in which everything may be looked for,' Paine concluded with triumphant anticipation.

The *Rights of Man* was important to Lord Edward for two reasons. In the first place it ordered and put into memorable phrases many of the beliefs that he had been voicing in the previous four years and had recently been airing to his family. In the second place it offered him a transition from belief to method, and from the moral to the political, in a way that might avoid the bloodletting that Lucy Fitzgerald feared. Lord Edward had been making his own journey back to Eden long before he read Paine. But Paine added to his belief that men were naturally good and free the insistence that men were naturally equal, that rights as well as moral values sprang from that original state. Lord Edward had years before identified the notion of primogeniture, whereby the eldest son inherited his father's title and wealth, as both a personal handicap and a general wrong. Paine argued simply that equality could sweep it away: no lords, no bishops, no kings, but only men and women existed in his republic. Paine explicitly aimed at transforming Rousseauian idealism like Lord Edward's into practical action. 'We find in the writings of Rousseau,' he wrote in the *Rights of Man*, 'a loveliness of sentiment in favour of Liberty which excites respect and elevates the human faculties; but having raised this animation, they do not direct its operations, and leave the mind in love with an object without the means of possessing it.' America and France, Paine explained, were those means; they offered models of practice to 'join to the theory'. Lord Edward had already been to America and seen there not only noble and primitive men, but also the settlers' 'equality of life'. He was soon closely following events in France. The *Rights of Man* transformed him from Rousseauist to complete Painite and from a radical to a republican. He was quickly aware of the implications of this, imagining himself, less than a year after the *Rights of Man* was published, training a regiment of those northern Irish dissenters who since the days of the American Revolution had been noted for their radicalism and sympathy for republican causes. In December 1791 when he was in camp at Portsmouth with the 54th Regiment of Foot, he wrote – only half-jokingly – to his mother, 'I own I do often wish, when I am drilling, that it was a parcel of good, stout Northern Presbyterians – this will shock Ogilvie's loyalty.'

Although he realised that Painite republicanism was quickly taking root in Ireland, Lord Edward was not quite ready to translate what he called Paine's 'delightful doctrines' into practical politics. Instead he became Paine's disciple. The *Rights of Man* made its author a celebrity, and Paine enjoyed becoming a figurehead. In the summer of 1791 he was living with the radical publisher Cleo Rickman, who recorded that 'Mr Paine's life in London was a quiet round of philosophical leisure and enjoyment. It was occupied in writing, in a small epistolary correspondence, in walking about with me to visit friends, occasionally lounging at coffee-houses and public places, or being visited by a select few.' First on Rickman's list of those counted as Paine's 'friends and acquaintance' was Lord Edward Fitzgerald. After him came a radical crowd that included 'the French and American ambassadors, Mr Sharp the engraver, Romney the painter, Mrs Wollstonecraft, Joel Barlow, Mr Hull, Mr Christie, Dr Priestley, Mr Horne Tooke, William Godwin [and] Thomas Holcroft.' Although Paine was its current focus, this group had not formed around him; its members were connected to one another by a variety of common radical causes and activities. Mary Wollstonecraft and the political writer Thomas Christie had both already published rebuttals to Burke and, along with the philosopher William Godwin, had worked for some time for Joseph Johnson, the printer who had initially agreed to produce the *Rights of Man*, before fear of prosecution led him to withdraw from the task. Joseph Priestley and Horne Tooke were veterans of radical pamphleteering; William Sharp had been a republican for some time and was active, like Tooke, in the Society for Constitutional Information, which, on 23 March 1791, voted its thanks to Paine 'for this most masterly book'. Soon afterwards Sharp made an engraving of Romney's portrait of Paine, which allowed his likeness to be displayed on the walls of thousands of parlours and inside the covers of scores of cheap editions of his works. Cleo Rickman had known Paine since the 1770s, when the latter was an angry and impecunious exciseman in Sussex. Since then Rickman had loudly advertised his radical affiliations and literary affections by baptising one of his children as Paine and calling the others Washington, Franklin, Rousseau, Petrarch and Volney.

Most of Paine's visitors were active as well as paper radicals; many had travelled to Paris in search of freedom's source after the revolution and many were to suffer for their beliefs. Christie had been in Paris as early as Paine, in 1789; the American Joel Barlow had lived there on and off for several years; George Romney went in 1790, Mary Wollstonecraft was planning to go soon. The Scottish poet John Oswald, whom Rickman described as 'Colonel' Oswald, was also early over. He joined the Jacobin Club and was appointed commander of the first battalion of pikemen. Oswald was to die in 1793 during the loyalist insurrection in the Vendée. Thomas Holcroft, the publisher, who had written excitedly to William Godwin when the *Rights of Man* came off the press, 'Hey for the New Jerusalem! The millennium!' was charged in 1794 with high treason in connection with his publications and his membership in the Society for Constitutional Information. William Sharp was hauled before the Privy Council and examined on similar 'treasonable charges' and Horne Tooke was tried for the same reasons and sensationally acquitted.

The Painites that Lord Edward now sought out and the Foxites among whom he lived were not discrete groups. Romney made most of his living from aristocratic patrons, many of them from the Foxite camp. There were Painites like Sharp who, though republican, believed in trying to reform the constitution, and there were Foxites like Lord Grey who formed the Association of the Friends of the People in 1792 to press for a franchise system closer to that advocated in the *Rights of Man* than in any strictly Foxite thinking. In 1791 all were optimistically delighted with developments in France; they believed that reform was imminent and inevitable, and gathered together round dinner tables to plan its coming. None the less Paine's circle differed markedly in outlook and background from the louchely privileged Foxites and the successful actresses and courtesans who accompanied their gambling and drinking. Most were the children of prosperous artisans or merchants. Romney was the son of a builder and cabinet-maker, Sharp of a London gunmaker; Christie and Wollstonecraft both had merchants for fathers; Oswald's mother kept a coffee-house; while Paine's father was a respectable but impoverished stay-maker, producing bone-stiffened corsets for women wealthier than his wife. Of Paine's British visitors in the summer of 1791, only Lord Edward Fitzgerald was an aristocrat.

It was not so much temperament, morality or personal habits that marked the difference between Foxites and Painites – for every glass of expensive champagne and burgundy that Fox consumed, Paine downed one of cheaper wine, brandy or rum – as their relationship to property and power. Many in Paine's circle were from dissenting families; they were therefore shut out from the established Anglican church, the universities and government office. If they had ambitions to govern as well as to renovate the country, they could do so only by means of a radical change that would shatter the power of the aristocracy in the House of Lords and the gentry in the House of Commons. The Foxites, in contrast, were born to aristocratic privilege and connected in a multitude of ways to those they opposed across the floors of the House. They were practical politicians, working within the existing political system. Although many were reformist and temperamentally rebellious, they were always only one election away from power. Few were prepared to jeopardise their chance of governing by advocating the abolition or radical reform of the institution in which they sat. Only Lord Edward actively espoused a philosophy which if implemented would have fatally undermined the class from which he came.

In 1791 few had digested the implications of Paine's work or had foreseen the impact that the *Rights of Man* would have upon its readers and upon the practice of politics. Believing that the high price of three shillings for the first part of the *Rights of Man* alone would deter any but prosperous purchasers, who would be immune to the siren call of republicanism, Pitt's Attorney-General declined to prosecute author or publisher for treason or seditious libel. Besides, a trial might not go the government's way and would be bound to attract attention to the work. Foxites were equally unresponsive, for different reasons. Fox admitted the beautiful simplicity of Paine's argument and found it sympathetic. But he judged it in the context of practical politics and preferred to concentrate on fighting government repression rather than to argue for wider liberties which he believed were impracticable. But there was no animosity between the two camps in 1791. Lord Edward could without anxiety believe in Paine and consort with Fox, and could walk from Rickman's house in Upper Marylebone Street, where Paine received visitors carefully dressed in ponytail, waistcoat, jacket and breeches, to Foxite haunts in Piccadilly and St James's without any sense of dislocation.

Far from severing his links with the opposition in the summer of 1791, Lord Edward was strengthening them in the most intimate way. When the *Rights of Man* appeared he was engaged in a long and passionate affair with Elizabeth, wife of the dramatist and prominent Foxite Richard Brinsley Sheridan. Over the years they had often been in one another's company – on the hustings, round the card table, in the theatre box. What precipitated the affair was not so much Lord Edward's disappointment over Georgiana Lennox as Elizabeth Sheridan's final, miserable rejection of her errant husband.

Elizabeth Linley was born at a time when a cult of domesticity was giving childhood a new prominence and prodigy children were becoming a source of wonder, imagination and riches for their families. The Linley children – Elizabeth, Mary, Thomas, Samuel, Maria, Ozias, Jane and William –

had all the prerequisites for being prodigies: talent, beauty and an ambitious, demanding father who was prepared to use his children's youth as a public spectacle and a commercial enterprise. Thomas Linley was already a successful singer and harpsichordist in Bath when Elizabeth was born in 1754. As a hard-working little girl, Elizabeth impressed onlookers as the image of what her ambitious parents denied her: childhood innocence. The portrait painter Ozias Humphrey, who lodged with the Linleys in Bath for two years from 1762, remembered how she sang to him 'so sweetly' as he painted, 'looking up at him, unconscious of her heavenly features'. Very soon she was appearing in public, selling tickets for her father's benefit concerts at the Pump Room, with her dark hair curling round her shoulders, her brown eyes and her grecian nose turned up towards the buyers, and with a little wicker basket in her hand.

By 1766 Elizabeth was singing in public, and a year later she appeared in a special play at Covent Garden for the four-year-old Prince of Wales, singing music by Johann Christian Bach. Astutely managed by her father and supported by a constellation of talented siblings, Elizabeth soon displayed the heady mixture of innocence and sexuality that was the essence of childhood stardom. Her voice was consistently described as 'angelic', 'sweet', 'soft . . . clear and affecting', but its effect was anything but spiritual. When she sang in Oxford in 1772 she produced in the undergraduates 'a sort of contagious delirium', while one young admirer wrote, after watching her rehearse, 'I am petrified; my very faculties are annihilated with wonder.' These contradictory attributes were cleverly exploited by the playwright Samuel Foote. In 1771 Foote produced a sensationally successful drama à clef, *The Maid of Bath*, about Elizabeth, in which the heroine's charms formed the plot and her virtue its resolution. *The Maid of Bath* ran to full houses in London every summer until 1777.

Elizabeth's own life, closely followed by the press, continued to blend innocence and sensation. Supposedly driven nearly to suicide by the attentions of a Captain Matthews in the spring of 1772, she made a spectacular escape to France. She was ostensibly seeking refuge in a convent, but was in fact accompanied by the twenty-year-old Richard Brinsley Sheridan, whom she married in a secret ceremony in Calais, ratified by a public marriage in England the following April. The *Bath Chronicle*, disappointed that Elizabeth's amorous affairs would, temporarily at least, be off the front page, milked the potential connection between scandal and celebrity to the last, writing, 'thus this charming siren has put it out of her power to listen to the addresses of any man.'

The *Chronicle* need not have worried. Elizabeth continued to make headlines and her life was always written and read as an enticing entanglement of innocence and experience, virtue and vice. Yet the public attribution of vice to Sheridan and virtue to his wife was never so simple as it seemed. Although Elizabeth stopped singing before her adoring fans after she married, a select few were allowed to hear her beautiful voice at twice-weekly subscription concerts in the Sheridans' house in London. This influential audience, disarmed by her voice, was eager to help Sheridan both in his career as a dramatist after the success of his play *The Rivals* in 1775 and as a politician in the 1780s. Elizabeth herself was active in her husband's service. She probably wrote parts of both *The Rivals* and the operetta *The Duenna*, and she read scripts and checked accounts for Drury Lane after her father and Sheridan took it over in 1775. She appeared on the hustings, gambled in the right circles and, after Sheridan's election as MP for Stafford in 1780, became a political hostess and habituée of Foxite circles. In 1775 Joshua Reynolds painted Elizabeth as St Cecilia accompanying a pair of warbling winged putti on the harpsichord, her beautiful Greek profile framed by a heavenly cloud. One bishop called her 'the connecting link between woman and angel', while another said that to see her was like looking into an angel's face. Elizabeth made no attempt to present another facet of herself, but as the 'saint' that Reynolds dubbed her, she was a shrewd, active and intelligent contributor to her own cult.

For more than a decade after their marriage the Sheridans were a successful, if not a contentedly happy, couple. Elizabeth tolerated her husband's infidelities, which were, for the most part, neither compromising nor threatening, and she put up with his drinking. But gradually the marriage emptied to its shell, brittle and cracking. In 1789 Sheridan began a passionate affair with Harriet Duncannon, carried on partly in the drawing rooms and bedrooms of the great Whig houses in London and the country, partly on the page. Schooled in the mutual duplicities of both the Anglo-Irish and Anglo-Saxon versions of the English language and professionally practised at charming comic dialogue, Sheridan excelled at saccharine *billets doux* and easily fell into the amorous baby-talk adopted by Lady Duncannon and her sister the Duchess of Devonshire. Some time in 1789, while they were staying in the same house, he wrote, as a lullaby, 'I must bid *oo* good Night for by the light passing to and fro near your room I hope you are going to bed, and to sleep happily, with a hundred little cherubs fanning their white wings over you in approbation of your goodness. Yours is the untroubled sleep of purity. Grace shines around you with serenest beams and whispering Angels prompt your golden dreams and yet and yet – Beware!! Milton will tell you that even in Paradise Serpents found their way to the ear of slumbering innocence.'

In fact the serpent left Harriet Duncannon alone. In 1790, when the affair became so public that Lord Duncannon thought it desirable to start separation proceedings, he was easily talked round by the Duke of Devonshire. It was the Sheridan marriage that nearly collapsed. When the affair was at its height Elizabeth wrote to her best friend, the austere and censorious Mehitabel Canning, 'The world, my dear Hitty, is a bad one, and we are both victims of its seductions. Sheridan has involved himself by his gallantries and cannot retreat. The duplicity of his conduct to me has hurt me more than anything else, and I confess to you that my heart is entirely alienated from him, and I see no prospect of happiness for either of us in the proposal I have made him of parting. Do not suppose that I will ever do anything to disgrace myself or my family.'

Elizabeth was persuaded out of a separation by Charles James Fox and the Foxite hostess, Mrs Bouverie. In the summer and autumn of 1790 she gambled heavily when she joined her husband at country-house parties, but wrote to Mrs Canning with a glimmer of hope amidst her despair, 'we are both now descending the hill pretty fast, and tho' we take different paths, perhaps we shall meet at the bottom at last, and our wanderings and deviations may serve for moralising in our chimney corner some twenty years hence.' Accustomed though she was to casting herself in a poor light in her letters to the upright Mrs Canning, Elizabeth felt far more guilty about her empty marriage and expensive gambling than Sheridan did about his affairs and deceptions. Still celebrated as an epitome of goodness, painted as St Cecilia, the Virgin Mary and the figure of charity, she found the disparity between her famous persona and her day-to-day life hard to bear with equanimity: unlike her husband she wished to behave as her many admirers thought she did.

By 1791, when Elizabeth and Lord Edward Fitzgerald became lovers, her desperate sense of being imprisoned by her reputation was obvious. Her marriage to Sheridan was over in all but form. The security that she had always derived from her family was shattered by the deaths of her siblings Thomas, Samuel and Mary and by watching her favourite sister and confidante, Maria, succumb slowly to consumption in 1787. Most of all she was lonely, lonely if she stayed in the country with her son Tom, lonely if she gambled in London drawing rooms. Lord Edward offered Elizabeth the adoration of one who believed her to be the person of virtue she no longer felt she was. He also gave her companionship and the chance to use her strong personality to take control of him. 'She managed me,' he told his mother, without regret. In the spring of 1791, Lord Edward's optimism lightened Elizabeth's gloom. His American journey had given him plenty to talk about and if he could not offer the wit of Fox or the brilliance of Sheridan, he could now offer something else: worldly experience and traveller's tales. The *Rights of Man* had given him a system to go with his beliefs; since Elizabeth had first met him in 1784 he had added maturity and confidence to his charm and the beauty of his grey-green eyes, long lashes, high forehead and thick, dark brown hair. Most of all, he offered a foil to her gathering gloom. Elizabeth Sheridan had come to feel that 'the world' was 'a bad one'. Lord Edward was convinced that it was governments and institutions that were bad. His conviction drew Elizabeth out of her lonely despair. She allowed him to love her and admitted that she loved him. In the summer of 1791, while Fox lost money at Ascot, went shooting in Northamptonshire, and made a triumphal tour of the north, and while Sheridan was down in Brighton giving political advice to the errant Prince of Wales, Lord Edward and Elizabeth Sheridan met and made love secretly, in London and the country.

By the late summer Elizabeth was pregnant. Almost immediately the symptoms of the consumption which had killed her sister began to show. As her belly swelled her body wasted away. The voice which had enchanted thousands, faded and broke. She coughed, spat blood and had fevers and chills. Already, by the autumn, when she was four months' pregnant, those around her were worried. 'I am glad you have seen my dear Eddy,' the Duchess of Leinster told her daughter on 17 October, 'for I feel uncomfortable about him. I am sure he frets about Mrs S. and that makes him bilious.'

In mid-December Lord Edward was able to reassure his mother that he was 'perfectly well' even if Elizabeth was getting no better. He had rejoined his regiment in Portsmouth and was drilling his men just as he had three years before in New Brunswick, 'up before seven, and in bed by half after nine, a great deal out of doors.' Soon, Mrs Sheridan had settled herself in Southampton, an easy day's journey west from the headquarters of the 54th Regiment. For the rest of the winter Lord Edward alternated between his regimental and his amorous duties, spending as much time as he could in Southampton, where Elizabeth was growing and dying before his eyes. Sheridan also visited his wife, at the beginning of March. At first he thought her better, but a night walk on the beach drove him to solipsistic misery and remembrance, and he wrote to Harriet Duncannon, 'How many years have pass'd since on these unceasing restless waters which this Night I have been gazing at and listening to, I bore poor E., who is now so near me fading in sickness from all her natural attachments and affections, and then loved her so that had she died as I once thought she would in the passage I should assuredly have plunged with her body to the Grave. What times and what changes have passed! . . . what has the interval of my life been, and what is left me – but misery from Memory and a horror of Ref[l]exion?'

Mary, the daughter of Lord Edward and Elizabeth Sheridan, was born in London, at the end of March. She was a beautiful baby, whom Lord Edward instantly adored. Elizabeth seemed eager for him to acknowledge Mary, and Lord Edward saw his daughter as a legacy from his dying mistress. In Southampton and in London, where they went at the end of April, they nursed it, 'kissed' and 'cried over it together'. As Elizabeth faded, their love grew, and she told Lord Edward that his devotion almost made up for her illness.

Weakened by pregnancy and childbirth, Elizabeth

Sheridan deteriorated fast. *The Times* told its readers on 19 April, 'we are sorry to learn that Mrs Sheridan's health is still in that precarious state, as to make a journey to Bristol Wells absolutely necessary as soon as she is recovered of her lying in.' At the beginning of May Lord Edward said good-bye to Elizabeth. While he stayed in London and prepared himself for her death, she travelled to the Hot Wells at Clifton, accompanied by Sheridan and Mrs Canning and watched by the press. Although, as Sheridan put it, Elizabeth was 'eager to live' and longing to be 'different . . . from what she has been', it was impossible to conceal from her the gravity of her illness.

As she died, Elizabeth seemed to those around her to regain her angelic persona. She was calm and uncomplaining, comforting her family and dwelling on religious subjects. She also became a musician again, the St Cecilia that her admirers remembered. 'Last Night she desired to be placed at the Piano-Forte,' Sheridan reported to Lady Duncannon on 14 May, and, 'looking like a Shadow of her own Picture she played some Notes with the tears dropping on her thin arms. Her mind is become heavenly, but her mortal form is fading from my sight.'

Although Sheridan did not mention it to his erstwhile mistress, some of Elizabeth Sheridan's last days were occupied with the question of her daughter Mary's future. Should she be entrusted to Lord Edward, who loved and would acknowledge her, or should she be passed off as a Sheridan, free from worldly censure but liable to be left in the country and starved of her putative father's affection? By coincidence, Lord Edward's aunt Lady Sarah Napier was nursing her sick husband near by. In conversations with Sheridan and Mrs Canning, Lady Sarah stressed the difficulties of bringing an illegitimate child into the world and cited her own illegitimate daughter, Louisa Bunbury, as an example.

Elizabeth was too ill to be completely clear about her

intentions for Mary. The day before she died, scarcely able to hold a pen, she wrote two declarations. The first was to be signed by Mrs Canning, and read: 'I have and do most solemnly promise my dear friend Mrs Sheridan to protect and guard her poor child thro' life and to do the utmost to breed her up like my own.' As if for herself, Elizabeth added, 'that is saying enough', and then went on to the second declaration, for Lord Edward, which ran, 'I here solemnly promise my dear Betsy never to interfere on any account with Mrs Canning in the education or in any other way of my poor child.' Her strength, grammar and punctuation faltering, Elizabeth wrote her last words, 'I cannot write all. I wish but he knows my heart. Swear or I shall not die in peace.'

At the beginning Lord Edward was stoical, remembering to comfort his mother about his own health and feelings. Six days after Elizabeth Sheridan died, Lord Edward wrote to the Duchess, 'My dearest mother, I just write a few lines to tell you I am tolerably [well], considering everything. Do not be too uneasy about me, dearest Mother. I bear it very well. I was well prepared. She is happy, much happier than any of us here. Why should one repine? But one is selfish, it is human nature. He that made her thought it was time to take her. He knows and does what is best, though we are too blind to see His reasons. We that remain feel the loss . . . it is oneself one feels for. All one's recollections of cheerful happy moments, when all was life; when every look was animation; when that mind and heart was alive to every fine feeling; when one saw it with all its fine beauties and its errors – Oh! they were small, if they were I loved them all – to have all this *nothing*! To see it a blank in the world, to see nothing to fill up that beautiful spot here below, Mother, for oneself this grieves one. Oh! may the little girl be like her.'

Lord Edward heard that Sheridan had Mary 'constantly with him' and in the loneliness of his grief felt forcibly, 'what a comfort it must be'. He made plans to go to Bristol himself, but was stopped by letters from his aunt Sarah, Mrs Canning and Mrs Bouverie. The first accused him of 'indiscretion' and allowing the story of Mary's parentage to leak out; the others probably explained the decision those around Elizabeth had already taken – that Sheridan should acknowledge Mary and Mrs Canning oversee her upbringing. Mrs Canning herself, shocked by Elizabeth's adultery, argued strongly against Lord Edward's going to see his child.

These manoeuvres deprived Lord Edward of a child whom he loved and had nursed, and left him alone without any memory of Elizabeth. At first he struggled against the decision, wanting his daughter, and not convinced that Elizabeth had come to a decision independently. Even his mother's advice to allow his daughter the warm covering of legitimacy was not enough to sway him. 'I see everyone is of one opinion about the child,' he wrote on 3 July. 'My opinion of [Elizabeth's] wishes on that subject is that from the state of her mind she could not judge exactly what was best, that she wished sometimes that I should have it, and at others that S[heridan] should have it; but that, at last, relying on Providence and all our loves for her and the dear baby, we should do what we thought best for it and her sake. It therefore comes to this – what is best for the child?' Lord Edward's reason told him one thing and his heart another, and although he bowed to the former, he was not reconciled to his own decision. 'It is a sacrifice, my dear, dear Mother, that costs me dear, very dear, – the loss of my child, all the dear delights of its loving me, of seeing, as I had flattered myself, my dear Betsy live, and training her through all her different stages of life, seeing her in her youth and fancying such had been her Mother before I knew her. In short, all the love of the Mother had centred in that child. The dear Mother had encouraged all my tender thoughts about it. I had seen it in her arms, kissed, cried over it together. She wanted me to love it, had made me nurse it before her, and now I am to give it up. Everything – all my heart – was centred in [it], but I do it for the best. God direct it may [be]. I tremble at it too. Will it find a tender father? Will it find hearts that will understand its feeling . . .?'

Lord Edward was buffeted one way by his longing to hold and love his child, another by the desire to be seen to be acting worthily. Fighting against his own tendency to 'think a thing right if to do it is a sacrifice of one's self in any degree', he tried to steer a reasonable course. But even after he decided to leave Mary in Bristol with Sheridan and Mrs Canning, he was still holding anguished debate with himself. 'I try to make up my mind about my little girl,' he wrote to his mother. 'To my own feelings I cannot, but I do think that, perhaps, it is better for it . . . Owning it one's child, and not giving it one's name is stamping it with what the *vile world* calls infamy . . . In short, upon the whole, I believe it is the best for the dear little thing to be as it is, and better for the dear, dear Mother's sake. I lose, to be sure, all the dear delights of its being mine, but I must and can make up my mind to do it. What have I not to make up my mind to? I am certain Sheridan will behave generously . . . Poor man, he has gone through a great deal. I feel for him thoroughly; he loved her and feels his loss. I love him for it. I hear he has the child constantly with him. What a comfort it must be! His task is now a dreadful one. But yet I envy it him. I once had a thought, but I have given it up . . . I have totally given it up.'

Despite his suspicion that Sheridan might not be a tender or sympathetic father figure, Lord Edward stopped there and sadly decided that his daughter should grow up as Mary Sheridan. After Elizabeth Sheridan's funeral, when such crowds of her admirers lined the streets that the carriage could hardly get through and filled Wells Cathedral with so much noise that the mourners' grief turned to indignation, Mary spent three months in Sheridan's household at Isleworth in Surrey. Then she was moved to Wanstead in East London, where Mrs Canning lived, and where

Sheridan, overcome by grief and remorse, took a house for Mary and his son Tom. As Sarah Napier told the Duchess of Leinster, 'He dwells sadly on the idea that if he had led a regular life suited to her cast of character she would not have died.'

By the autumn Sheridan had recovered enough to plunge himself into theatre business and entertaining at Isleworth. Between dreams of rebuilding his burnt-out theatre at Drury Lane and plans for redeeming his dissolute life and wasted youth, there was little time left over for the nursery in Essex. 'The last time I saw him, which was for about five minutes, I thought he looked remarkably well, and seemed tolerably cheerful,' Mrs Canning wrote soon after the children had moved to Wanstead.

Sheridan saw Mary infrequently, Fitzgerald never. 'I will not attempt to see it for a year or so,' he told his mother when he had finally decided not to interfere in the arrangements made for Mary's upbringing. To his mother's hope that he would find new love and tranquillity in a wife and household, he responded with contemptuous despair and continued grief. 'I am obliged to you for your wish, but I do not think you will see it accomplished. I require more than I have a right to expect. I don't mean there are not women such as I mean, but I mean they are in a higher class of women than I in the class of men, and it is not my fortune that will persuade them. No, dearest Mother, the remembrance of my dear, dear amiable Betsy must be well, very well, got over before I can give myself up so entirely to another as my idea of marriage requires. Time I know does a great deal and I dare say I shall have the appearance, and at times in reality, shall forget her and shall love others, but she will return to me . . . When I look back on my own conduct and see, loving her as I did – and, God Knows, do – how often I was near destroying my own happiness, I know I am not fit for marriage.'

After Elizabeth Sheridan's death Lord Edward plunged

himself into politics, finding hope again in developments in France. But as he began again to visit Paine and his radical friends, it soon became obvious that the political climate in both England and France was darkening. In February 1792 the second part of the *Rights of Man*, which Paine confidently subtitled 'combining principles and practice', had been successfully published, despite government efforts to buy and suppress the manuscript. Besides outlining a system of representative, republican government which would rule the nation for the common benefit of society, the second part of the *Rights of Man* proposed a radical redistribution of government income to benefit the poor and support their old age rather than to fight wars and maintain sinecures. Within days of its publication, the government had dispatched a spy to watch Paine's movements and check on his associates. The book and its doctrines spread swiftly up through Britain and across the Irish Sea, where it was read by Catholics and Dissenters alike and had soon sold several thousand copies. At the same time the French government seemed to be signalling its desire to test the universality of its revolution by exporting it beyond its own borders. On 20 April France declared war on Austria, and a month later Pitt's government issued a proclamation against 'wicked and seditious writings'. Convinced that republicanism, fuelled by French example and perhaps also by French money and military expansion, threatened both the monarchy and the Houses of Parliament, the government began a two-pronged campaign of repression and propaganda. Spies followed suspected republicans and infiltrated political societies that promoted radical change. At the same time, loyalist sentiment was encouraged and publicised through government-financed journals and newspapers, the support of anti-revolutionary 'Loyal Associations', and the discreet distribution of money to writers, informers, rioters and those who would burn effigies of Paine in town squares and on village greens.

This spectacularly successful campaign, combined with

events in France and the spontaneous growth of loyalist societies, not only averted any potential threat of revolutionary activity on the British mainland by the end of 1795, but also defined a distinctly British identity as everything that was not French. But in 1792, John Bull was not yet marching – honest, plain, reserved and triumphant – against the immoral, effeminate, overdressed, underfed, loose-tongued Frenchman. Painite doctrine seemed to be sweeping all before it, so it was imperative that the first target of the government campaign should be Paine himself.

On 21 May Paine was issued with a summons to appear in court on a charge of seditious libel. Although this was put off a fortnight later, it was reinstated after the flight of Louis XVI from Paris on 21 June and the overthrow of the French monarchy on 10 August. Meanwhile spies watched Cleo Rickman's house in Marylebone, Paine was followed on the street and the government put out rumours that he was about to be arrested. Paine decided not to test their veracity. In mid-September, after government officials had ransacked his luggage and gone through his papers, a harassed and anxious Paine crossed over to France, where he had been elected *in absentia* to represent Calais in the new National Convention. By 19 September, after a triumphal progress through the country, he was in Paris, ready for the opening meeting of the Convention the following day.

On 22 September the new Convention that Paine attended voted to date all documents 'First Year of the Republic'. Six weeks later the Duchess of Leinster received a letter from Lord Edward headed, 'Paris, Tuesday, October 30th. 1st Year of the Republic, 1792,' making it quite clear that he was happy to comply with the Convention's decree. 'I know you will be surprised to hear from me here – do not be uneasy,' Lord Edward told his mother, and added, 'This town is as quiet as possible, and for me a most interesting scene. I would not have missed it at this period for anything.' But it was not the tumult of Paris that might have disturbed the Duchess, so much as the way he began his letter. If Lord Edward had not already told his mother he had become a republican, he was as good as telling her now.

When they arrived in Paris, Lord Edward and Tony made straight for Paine's lodgings at White's Hotel, in the Passage des Petits Pères, close to the Palais-Royal, and right at the heart of the revolutionary city. The Palais-Royal was owned by Louis XVI's cousin, the duc d'Orléans, now called Philippe Égalité. Long before the revolution, the duc d'Orléans had turned its arcades and gardens into a commercial pleasure garden of shops and coffee-houses, where prostitutes and street sellers mingled with bourgeois Parisians parading the latest fashions *à l'anglaise*, buying luxuries from the shops built into the arcades or sitting surveying the scene from café tables scattered across the open space. Lord Edward knew the Palais-Royal well; he had visited it as a child and used it as a young man. 'Henry and I are just come from the Palais-Royal, where we went *pour nous dissiper*', he had written to his sister Sophia from Paris on the way back from Spain in the autumn of 1787. Since then revolutionary spectacle had come to compete with boutiques and prostitutes for crowds and customers. Large audiences of all sorts of Parisians gathered to see orators like the electrifying Camille Desmoulins jump on to the tables and harangue their captivated audience. It was under the arcades of the Palais-Royal that the rhetoric of revolution had first been practised and where the language of liberty and equality had leapt like a fire from mouth to mouth and lip to lip.

By the autumn of 1792 the open excitement of the first years of the revolution seemed to have been replaced by a tenseness, an expectation of violence which the government was trying to harness, and which was symbolised in the swift and hissing guillotine that had recently been set up on the place du Carrousel, in front of the Tuileries. Observers like the young pamphleteer Mary Wollstonecraft, who arrived in

Paris just after Lord Edward, found the atmosphere frightening and the streets of Paris heavy and dour with the threat
of bloodshed. But for Lord Edward Paris was familiar, part
of his happy childhood and the city of his growing up.
Instead of shrinking into himself as many English visitors
did, he walked exuberantly through the streets, chatted
uninhibitedly in coffee-houses and went to the theatre in the
evening.

If he noticed any violence in the air, Lord Edward did not
mention it to his mother. He contented himself with saying,
'the energy of the people is beyond belief,' and would have
dismissed any setback as trivial when weighed against the
immense good the revolution had secured. But many now
felt that the revolution had gone too far. On 10 August the
monarchy had been overthrown. Louis XVI was no longer
the father of his people and the head of state. He was a citizen, Louis Capet, immured in the Temple prison, with his
future hanging in the balance. This event, rocking the established monarchies of Europe, was compounded by the
September massacres, when hundreds of prisoners – priests,
beggars, criminals, prostitutes and lunatics – were brutally
butchered by rampaging mobs, and by a series of military
victories and manoeuvres in which the French army moved
out beyond the borders of the nation for the first time. To
many horrified British observers it seemed that Edmund
Burke's predictions of blood and mayhem, which had read
like deranged and paranoid ravings in the sunlit climate of
1790, were now coming true. It appeared too that the revolutionary army had now begun to embody the international-
ist spirit of the revolution. By occupying lands beyond the
Rhine and invading The Netherlands early in November, the
new republic seemed to wish to spread the sanguinary chaos
of democracy across the monarchies of Europe where deference and stability still reigned.

The September massacres fractured the parliamentary
opposition in London, terrified men of property and immea-

surably strengthened the hand of the government. The opposition was irretrievably split between those who now argued that revolution was inextricably connected to violence – indeed, that violence defined revolution – and those, like Fox, who tried to tread the knife-edge between condemning the massacres and maintaining support for the revolution and the humbling of the King. But fewer and fewer sided with Fox; while he maintained his robust good humour with lazy days of cricket, wine and poetry, his support dwindled and fell away. Great gaps appeared on the opposition benches, until, by 1794, Fox could command only fifty or so MPs.

'We live in times of violence and extremes,' Fox wrote sadly to his nephew at the beginning of 1793. With extremity came polarisation. The habit of thinking in, and defining by, oppositions was now politicised and infused with patriotism. By many, the good was henceforth associated with England, the bad with France. Everything – politics, religion, dress, manners, reading habits, taste, sexual behaviour and sexual attitudes – was put in the implacable scales, until no area of life was free from narrow political definition. Early casualties were the linked beliefs in the essential unity and the essential goodness of man, beliefs that could easily be ridiculed in the face of Parisian massacres and French aggression.

No one better illustrated this implosion of Enlightenment optimism than Lord Robert Fitzgerald. Always lukewarm about the revolution, he moved from detachment to horror after he left his post in Paris and moved to Switzerland in the middle of 1792. By 1795 he had come to the conclusion that the world was 'inhabited by two sets of human beings, by men and Frenchmen.' 'Misery and wretchedness' may have come out of the revolution, he told Lord Grenville, but it 'has also been productive of some good in opening the eyes of men to the real character of Frenchmen and of exhibiting to the world in its true colours that horrid mess of infamy, perfidy and wickedness of every description which had been long concealed under the veil of politeness and urbanity, to the great misfortune . . . of those who mistook the appearance for the reality.' The French, Lord Robert concluded, had become 'agents of the devil', 'openly disavowing God and the Truth!'

As the rhetoric hardened and France slid towards all-out war against the monarchies to the east and west of her, fewer Englishmen travelled to Paris. Those who did knew they were courting the attention of government spies and postmasters, especially if, like Lord Edward, they flaunted their allegiance to Paine; so Lord Edward hastened to reassure his mother in Tunbridge Wells that Paris was tranquil and safe, that he was there to distract himself from thoughts of Elizabeth Sheridan and enjoy the company of Tom Paine. 'I lodge with my friend Paine – we breakfast, dine and sup together. The more I see of his interior the more I like and respect him. I cannot express how kind he is to me; there is a simplicity of manner, a goodness of heart and a strength of mind in him that I never knew a man before possess. I pass my time very pleasantly, read, walk and go quietly to the play. I have not been to see anyone, nor shall not. I often want you, dearest mother, but I should not have been able to bear Tunbridge for any time. The present scene occupies my thoughts a great deal and dissipates unpleasant feelings very much. Give my love to Ogilvie and the girls. I think he would be much entertained and interested if he was here. I can compare it to nothing but Rome in its days of conquest – the energy of the people is beyond belief . . . I go a great deal to the Assembly – they improve much in speaking.'

However wary Lord Edward may have been of government officials who might read his letters, he was confident of his mother's approbation. The Duchess of Leinster longed to indulge her favourite son's every wish and was disposed to like what he liked. When war broke out between France and Austria she was happy to humour her son's delight in

French military success and flirtatiously to side with him against an unyielding William Ogilvie. 'Dearest Mother, I got your dear letter yesterday,' Lord Edward wrote towards the end of November. 'You were quite right about my joy at the taking of Mons, and the success of the battle of Jemappes. I was in the house [the Convention] when the news came, and saw Baptiste received. It was an animating scene – as indeed everything that passes here now is. You who know the French may conceive it. I am delighted with the manner they feel their success: no foolish boasting or arrogance at it, but imputing it all to the greatness and good-ness of their cause, and seeming to rejoice more on account of its effects on Europe in general than for their own indi-vidual glory. This, indeed, is the turn every idea here seems to take. All their pamphlets, all their pieces, all their songs, extol their achievements but as the effect of the principle they are contending for, and rejoice at their success as the triumph of humanity. All the defeats of their enemies they impute to their disgust at the cause for which they fight. In the coffee-houses and play-houses, every man calls the other *camarade, frère*, and with a stranger immediately begins "Ah nous sommes tous frères, tous hommes, nos victoires sont pour vous, pour tout le monde"; and the same sentiments are always received with peals of applause. In short, all the good enthusiastic French sentiments seem to come out; while, to all appearance, one would say, they had lost all their bad . . . I am glad Ogilvie warms up a little. I knew he would. I am sure you enjoy the success, for you and I always had a proper liking for the true French character.'

Lord Edward, with all his uneasiness about father-figures and patriarchal authority, and his new disdain for monarchi-cal states modelled on the family, had noticed with approval in his letter the French called one another and their sympa-thisers 'camarade' and 'frère'. Years before French writers found a solution to the problem of finding a rhetoric to inspire love for the Republic, Lord Edward had told his mother that the Indians spoke the language of *fraternité*, telling him they were '"all one brother" – all "one Indian."' Now in France, where the King was no longer the father of his people and the patriarchal model of the state seemed to have been replaced by a free brotherhood of equals, he was delighted to find the language of the new, republican family spoken on the streets. It confirmed for him that Paris was just the latest, and best, manifestation of the brave, and fatherless, new world created at Frescati and purified in Canada.

Because he lived his political convictions so transparently, and because he was an aristocratic convert to republicanism, Lord Edward attracted the revulsion of men of property horrified at finding the viper of democracy in their midst. Rumours about his activities in Paris were soon circulating round the drawing rooms of St James's and at house parties in the country. Before the end of November it was widely reported that he had joined the Jacobin Club and given money to pay for a French force to invade Britain from The Netherlands. From his elegant mansion of Stowe, in Buckinghamshire, the Marquis of Buckingham wrote to Lord Grenville, 'I have received three letters this morning from persons all unconnected with each other, expressing the universal indignation of all London at the names of the officers who subscribe to the French cause, and the universal expectation that they will be dismissed. Both Lord Semphill and Lord E. Fitzgerald have long before been mentioned to me as speaking openly the most direct treason. They subscribe 2£ 11s; the sum excited my curiosity, as I found several others had done the same, and I . . . was told that the sum was meant to cover two muskets at 25s each, and one shilling for the expenses to Ostend.'

But Lord Edward had no intention of placating his critics in England. On the contrary, he now prepared to take his commitment to fraternity to its logical conclusion. In the *Rights of Man* Paine had already ridiculed titles. There were no titles in the Garden of Eden, he wrote, and 'through all the vocabulary of Adam there is not such an animal as a Duke or a Count'. 'The Patriots of France have discovered in good time that rank and dignity in society must take a new ground,' Paine concluded. 'It must now take the substantial ground of character, instead of the chimerical ground of titles; and they have brought their titles to the altar, and made of them a burnt-offering to Reason.'

Soon after he arrived in Paris, Lord Edward did the same. On 18 November, at a dinner in White's Hotel to celebrate recent French victories, he proposed several of the toasts, among which one ran ominously, 'The armies of France: may the example of its citizen soldiers be followed by all enslaved countries, till tyrants and tyranny be extinct.' Then Lord Edward and Sir Robert Smith renounced their titles. As they swilled the wine around their glasses and drank to 'the speedy abolition of all hereditary titles and feudal distinctions', Lord Edward Fitzgerald, fifth son of Ireland's premier peer, nephew of the Duke of Richmond and great-great-grandson of Charles II, became, as he told his mother, 'le citoyen Edouard Fitzgerald'. It only remained for him to find his own field of action, his own 'enslaved country' and his own 'citizen soldiers': he had become a revolutionary.

In the consuming excitements of Parisian politics Lord Edward's grief for Elizabeth Sheridan faded. A new peace of mind allowed him to enjoy people as well as politics. Through Paine he made contact with a number of radical Irishmen living in Paris. He also struck up a friendship with John Hurford Stone, who at twenty-six was exactly his age and whose immoderation matched his own, and he visited his old mistress Françoise de Lévis. Madame de Lévis's husband was to be one of the French Revolution's great survivors, turning himself from royalist to republican and back again with suave indifference. She herself was already successfully playing the part of the *citoyenne*, dining off soup

and fish, with a reduced income, a small staff and a knowledge of the streets of Paris acquired by walking instead of
driving to engagements and soirées.

Madame de Lévis was one of many Parisian aristocrats
who had prudently given up their carriages and adopted
what Lord Edward described to his mother as 'very plain
dress'. Dr John Moore, whose son was to die at Corunna
defending the British monarchy against the French republic,
ascribed this change to Gallic dissimulation when he noticed
it in Paris at the end of 1792. But some aristocrats dressed
down with relief, some with conviction, others for survival.
Everyone understood that each item of clothing, from the
tricolor cockades and ribbons to the simple cottons worn by
women, and from cloth coats and high hats to the breeches
and long boots *à l'anglaise* of the men, expressed a political
attitude. Clothes declared allegiances, and with their English
and Roman references, offered a stitched summary of the
revolution's pedigree.

Before the revolution aristocratic reformers had adopted
the dress and colours of the English opposition, simple to
indicate liberty and openness, buff and blue to show
American sympathies. Elements of this style remained, but
'Roman' haircuts for men – copied from the style worn by
the actor Talma playing Titus in Voltaire's *Brutus* in 1791 –
and 'grecian' hair for women, were new, as were refinements
such as the protruding shirt collar. Madame Tussaud, whose
sense of the symbolic led her to buy the guillotine that killed
the King, noticed that the duc d'Orléans set the high fashion
for dressing low. In the 1780s he had dressed his household
in Foxite buff and blue. Now, in 1792, he himself wore 'a
short jacket, pantaloons and a round hat, with a handkerchief
worn sailor-fashion loose round the neck, with the ends long
and hanging down, the shirt collar seen above . . . the hair cut
short without powder à la Titus, and shoes tied with strings.'

Lord Edward quickly grafted this new sartorial republicanism on to his habitual 'opposition' outfits. He took to

wearing his collars high, his hair short and unpowdered and his jackets simple. His enthusiasm for 'dressing down' was soon such that one observer noticed his 'peculiar dress', and his outfits were scrutinised for their political signals wherever he went.

In the evenings Lord Edward whiled away time at the theatre, where, although everyone was now a citizen, the rich who remained in Paris still crowded into the tiered boxes and watched the people and the play through gaps in the iron fretwork erected years before to put a barrier between them and the eager gaze of the multitude below. But the metallic grilles were lacily see-through: the rich wanted to be seen as well as to see. On 21 November Lord Edward accompanied his friends Reid and John Stone to *Lodoisha*, a new and fashionable opera by Cherubini. While the singers worked their way through the newest Italian elegances of phrase, Lord Edward in his box scanned the faces behind the *loges grillées*. He was startled to see, staring out, a face like Elizabeth Sheridan's, with white skin, dark eyes, high forehead and the same black-brown curls, not falling loose as Elizabeth's had done but put 'close up' in democratic style. John Stone knew this face well. It belonged to Pamela, daughter of the renowned educationalist Madame de Genlis.

The close attention that Lord Edward paid to Pamela's face for the rest of the performance would not have surprised her. Scores of men and women had already exclaimed over her beauty, unusual bearing and distinctive style of dress. She was described by the comte de Neuilly as 'an entirely divine creature with a pale oval face, the most beautiful eyes in the world, although of different colours, charming unpowdered brown hair which she wore in curls, with a nonchalant graceful bearing and always dressed in simple but exquisite taste.' But she excited interest beyond her white skin, neat figure and long dark eyelashes because she belonged to an extraordinary household and because her origins, even her name, were uncertain and mysterious.

Pamela had grown up in the extended household of Louis XVI's cousin Philippe Égalité, duc d'Orléans, and his mistress Stéphanie-Félicité, Madame de Genlis. Madame de Genlis, an aristocrat from Burgundy whose husband was a royal servant, had ascended the treacherous slope of courtly success using the well-tested footholds of good looks, wit and a royal lover. Leaving her long-suffering husband toiling in royal ante-chambers, Madame de Genlis had become, by the mid-1770s, the accepted mistress of Louis-Philippe-Joseph, duc de Chartres and future duc d'Orléans, the beloved lady-in-waiting of his wife and the effective manageress of the Palais-Royal. At the same time she began to publish the first of scores of dramas, novels, tracts, reflections and maxims, which won her widespread fame as a female interpreter of Rousseau and a follower of the English novelist Samuel Richardson.

For twenty years, Madame de Genlis enthralled her royal lover, maintained an amicable friendship with his wife and was adored by the assortment of children she gathered around her. In 1779 she was given charge of the duc's two-year-old twin daughters, and three years later they were joined in their picturesque school-house pavilion, in the convent of Bellechasse, by his sons (the eldest of whom was the future monarch, Louis-Philippe), Madame de Genlis's niece and a few courtiers' daughters. Madame de Genlis's educational method was derived mostly from Rousseau but incorporated elements of earlier educational theorists, particularly Fénelon and Madame de Maintenon. Much attention was given to female accomplishments: at Bellechasse and during the summers at the duc's châteaux of Raincy and Saint-Leu, the girls studied dancing, singing and the harp, an instrument which encouraged the striking of dramatic attitudes and the display of fashionably naked arms. They learned English, German and Italian, and innumerable crafts, constructing portfolios, ribbons, wigs, marbled paper and artificial flowers. The Orléans princes, true to Rousseau's prescriptions, learned joinery and gilding alongside the more traditional skills of fencing, riding, classical languages, geography, history, science, law and mathematics. Any moment left over – Madame de Genlis did not believe in wasted time or holidays – was devoted to gardening, gymnastics and visits to workshops, manufactories and the theatre.

One of Madame de Genlis's more practical maxims was that one should always tell the truth except when one has something to hide. Her autobiography, in which memories and imaginings were woven together into a seamless garment with which to shroud her ambitions and indiscretions, gave its readers an example of this aphorism in practice. In her memoirs and her conversations Madame de Genlis offered two complementary explanations for the sudden arrival of Pamela in the Orléans household in the spring of 1780. In the first place she wanted a child to talk English to her pupils; in the second she longed to follow Rousseau's prescription of separating a child from its parents and placing it under the care of a tutor who could educate it into the natural and original goodness of mankind. Accordingly, the duc asked Nathaniel Forth, his agent in London – and the British government's agent in Paris – to search for a six-year-old child with dark hair and a white skin, and, after some searching, Forth produced Pamela. As Madame de Genlis explained, 'She was the daughter of a man called Seymour, who was of good birth and who married, despite his family, a person of the most inferior class who was called Mary Sims and took her to America to Newfoundland to a place called Fogo. Pamela was born there and they named her Nancy. Her father died and her mother went back to England with the child, aged eighteen months. As her husband was disinherited, she found herself in distress and was forced to live by the work of her hands. She established herself at Christchurch. It was there that, four years later, Mr Forth went, charged by the duc d'Orléans to look for and send us a little English girl. He found this child there, and obtained her from her mother.'

To her dying day, Madame de Genlis never deviated from this account of Pamela's origins, although she sometimes claimed that her father was not called Seymour but William Brixey. In her support she would cite her passion for Rousseau, her penchant for adopting children and the need for her pupils to learn perfect English. It was her misfortune that few, certainly not Pamela herself, believed her story. Observers pointed out that Pamela had the opal-white skin of the Orléans family and that her hazel eyes and forehead were very like those of Madame de Genlis. Horace Walpole, a man always inclined to accept and relish seamy or scandalous explanations for mysteries, met Pamela in 1785 and told his eager correspondents that Madame de Genlis – whom he called 'the scribbling trollope' – had 'educated' Pamela 'to be very like herself in the face'. People remembered that in the spring of 1773, one date given for Pamela's birth, Madame de Genlis had first been confined with a mystery illness and then travelled to Spa in Belgium for her convalescence. There she had appeared at dinner in a *pet-en-l'air*, a corsetless petticoat normally only worn for lounging about in the morning, whose loose pleats would discreetly envelop the sagging folds of a post-natal stomach. One of the pupils at Bellechasse recorded that soon after the little girl arrived in the household both Christian and surnames were chosen for her; Pamela in homage to Richardson's beautiful servant girl whose virtue brought her the reward of marriage into the gentry, and Seymour, the family name of the Dukes of Somerset, which conjured up an aristocratic origin to balance the humble if romantic timbre of Pamela. Madame de Genlis never denied that Pamela was a surrogate name, but insisted that Seymour was her father's name – except when she said it was Brixey. Her given first names of Stephanie Caroline Anne (sometimes reversed as Anne Caroline Stephanie) contained by chance both Madame de Genlis's own name of Stéphanie and also that of her daughter Caroline. Finally, those inclined to read the guilty secrets of a life into a writer's work could point to Madame de Genlis's novel *Les Mères rivales*, which told the harrowing story of a mother forced to farm out her illegitimate daughter whom she loved to distraction but could never acknowledge.

Pamela always believed that she was the daughter of Philippe Égalité and Madame de Genlis, shipped to England by her parents when young and brought up by Mary Sims in Christchurch under the watchful eye of the duc's agent, Nathaniel Forth. She told the story of her arrival at the Palais-Royal as a homecoming rather than as the start of a new life. After she arrived in Paris, she said, she was taken to a side entrance of the Palais-Royal where Philippe Égalité himself was waiting. The duc took her in his arms, kissed her repeatedly and then carried her along several dimly lit corridors to the apartments of Madame de Genlis. As he came into the little room he announced triumphantly *'voilà notre petit bijou'*. Pamela sat between the duc and Madame de Genlis on the sofa, while they embraced her in turn, and wept 'a great deal'. The next day the little girl was officially introduced to her new world. Unaware that she was supposed never to have seen Madame de Genlis before and confused by the milling crowd of chattering courtiers, she rushed up to her 'Maman' and buried her head in her lap. Madame de Genlis insisted that Pamela's natural sagacity had drawn her to her.

In the fervid atmosphere of the court the rumours flourished. As Pamela grew, so did the mystery of her origin. Had she been plain or awkward many would have been willing to believe the story of her humble origins. But she grew up into a beautiful girl who amply fulfilled Madame de Genlis's desire for the embodiment of Rousseauian purity: she was graceful and demonstrative, educated into feeling rather than book learning and seemed to have a natural aptitude for story-telling, dancing, *tableaux vivants* and fashionable 'attitudes'.

Her '*Héloïse*', a pose of passionate ecstasy that encapsulated the spirit of Rousseau's famous novel, drew gasps of admiration from onlookers, and showed that, as a young girl, Pamela did everything she could to please the woman she wanted to believe was her mother but who refused to acknowledge her. By the time she was nine or ten, Pamela's beauty was legendary and the mystery of her origin surrounded her like an impenetrable, shimmering cloud; her looks and her story were her definition and her fate: they became her.

As early as the mid-1780s Pamela's life story was dependent more upon attitudes towards Madame de Genlis than upon anything that she herself did. In 1785, at the height of her fame as an educationalist, Madame de Genlis travelled to England to accept an honorary degree from the University of Oxford. Pamela went too, accompanying her 'Maman' not only to the court and London's grandest drawing rooms, but also to the grave of Samuel Richardson, where Madame de Genlis paid homage to her great precursor. Most people politely accepted the story of Pamela's origin as a fiction, privately revelling in her close connection with the French royal family. Some, including the diarist Fanny Burney, gave Madame de Genlis the benefit of the doubt. Although Pamela's beauty might hint at nobler origins than Madame de Genlis's version suggested, it was plausible that a great educationalist and high priestess of sensibility would want – as others had done – to test the efficacy of Rousseau's theories by adopting and nurturing a child of nature. Twelve-year-old Pamela was a creature of transcendent beauty, a living proof of Rousseau's emphasis on naturalness, simplicity and the separation of children from their parents.

At the end of 1791 Madame de Genlis and Pamela were back in England, this time quasi-refugees from the revolution in France and accompanied by several members of the Orléans household, including Adèle, the legitimate daughter of Philippe Égalité. But now Madame de Genlis was shunned by the court and in Pittite assemblies, where she was openly described as the mistress of Philippe Égalité and the power behind his treacherous behaviour and republican sympathies. Stories were passed round about her own fondness for gestures of revolutionary solidarity, the most widespread of which was that she liked to flaunt a piece of polished Bastille stone between her breasts, as if the revolution were her own suckling child. After learning of Madame de Genlis's dangerously democratic household at Bury St Edmunds in Suffolk, Fanny Burney confided to her diary that she had been horribly deceived. 'They form twenty, themselves and household. They keep a botanist, a chemist and a natural historian always with them. They are supposed to have been common servants of the Duke of Orléans in former days, as they always walk behind the ladies when abroad; but to make amends in the new equalising style, they all dine together at home . . . What a woeful change from that elegant, amiable, high-bred Madame de Genlis I knew six years ago, the apparent pattern of female perfection in manners, conversation and delicacy.' Those who wanted to preserve Pamela's purity and natural goodness were now eager to look beyond the Palais-Royal for her birthplace and to publicise their belief that Pamela could not be the daughter of a couple whose conduct traduced familial and monarchical values: far better that she were an English girl, of respectable lineage, than the product of French democracy.

Madame de Genlis and her entourage were still welcomed by the dwindling band of opposition politicians and radicals. The poet Samuel Rogers invited the whole party to an assembly and recorded that Pamela was 'radiant with beauty' and that John Stone, Talleyrand, Sheridan and Fox were among the guests. Lord Edward was invited to several similar gatherings, but he apparently refused to attend. Sheridan, though, was a willing guest, and was immediately struck by Pamela's likeness to his ailing wife. After Elizabeth Sheridan's death in May 1792, the playwright invited Madame de Genlis to his country house at Isleworth, on the southern bank of the Thames above London. There he assuaged his grief in Pamela's beauty, seeing in her a chance of creating a happier version of his first marriage. A rumour circulated that he had proposed to Pamela. Though never confirmed, it added one more legend to those that surrounded her.

Lord Edward had had several opportunities to meet Madame de Genlis and Pamela in London, but had turned them down. Trained by the Duchess of Leinster to value expression of feeling rather than the exercise of intelligence, he professed a dislike of 'blue stocking' women, who, he thought, defined themselves by intellect alone. Besides, according to his younger sister Sophia, he did not take Madame de Genlis seriously as a theorist, calling her most popular work on education, *Adèle et Théodore*, 'all perfect nonsense'. The Duchess of Leinster, however, as a confirmed Rousseauist, admired Madame de Genlis 'to the greatest degree', Sophia noted in her diary for 1792. Lord Edward enjoyed pointing out that while Madame de Genlis was noted for the moral purity of her works, her life was by no means 'free from censure', as Sophia put it.

After seeing Pamela at the theatre, Lord Edward dropped his objections to her 'Maman', sent Reid and Stone round to their box, introduced himself, and was invited with Reid to dinner the next day. They found Bellechasse turned upside-down and its inhabitants in a chaos of packing. The convent itself had been emptied of nuns and filled with soldiers. The garden was piled high with forage for their horses and the convent's outbuildings had been transformed into munitions dumps. Inside the single-storey pavilion, where maps still hung on the staircase walls and portraits of emperors and kings still stared down from the sky-blue walls of the schoolroom, servants were sifting through the goods of the entire extended family. Madame de Genlis was preparing to leave Paris. Because of her royal connections and stay in England,

Adèle, Philippe Égalité's daughter, had been put on a list of undesirable émigrés who threatened the revolution and were ordered to leave France. The whole school was going with her: nineteen-year-old Pamela, seventeen-year-old Hermine, Madame de Genlis's other adopted daughter, her niece Henriette de Sercey, her nephew César du Crest, Myris the resident painter and the 'Gouvernante' herself. For two days after Lord Edward went to dinner at Bellechasse, Orléans family servants dismantled the school-room and packed goods and clothing into trunks. On 25 November the party lumbered out of the convent gates in the rue de Bellechasse, crossed the Seine and set off north, making for Tournai, near the border in Belgium. On the road they were overtaken by Lord Edward. Overcome by Pamela's beauty and enamoured of everything she represented, he had fallen desperately in love and was determined to propose to her.

Lord Edward was well aware both of Madame de Genlis's account of Pamela's origins, and of Pamela's supposed connection with the Orléans family. He believed that she was illegitimate rather than adopted, but that gave him little cause for alarm. His mother's family, the Lennoxes, were descended from just the sort of illegitimate royal child that he believed Pamela to be. He was familiar, too, with the ways in which natural children of aristocrats were treated. His uncle, the Duke of Richmond, had several. Those who were of humble origin – the children of his local mistress Mrs Bennett – the Duke more or less openly acknowledged, giving an annuity to their mother and leaving the three girls ten thousand pounds apiece in his will. But his daughter by his French mistress Madame de Cambise was treated differently. In the first place the Duke wanted the child with him; in the second her mother had to be protected from exposure in the press and censure from her own circle. Henriette le Clerc, as she was named, was Pamela in reverse, kept in France until a few years old and then brought over to England by Lord Edward's aunt Lady Louisa Conolly and installed, as an adopted orphan, with the Duke of Goodwood. Richmond eventually left Henriette his personal papers, but he never openly acknowledged her as his child.

If Pamela's origins were no worry for Lord Edward, neither was the identity of her putative father. By the end of 1792, Philippe Égalité had been rejected by most French aristocrats and denounced across Europe as 'unnatural' in his support for the abolition of the monarchy headed by his cousin. But to Lord Edward a connection with the Orléans family would be a proclamation of his radical sympathies and a declaration of his republicanism. Pamela's illegitimacy, and her occluded relationship with the man she believed her father, made her almost an embodiment of the fatherless republic itself, and was a positive attraction for a man who had in so many ways renounced his own father. Besides, he and Pamela shared a Rousseauian education and were both imbued with a belief in the expression of feeling and emotion. And then, she reminded him of Elizabeth.

Pamela was beautiful and accomplished, if educated into an over-demonstrative flightiness. She was also available, her marriage prospects shattered by her connection to the Orléans family, damned as an aristocrat by many republicans and a republican by many aristocrats. Lord Edward knew that his own relative poverty – now compounded by his having just been dismissed from the army – would be unlikely to secure him an English bride from his own circle. But Madame de Genlis made it clear that he could have Pamela, and seemed happy enough to accept his opposition contacts and royal blood in return. She did nothing to discourage Lord Edward's attention and, after little more than two weeks, gave her consent to his proposal of marriage to Pamela.

Once his proposal had been accepted Lord Edward should have written to tell his brother, as head of the family, of his intention of marrying. But the Duke of Leinster was in Carton and far beyond the reach of Lord Edward's pen or thoughts. Lord Edward's concern was for his mother's approbation and permission. As soon as Madame de Genlis had given her consent he dashed off to the Duchess of Leinster, who was in Tunbridge Wells on a matrimonial errand of her own, trying to catch husbands for her youngest daughters.

The Duchess of Leinster did not demur at her favourite son's choice of bride. The tide that had turned against the French Revolution in the autumn was running fast now; Louis XVI was being tried before the Convention and in less than a month would be found guilty and condemned to the guillotine. A family alliance with France's foremost aristocratic republicans would do nothing to help the marriage prospects of her daughters or the careers of her sons. But the Duchess knew Lord Edward was obstinate and she was an admirer of Madame de Genlis. She already knew of Pamela as a legendary figure and obviously believed that she had royal blood. Despite her own marriage to William Ogilvie the Duchess urged her children to pursue money and social standing unashamedly and would have demurred at her son's choice had she really believed Pamela to be the child of a woman so poor that she had accepted a sum of only twenty-four pounds to give her up. Besides, her beloved Edward was twenty-nine years old, and it was time he settled down. The only pity was, the Duchess exclaimed, that Pamela herself was not richer, especially as Lord Edward was both careless and generous with money. 'My mother remonstrated upon that subject, and I believe advised him to consider well whether he could live and be happy upon a little,' Lady Sophia Fitzgerald wrote in her diary. Lord Edward was unmoved, pointing out that Pamela would have a provision from the duc d'Orléans of seven thousand livres a year. His mother gave her consent, persuaded Ogilvie to part with twelve hundred pounds as a wedding present, and sent Lord Edward joyfully back to Tournai.

The Duchess had no qualms that the special place she held in her son's heart could be usurped by Pamela. Her confidence was confirmed by the letter Lord Edward wrote while the marriage settlement was being finalised, in which he described his wife as a present for his mother, another young satellite that would move and turn in the sphere of her influence. 'I now only long for the moment of giving you the dear thing to love as you do me, which I know you will. She is dreadfully frightened at the thoughts of going among you all . . . Ciss and you are the two she seems to depend on; Charlotte and O. she is afraid of. God bless you, dearest Mother, you are the best of Mothers, and I love you better than ever.'

As soon as the marriage contracts – in which both he and all the Orléans family were described according to revolutionary protocol as '*citoyens*' and '*citoyennes*' – arrived in Tournai, Lord Edward and Pamela were married. He represented himself alone, but Pamela had a panoply of witnesses from the Orléans household, including Madame de Genlis, Philippe Égalité and the future King of France, Louis-Philippe, who dutifully signed the register with the correct republican formulation, 'L. Philippe Égalité'.

For his family, Lord Edward's marriage was a bravura romantic gesture; he had gone to Paris to revel in politics and had fallen in love; he had left Paine behind in the revolutionary maelstrom and emerged married, and with Pamela. 'Edward Fitzgerald has acted a romance throughout all his life, and it is finished by his marriage to Pamela Seymour,' Sarah Napier told her old friend Susan O'Brien, a convinced Pittite who already disapproved of Lord Edward's political opinions and associates. Lord Edward himself lent credence to the idea that the attraction of Pamela lay solely in her beauty, her unselfconscious charm, her distinctive sense of style and her likeness to Elizabeth Sheridan. When he wrote about Pamela to his mother or sisters, he always emphasised her position as his wife and her beauty: she was his 'dear little wife', 'the dear, little, pale, pretty wife' who was so young that she grew 'both broad and long' after the wedding, maturing into a woman and a wife at the same time.

Lord Edward was careful to separate Pamela from politics. When he left his mother in Tunbridge Wells to return to Tournai for his wedding he wrote, 'Dearest Mother, I wish you would tell Leinster all about this, for you may guess I am not in a writing mood. You can now also tell all friends, for there is no occasion that they should think I am carrying on treasonable practices, which they will certainly impute this second journey to.' But Pamela was the Revolution; marrying her bound Lord Edward to what she represented; and that was, in itself, a kind of treasonable activity. For which King-loving British patriot would join his life to the daughter of a man who, soon after the wedding took place, would sit in judgment on his own King, his cousin, and would shortly vote for his death? But this was both a political love affair and a political marriage. So coming out of Paris Lord Edward did not leave Paine behind; he brought Paine out in Pamela, and his wife was, as she would soon discover to her cost, a living symbol of the Revolution he espoused.

Before he left Paris, and in the first heat of his love for Pamela, Lord Edward had talked to his fellow Irishman and republican Henry Sheares and to Tom Paine about the possibility of bringing the French Revolution to Irish soil. His new fervour had made him dismissive of any more attempts at parliamentary reform in Ireland. He was now thinking as a revolutionary soldier and was convinced that an armed struggle against the Dublin government and the British Crown would be necessary to create an Irish republic free from the English connection. He remembered the great Volunteer conventions of the 1780s, where massed ranks of armed men stood under fluttering flags and the assembled crowd had jostled and pushed to get good views of speakers calling for political reforms. He knew of the enthusiasm with which many of the fiercely independent Volunteer forces had greeted the French Revolution. In Belfast, the centre of radical activity, portraits of Franklin and Washington, Mirabeau and Dumouriez were painted on signs suspended above the streets. In 1792 a great Bastille Day pageant was celebrated there. Tricolors were hung from windows and a banner showing the French fortress engulfed by fire and *sans-culottes* was paraded above the crowd by uniformed Volunteers on a cart drawn by four horses. Lord Edward decided that the fervour of the Volunteers might be turned into a hunger for revolution. He told Paine that with French money pushing them on, a force of four thousand disaffected Volunteers could overwhelm the understaffed Irish garrisons in three months. Paine was impressed, and agreed to put a request for French backing to his Girondist ally in the Convention, the Foreign Minister Lebrun. After planning a means of secret communication between Paris and Dublin, Lord Edward set off for Tournai, Tunbridge and marriage.

Lord Edward left Paris for London with a new sense of purpose and as a practical politician. Whereas in earlier years his habit on returning from journeys or postings was to linger with his mother, bathing in her adoration, getting answers at last to his endless epistolary questions and sleeping off lazy afternoon dinners on drawing-room sofas, this time he did not even stay at her house in Harley Street. He took lodgings instead at the York Hotel in Albermarle Street, a stone's throw from his father's old London house. There Pamela could have some respite from the attentions of her husband's family. But, just as important, there, or in the taverns nearby – like The White Bear in Piccadilly, where Paine had often sat over brandy with his friends – Lord Edward could receive communications from France and meet English republicans who might help advance his plans. But he and Pamela did not stay long. On 26 January 1793, eight days after Louis XVI was condemned to death in Paris, the Dublin press announced: 'Yesterday morning, arrived the Princess Royal, Captain Browne, from Parkgate, with the Right Hon. Lord Edward Fitzgerald, his lady and suite, and several other persons of quality.'

CHAPTER
THREE

◆

REPUBLICAN AND
MARRIED MAN

Dublin, Ireland, 26 January 1793

Lord Edward and Pamela stepped off the Parkgate packet straight into scandal in Dublin. They installed themselves in Leinster House with Tony, Pamela's trunks and trousseau, her French maid Sophie and Lord Edward's modest belongings. Leinster House was dark and forbidding. Although trees dotted the grass of the back lawn and the fields beyond the new Circular Road were clearly visible from the upper windows, it had a cold, stony air, especially in winter, when the trees were leafless and the houses of Merrion Square and Kildare Street seemed to creep towards the façades. But it was convenient for parliament, a short walk down Kildare Street and along College Green.

When Lord Edward arrived, parliament had just assembled. A few days later, in the middle of settling Pamela and Tony into a world which, for different reasons, was hostile to them both, he took his seat in the newly remodelled chamber. Straight away he was plunged into a debate on a government proclamation banning assemblies of just those Volunteers whom he dreamed of recruiting into his rebel army. Alarmed at the republican language of recent Volunteer statements, and appalled at the decision by some Dublin Volunteers to celebrate recent French military victories, the House warmly supported the ban. Most opposition members, and even Henry Grattan, whom Lord Edward remembered from his last stint in parliament as the greatest of all opposition figureheads, came over to the government side. When those he sat among rose one after the other, condemned the Volunteers and declared them some of the King's worst subjects, Lord Edward was abruptly brought out of the elation of his Paris days and into the gritty compromises of Ascendancy politics. The disappointment overwhelmed him, and jumping up from his seat in great agitation he shouted out to the Speaker, 'Sir, I give my most hearty disapprobation to this address, for I do think that the Lord Lieutenant and the majority of this House are the worst subjects the King has.'

Straight away there was chaos. MPs all round the circular chamber started shouting 'To the bar' and 'Take down his words'. The Speaker ordered the House cleared; visitors and jotting transcribers were hurried out of the public gallery under the new square glass roof, and parliament went into closed session. For three hours members tried to get Lord Edward to withdraw his remarks. Some threatened punishment – suspension or expulsion, perhaps – others asked him simply to say, officially and for the record, that he was sorry. Eventually Lord Edward declared, with the sarcastic humour which he occasionally showed at times of stress, 'I am accused of having declared that I think the Lord Lieutenant and the majority of this House the worst subjects the King has. I said so, 'tis true, and I'm sorry for it.' This linguistic juggling enraged MPs who quickly and unanimously passed a resolution 'that the excuse offered by the Right Hon. Edward Fitzgerald . . . for the said words so spoken, is unsatisfactory and insufficient' and ordered 'that Lord Edward Fitzgerald do attend at the bar of this House tomorrow'.

The bar in parliament was both the wooden rail which separated MPs from the public, and a symbolic boundary between ostracism and acceptance, separation and belonging.

The day after his outburst Lord Edward was brought to the bar by parliamentary officials. His fellow members sat on the other side of it and listened to what he had to say in expiation of his conduct. Lord Edward said enough to open the bar and sit in the House once more, but fifty-five MPs were so suspicious of his motives and demeanour that they voted against accepting his apology.

A week later he was attacking the government again, and again the object was the forces he was planning to recruit for rebellion. In response to calls from the newest radical political society, the United Irishmen, the Volunteers planned to turn themselves into a permanently armed body that could press for reform. Soon after war with France was declared the Dublin government moved to clamp down both on the Volunteers and on the Defenders, armed Catholics in the countryside. An Arms and Gunpowder Bill was introduced that banned the movement of arms from place to place. Recognising that this would hinder the training of his 'citizen soldiers', Lord Edward spoke vehemently against the Bill, saying it infringed 'the liberty of the subject'. He was almost the only MP who voted against it. Later, speaking against a Bill brought in to quell a spate of rural disturbances, Lord Edward went so far as to threaten the government, declaring that nothing could 'restore tranquillity to the country, but a serious, a candid endeavour of Government and of this House to redress the grievances of the people. Redress those, and the people will return to their allegiances and their duty; suffer them to continue and neither your resolutions nor your bills will have any effect.'

Lord Edward's minatory outbursts, stories about his activities and associates in Paris, and the presence of Pamela made him an object of fascination and fear to his former Dublin acquaintances. They had known him to be a radical but remembered him from his previous stay in Ireland also as a raffish half-pay officer who drank a good deal, gambled and raced horses at the Curragh and flirted desultorily with the prettiest girls in the drawing room. The transformation in Lord Edward, who now scorned his horses and strode purposefully through the Dublin streets with his conspicuous quick 'elastic step', his modest dress and cravat of ominous hibernian green shocked a former friend, Robert Jephson. 'He is turned a complete Frenchman, crops his hair, despises his title, walks the streets instead of riding and thence says he feels more pride in being on a level with his fellow citizens,' Jephson explained, aghast. Rumours that Lord Edward was an agent of the French seemed to be confirmed by an incident at the Smock Alley Theatre, where he had gone with Pamela to see the celebrated Mrs Abingdon soon after war was declared against France at the beginning of February. Although the theatre audience was mixed and could not be counted on to support any government policy, one of the actors added an impromptu, 'Damn the French' to his lines, which brought a 'moderate clap', according to the Countess of Roden. But Lord Edward jumped up in his box and started hissing at the stage, defending both the Revolution and his wife. In the theatre his radical gesture found support; the men and women in the pit below him stood and applauded loudly. 'I never saw anything so delighted as they were with it,' noted Lady Roden, adding that Lord Edward himself, like a serpent on the attack, 'looked bursting with rage and venom.' 'I think he will come to some untimely end,' she concluded with sensational relish.

Many of Lord Edward's former friends who were inclined to give him the benefit of the doubt about his political views were checked by the presence of Pamela. To Ascendancy society Pamela seemed to be every bit as much of a symbol of the Revolution as she was to Lord Edward himself. Her poor English was regarded as a sign of commitment to France, her disdain for the niceties of dress was taken as deliberate subversion and she had an irremediable defect in Ascendancy eyes which was unmentioned but universally noted: she was a Catholic. Scarcely more than a child, used to being praised for her expressiveness and beauty, she had no aptitude for social politics and no talent for scotching the rumours that circulated about her beliefs. Instead of insinuating herself quietly into the heart of Ascendancy society, she went to balls dressed in the latest revolutionary fashions; and instead of receiving guests herself, she cheerfully accompanied Lord Edward on his demotic rambles through the Dublin streets. Stories about her imprudent behaviour quickly reached the Duchess of Leinster in London. Lady Lucy Fitzgerald reported that soon after the execution of Louis XVI, when mourning dress was adopted by most people connected with the government in Dublin, Pamela flamboyantly compromised the sombreness of her black gown by putting pink ribbons in her hair. Shunned by her horrified hosts and fellow guests, 'she came home to Edward, who was in bed, quite in a rage, pulled open his curtains and told him, "Edward, *je ne veux plus aller au Bal: des gens d'une telle impolitesse!*"' Rumours spread that she had approvingly described some of her own red ribbons as 'la couleur du sang des aristocrates' and that a necktie she wore had been dipped in the blood of the murdered French king as it dripped from his guillotined head.

Lord Edward's family dismissed these stories, dwelling insistently instead on the couple's endearing eccentricities. 'It is a comical scene between Edward and her,' the Duchess of Leinster reported the Duke of Leinster as saying, 'for that they quarrel like two little children, making it up the next minute and doting upon one another, all in a good humoured way.' But they did react to the Francophobic mood in Britain by beginning to question the very aspect of Pamela's legend that had initially justified her entry into the family: her link with the French royal family. Sarah Napier, describing Pamela for Susan O'Brien, now stressed that she was quite unlike the deceitful Madame de Genlis. 'I hope we have got our lovely little niece time enough out of her care to have acquired all the *perfections* of her education, which are certainly great, as she has a *very uncommon*, clever, active mind, and turns it to most useful purposes, and I trust our pretty little *Sylphe* (for she is not like other mortals) has not a tincture of all the double-dealing, cunning, false reasoning and lies, with which [Madame de Genlis] is forced to gloss over a very common ill-conduct . . . I never saw such a sweet, little, engaging, bewitching creature as Ly Edward is, and childish to a degree with the greatest sense. The upper part of her face is like poor Mrs Sheridan, the lower part like my beloved child Louisa. Of course I am disposed to dote upon her. I am *sure* she is not *vile Égalité's* child; it's impossible.'

In London the Duchess of Leinster responded to rumours of Pamela's revolutionary sympathies and Lord Edward's treasonable outbursts in the way that she would time and time again in the years to come: by denying everything and insisting that her family display her own certainties. Lord Edward replied in a way that would become characteristic too. He sent his mother a long letter of half-truths designed to allay her fears by contradicting hearsay, announcing his withdrawal from political dispute and avowing his domestic happiness. Pamela had settled down well, he implied in early April. 'Everybody seems to like her, and behave civilly and kindly to her.' His grievances against his old friends were not on her account. 'My differing so very much in opinion with the people one is unavoidably obliged to live with here, does not add much, you may guess, to the agreeableness of Dublin society. But I have followed my dear mother's advice, and do not talk much on the subject, and when I do, am very cool. It certainly is the best way; but all my prudence does not hinder all sorts of stories being made about both my wife and me, some of which, I am afraid, have frightened you, dearest mother. It is rather hard that when, with a wish to avoid disputing, one sees and talks only to a few people of one's own way of thinking, we are at once all set down as a nest of traitors. From what you know of me, you may guess all this has not much changed my opinions. But I keep very quiet, do not go out much, except to see my wife dance, and, in short, keep my breath to cool my porridge. Your affectionate son, E.F.'

In fact, as his mother knew, Lord Edward had been doing anything but staying quietly at home. In February, only a month after his angry outburst in parliament, he was exciting attention far away from Dublin, in Dungannon, County Tyrone, where a Volunteer Convention was held at which delegates from a number of political societies and the Volunteers met to consider the question of reform. Although his name was not mentioned in press reports, as the Duchess thankfully noticed, Lord Edward's presence was noted in London. 'The Dungannon proceedings are, as you will see, in all the papers, and Edward's name not mentioned,' the Duchess wrote to her daughter Sophia, adding, 'He had, in truth, nothing to say to them in any way whatever, and was only led to go there from mere curiosity; but it was an imprudent one at this time, as anything he does is so misrepresented, and it is plain to see nobody believes one word one says in his defence.'

The Convention in Dungannon had been designed to recall the great Volunteer Conventions that had pushed for reforms a decade earlier. But times had changed. Although the Convention applauded the Volunteers, it refused to condemn the war against France, declared its attachment to the existing constitution and condemned republican forms of government. Any hopes that Lord Edward brought with him from Dublin would have been firmly quashed.

Lord Edward was quick to shift towards men more likely to be sympathetic. By the time of the Dungannon Convention he had probably already realised that his defence of the Volunteers in the House of Commons was an anachronism; their radical energy was already spent and it was not from among them that a republican army might be recruited. His interest shifted swiftly to a more promising group of men, members of the Society of United Irishmen, founded in Belfast in October 1791, 'to forward', as its members' oath said, 'a brotherhood of affection, an identity of interests, a communion of rights, and a union of power among Irishmen of all religious persuasions.'

Less than a month after he had landed in Dublin, only a couple of weeks after his outburst in the House, Lord Edward was travelling to Dungannon with a leading member of the Dublin Society of United Irishmen, Archibald Hamilton Rowan. Rowan was a country gentleman and former Volunteer who had written and distributed the address from the United Irishmen that had given the Castle an excuse to suppress the Volunteers. In December, just before Lord Edward arrived back in Dublin, the government had issued a warrant for Rowan's arrest and, although the warrant was widely regarded as toothless, an aura of sedition henceforth hung around him. It was thus Lord Edward's companion, rather than his presence at the Dungannon Convention, that alarmed his mother and aroused talk of his treacherous leanings.

If he had not already written to them before he left Paris, it was easy enough for Lord Edward to find the United Irishmen. Two acquaintances from his Paris stay, John and Henry Sheares, could have given him introductions to the Society's principal officers in Dublin. Henry Sheares, a frugal lawyer who lived modestly surrounded by stacks of books, was an ardent republican. Like Lord Edward, and with his brother John, Sheares had joined the Jacobin Club in Paris. After Lord Edward had impulsively left Paris for Tournai in December 1792, the Sheares brothers had stayed on and, as members of the French National Guard, attended the King's trial. Before he left Paris John Sheares had stood in the great silent crowd in the Place de la Revolution when Louis XVI was trundled in to the guillotine, and it was rumoured that he was one of those swift citizens who

dashed forward with outstretched arms to dip their handkerchiefs and neckties in the monarch's blood. Like Pamela's
red ribbons, John Sheares's red handkerchief symbolised his
connection with the revolution and he enjoyed flaunting it,
once waving it under the nose of the inexperienced Daniel
O'Connell and saying it was stiff with the King's life-blood.

The United Irishmen held open meetings of anything
between a few dozen and two hundred men in Tailors' Hall,
an old guild hall in the decaying area of the city near Christ
Church where effluent, rats and children all ran together
through a warren of stinking, narrow streets. But members
also often met in committees in their own homes, which
were mostly in more prosperous areas of the town.
Although he was not yet a member of the United Irishmen,
Lord Edward was soon acquainted with several of its most
prominent figures in Dublin: Oliver Bond, a wealthy
woollen draper and the Society's newly elected secretary;
Simon Butler, the Society's first president, a lawyer from an
aristocratic family; Thomas Addis Emmet, a brilliant young
barrister who had already proved his credentials by appearing on behalf of the radical demagogue James Napper Tandy
in an action against the Lord Lieutenant; Dr James
Reynolds, a physician from County Tyrone; Edward
Lewins, one of the few Catholics high up in the organisation, a good French speaker once destined for the priesthood
who was now a Dublin attorney, and Wolfe Tone, the brilliant, witty and mercurial lawyer who had been one of the
moving spirits behind the Society's foundation.

Matilda, Tone's wife and keeper of his flame, claimed in
her old age that in the spring of 1793, 'Lord Edward
Fitzgerald and the Sheares brothers who had just come from
Paris were *playing revolution* and did mischief.' But if Wolfe
Tone himself thought the trio's revolutionary enthusiasm
was impolitic and likely to lead to government reprisals
against the Society, some of his colleagues in Dublin were
prepared at least to listen to their urgent demands for action.

In the spring, Paine's negotiations with the French Foreign Minister Lebrun dramatically bore fruit. An American, Eleazer Oswald was commissioned by the French government to go to Ireland 'to sound out the dispositions of the Irish people' towards French military intervention. After one of the circuitous journeys favoured by secret agents, which took him to Ireland via northern Europe and Norway, Oswald arrived in Dublin on 8 May. He immediately contacted Lord Edward, who had just left the gloom of Leinster House for the spring flowers of Frescati. South of the city, down the notorious Black Rock road where loose stones damaged horses' hooves, flew into riders' faces and overturned numerous carriages, Lord Edward was less conspicuous than on the streets of Dublin. He could receive visitors in relative secrecy there, and he need have no fears of compromising his brother by plotting against the government in the family mansion.

Lord Edward took Oswald to talk to senior United Irishmen by turns: Simon Butler, Oliver Bond, Rowan, Reynolds and perhaps Edward Lewins and Emmet. They were suspicious of Lord Edward and, though they cautiously welcomed offers from France, made it clear that Ireland was not ready for rebellion. Lewins later recalled that 'Thomas Paine sent the American Oswald to Lord Edward Fitzgerald with an offer of 20,000 men, arms, munitions and money . . . to help the Irish shake off the English yoke and to establish their independence. Ireland was not then sufficiently prepared for such a revolution and the proposal was rejected.' Oswald went back to Paris, Lord Edward to Frescati.

As usual when he was disconsolate or lonely, Lord Edward dug himself into feeling at home at Black Rock, re-creating with soil and seedlings a version of the garden he had loved as a child. As soon as he had reached Frescati he had thought of his mother, writing to her on 6 May, 'I dote on being with you anywhere, but particularly in the country, as I think we always enjoy one another's company there more than in town. I long for a little walk with you, leaning upon me – or to have a long talk with you, sitting out in some pretty spot, of a fine day, with your long cane in your hand, working at some little weed at your feet, and looking down, talking all the time.' The Duchess's book room, where he sat in the bay window to write to her, had a plant-filled passage from it that led out to the garden. With the doors and windows open, and the pots of spring plants in the passage just watered, bird song and the scent of the flowers drifted over Pamela at her needlework and Lord Edward at his desk. 'The room smells like a green house,' he wrote, and, seeing his mother's tiny neat handwriting on a letter to Pamela in front of him, added on cue, 'you may judge how I love you at this moment.'

Two days later, with Pamela recovering from an illness in the book room, Lord Edward turned his attention to the part of the garden nearest to the house, where myrtle and bay trees grew against the back wall between the stuccoed cream façade and the green lawn. Lord Edward made the gardeners cut and roll the grass, but he weeded and planted the flower beds himself. First, with lingering Foxite loyalty, he mixed blue gentians and yellow primroses. Then he planted clumps of lily-of-the-valley under the evergreens and beneath a towering elm. 'I have got the beds well dressed, and the whole thing looks beautiful, and I mean to keep it as neat as possible while here. In short, dearest mother, I only want you here, and [my] little wife well; for, in the midst of the feelings of the fine weather, I want her to enjoy them with me.'

The soil at Frescati, like that all around Dublin, was poor, heavy and clayey. Despite the best efforts of the gardeners to lighten it with lime, limestone gravel, coal-ashes from the fireplaces, sand, and even street sweepings, only sturdy European plants flourished in it; alpines like the yellow-eyed auriculas that Lord Edward treasured had to be grown in the greenhouses and then moved indoors to flower. The garden itself was a mixture of formal planting, informal walks and what Lord Edward called a 'wilderness'. Close to the house there was an old-fashioned, formal rosery and several beds of flowers and shrubs that rose in mounds from the lawn and were bordered by low, green-painted palings. Further away were gravel walks and a wild area. Here meadow plants and grasses were probably allowed to flourish into an appearance of neglect and naturalness. Hedgerow climbers twined together to make a secluded bower very like 'Elysium', Julie's ominously named garden in *La nouvelle Héloïse*, where Saint-Preux saw 'roses, raspberries and gooseberries; little plantations of lilac, hazel-trees, alders, syringa, broom and trefoil dispersed without any order or symmetry, and which embellished the ground, at the same time as it gave the appearance of being overgrown with weeds.'

Rousseau's garden was a harbinger of the end – Julie's death was imminent when Saint-Preux made his way there. But it was also a return to the beginning, to a longed-for political paradise where everything was, as he put it, 'natural and simple', unlike aristocratic gardens and governments where everything was corrupt and contrived. As usual, the Duchess of Leinster only transplanted part of Rousseau to Black Rock. Frescati was an Eden, and it had its wilderness and hay-field. But it also had greenhouses, pots of tender flowers and carefully planted beds. The Duchess stopped short of political symbolism; unlike her son, she would never have wielded a spade herself or made any comparisons between a garden and a state.

Disappointed both by the reception of Oswald by the United Irishmen and by the parliament's lack of interest in substantial reforms, especially complete emancipation for Roman Catholics, Lord Edward lived almost continuously at Frescati in the early summer of 1793. In the absence of revolution, the garden had to do duty for the new kingdom.

The spring shrubs were all out; pale roses, white viburnums with their heavy scent, the cornucopias of lilac blooms with pink tops that curled like calves' tongues towards the sky. It was a 'heavenly' place, he told his mother, and of course he loved it because she had made it. 'All the shrubs are out, lilac, laburnum, syringa, spring roses, and lily-of-the-valley in quantities – four pots full now in the book room . . . I believe there never was a person who understood planting and making a place as you do. The more one sees Carton and this place, the more one admires them; the mixture of plants and the succession of them are so well arranged.'

Lord Edward stayed at Frescati week after week partly because he was isolated, socially and politically. As news of Robespierre's *coup d'état* reached Ireland, and as prospects of an early peace faded, caution filled the hearts of reformers and the widespread dislike of France amongst supporters of the Castle and Westminster governments turned to hatred. Pamela became an object of fear as well as scorn. Lord Edward was shunned by old acquaintances, and with the United Irishmen in disarray, suffering falling membership and a crisis of confidence, many of his new associates were wary of him too. The Duchess of Leinster relayed to Lucy Fitzgerald with relief at the beginning of August the Duke of Leinster's report that 'tho' great pains have been taken with Dr. Eddy to draw him into the political societies he has kept out of them all. Are you not delighted at the Dr. Angel's prudence. I am certain too it has all been owing to his fear of vexing me Dear fellow!'

But Lord Edward stayed aloof from the United Irishmen not because he was prudent, but because they were. At this vulnerable moment he made friends with Arthur O'Connor, a radical MP from County Cork exactly his own age. O'Connor had a way with women and words, a swarthy complexion, a saturnine, intelligent expression, and an ability to laugh at his own beliefs that some saw as subtlety, others as a lack of commitment. Until 1793 he had an unremarkable career as a barrister and Member of Parliament. He lurked on the fringes of the Foxite opposition in London, and in 1787 met the Duchess of Leinster there. But in Dublin he often voted with the government and was not regarded as a radical until he professed his disgust at his fellow MPs, wearing mourning for the executed Louis XVI in February 1793. From then on O'Connor consistently demanded Catholic emancipation and denounced the government with an articulate vehemence that overwhelmed and impressed Lord Edward. According to his sister Lady Lucy, Lord Edward called O'Connor a soul 'twin to his own'. Whatever the cause, he was dazzled by O'Connor and felt that, at the age of thirty, he had at last found a male friend he could trust with his secrets. The two were soon seen together everywhere, and Lord Edward was especially delighted that his new companion seemed to be able to express so eloquently and succinctly his own political views.

At the end of the parliamentary session, in the late summer, Lord Edward and Pamela joined Mr Ogilvie, the Duchess of Leinster and the four youngest Fitzgerald and Ogilvie girls at the quiet spa town of Malvern in Worcestershire. The Duchess had first gone to Malvern thirty years before, pregnant with Edward and worried about the health of her son Charles. Charles had recovered, so Malvern held no miserable memories for the family. Even so, bad news and spa towns inevitably went together; this time it was Lord Edward who was stunned by an unexpected message. Its subject was little Mary Sheridan, his daughter by Elizabeth; Mary was now eighteen months old. Her nurse observed that she had 'all the airs and phantasies of any woman of fashion in Grosvenor Square.' William Smyth, tutor to Mary's half-brother Tom Sheridan, called her 'a child of the most extraordinary beauty that I have ever seen', and noticed how Sheridan, who was always distracted and overworked, 'never came to Wanstead without bringing some cap or riband or toy for this beautiful infant'. He would 'stand looking at it, and talking with the nurse, and endeavouring to engage its attention for the hour together'.

One evening in November, when Sheridan was down at Wanstead for a ball, Mary became seriously ill, convulsed by fits brought on by dehydration or a very high temperature. In the drawing room Smyth and the guests were dancing. Suddenly, Elizabeth Sheridan's old friend Mrs Canning pushed open the door at the end of the room and shouted to Smyth as he stood at the head of the line of dancers, 'the child, the child is dying'. Rushing upstairs, Smyth found Mary lying weakly on her nurse's lap and Sheridan gazing at her in horror and despair. A doctor was brought down from London, but to no avail. The fits returned and Mary died. Later Smyth lay in bed listening to Sheridan crying uncontrollably in the next room.

Mary's little body, which Lord Edward had hugged and kissed only the year before, was sent down to Wells in Somerset to be buried in the cathedral next to her mother. But her father was taken up with politics and with Pamela, and he did not mourn his daughter for long. He remembered the autumn visit to Malvern as quiet and cheerful, writing to his mother when he returned to Ireland, 'no party will ever be so pleasant to me'. Besides, he had other distressing news to cope with; Philippe Égalité had been guillotined on 6 November, to prolonged applause from the watching crowd. Pamela did not yet know what had happened. Lord Edward had been harbouring the news for weeks. He had written to Madame de Genlis in Switzerland, hoping that a letter from her would spare him the terrible task of telling his wife that the man she believed was her father was dead. But no reply had reached Dublin by the middle of January. So, just before they were to spend a week at Carton, where guests who knew and approved of Égalité's demise would come and go, and newspapers exulting in the grisly news would litter the library, Pamela was told. 'Dearest little Pamela was better when she left Carton,' Sarah Napier reported to the Duchess of Leinster, but added, 'I fear her nerves will not soon recover the shock.'

The Reign of Terror that swept away Philippe Égalité struck fear into more hearts than those already hostile to the revolution. Moderate people of all sorts in Ireland now became afraid. They thought about the fearful phalanx of policemen and officials of the Committee of Public Safety who arrested the unsuspecting at the dead of night; they imagined slimy cells of the Luxembourg prison where whole families were immured without warning, heard the laden tumbrils creaking through deserted early-morning streets and saw the efficient guillotine that worked day after day like the machines in Pandemonium. Panicking, they made monsters in their imaginations of all republicans and of all Catholics who might bring the French to the shores of the British isles. Half in scorn, half in pity, Lord Edward described for his mother the fears of his uncle Thomas Conolly, who had raised and commanded a militia corps in Derry to demonstrate his loyalism and preserve his huge estates in the north of the country. 'His militia has frightened him: he swears they are all republicans, as well as every man in the North. He concludes all his speeches by cursing Presbyterians: he means well and honestly, dear fellow, but his line of proceeding is wrong.' Conolly's fear had passed to his wife, Louisa. 'When she wakes she expects Robespierre or Danton to guillotine her before night,' Sarah Napier tartly reported.

On Lord Edward, however, the Terror had no effect. He never wavered in his republican conviction and, although he continued to attend parliament, he had given up any hope that it would go any way toward implementing even the sorts of reforms that the United Irishmen were then demanding: votes for all men, yearly parliaments and reform of electoral districts. For over a year he had seen the solution to all Ireland's political problems in a revolution which would express the popular will. Unfortunately the people seemed quiescent, as he hinted to his mother; 'if the people don't help themselves, why, they must suffer. There is not a person that doesn't abuse this war, yet no man will take measures to stop it.' 'Politics do not go on well, I think,' he concluded, and turned back to Frescati and his gardening.

It was in the Frescati garden that Lord Edward first put his levelling doctrine to work, placing himself, half humorously but with symbolic deliberateness, under his gardener Tim, and digging the soil himself. This direct contact with the land may have been tolerated in the children of confirmed Rousseauians, but was unprecedented and despised in an adult. In Ireland, where Catholic cottiers who laboured in the fields and tilled their own patches of potatoes were held in fear and contempt by Protestant landowners, it was particularly inflammatory. But this was more than a flamboyant gesture; in taking the part of Adam, Lord Edward was planting the seeds of a new kind of politics which would soon absorb much of his time: going among ordinary people, talking to them, drinking and dancing with them, listening and persuading, seeking not their votes but their commitment to his cause.

For now, he was happy to labour among the flowers, knowing that his mother was reassured by horticultural chat. 'I have got an under-gardener (myself) to prepare some spots for flowers, and to help Tim. I have been hard at work to-day and part of yesterday (by the by, the weather so hot I go without coat, and the birds singing like spring) clearing the little corner to the right of the house, digging round roots of trees, raking ground and planting thirteen two-year-old laurels and Portugal laurels . . . I mean from thence to go to the rosery and then to the little new planted corner. I am to have hyacinths, jonquils, pinks, cloves, narcissus . . . Bless you all: this is too fine a day to stay longer writing. I wish to God you were here.'

Although he toyed with ideas of staying on at Frescati, Lord Edward was looking for a house of his own. He needed a place where he could meet his new political associates without compromising his family. Besides, William Ogilvie, who was always an astute businessman, had wanted to let or sell Frescati for some time, and now had hopes of a tenant, the Lord Lieutenant himself. Disgusted that his republican garden might become the playground of the King's appointees, Lord Edward laid down his spade and thought seriously of moving. 'I have left off gardening,' he told his mother on 19 February 1794, 'for I hated that all my troubles should go for that vile Lord Westmorland, and my flowers to be for aides-de-camp, chaplains and all such followers of a lord-lieutenant.' He transferred his energies to politics and to Pamela, who was expecting a baby in the autumn. Lord Edward started to look after his wife immediately her pregnancy was certain. 'She is quite well, eats, drinks, and sleeps well; she works a great deal and I read to her,' he wrote, and described his unborn baby as if it were growing in his garden, calling it 'the little young plant that is coming'.

With the end of the parliamentary session on 25 March Lord Edward turned back to the increasingly secret world of the United Irishmen. A second French agent, William Jackson, arrived in Dublin on 3 April charged with finding out if a French invasion force would be welcomed and supported. Jackson was a resident of France whose colourful past – he had been a tutor, Anglican curate, firebrand preacher, radical journalist and secretary to the notorious Duchess of Kingston who was tried for bigamy in the House of Lords in 1776 – aroused the suspicions of many United Irishmen who thought he must be a British spy. Lord Edward, who had not known Jackson in Paris, was not convinced by his introduction from their mutual acquaintance John Hurford Stone, and refused to meet him.

Jackson was not a spy, but he was accompanied by an old friend, John Cockayne, a London solicitor so appalled by Jackson's beliefs that he had already contacted William Pitt and was passing every detail of the mission to the government of Westminster. So a miserable irony arose. Jackson, whom many suspected of double dealing, was a sincere revolutionary; Cockayne, whom no one took much notice of, was betraying them all to London.

When they arrived in Dublin Jackson and Cockayne took lodgings in Dame Street, close enough to the Houses of Parliament to look as if they had legitimate business, but convenient for United Irish meetings near Christ Church Cathedral. But Jackson had great difficulty meeting United Irish leaders, and the only one to trust his story was Hamilton Rowan, who was already in gaol awaiting trial for sedition. Jackson visited Rowan in his cell and the two agreed that a statement on Ireland should be written by Wolfe Tone and sent to France. Tone's statement, hurriedly written on 14 April, and copied and embroidered by Rowan, depicted an Ireland ripe for rebellion and eagerly awaiting French help. Jackson was delighted when he read it and decided to send it off to France by putting it into the ordinary post. Its inevitable interception put Tone and Rowan under immediate suspicion of treason and allowed Jackson to be arrested and confined in Dublin under heavy guard.

In the wake of the arrest the Dublin government suppressed the United Irishmen. As a result it became the secret society its most conspiratorial members had always wanted, irrevocably pitted against the government, an obvious refuge for revolutionaries and disaffected republicans. When they went underground the United Irishmen lost their public platform from which to press for change. They developed all the hallmarks of a secret society: passwords, handshakes and an increasingly sophisticated campaign of propaganda aimed at the whole population, from the newspaper-reading merchants and artisans of the towns to the illiterate cottiers in the countryside for whom ballads and sentimental songs were written and sung. Carters in the movement took newspapers from place to place in their wagons. Pedlars carried boxes fitted with secret drawers where broadsides and song sheets could be concealed. As they walked the country lanes they pinned messages and exhortations to gates and trees; when they arrived in towns they added handbills to their wares. In every militia regiment, at every country fair or rural festival, United Irishmen circulated secretly, shaking hands and spreading the word, gathering support and giving back a buzz of action and resistance, explaining where meetings were held and how members could be found. In suppressing a movement in which many members argued for constitutional reform, the government created something much more dangerous: a secret and exciting world of rumours and revolutionary cells. In 1794 the United Irishmen were disunited and feeble. A year later they were flourishing in their dark underground habitat, skilfully tunnelling, the government knew not where, under the pillars of the social order, acquiring the confidence and the means to bring Dublin Castle crashing down.

No one knew better than Castle officials that the United Irish leaders would take easily to this world of conspiracy and fear. It was a state of mind that had governed Ireland for centuries. Having suppressed the United Irishmen, the Dublin government immediately took steps to infiltrate it, creating in the process a mirror world of spies and informers who operated, like those they stalked, in a twilight world of disguise, secrecy and betrayal. Many spies operated in both worlds, living one day in the cells of the United Irishmen, known only to the few but part of a silent, waiting army; the next entering the Castle world, an initial in a government ledger, reporting to Castle officials in dingy backrooms and quiet side streets. Few spies were unmasked, but equally few reached the top of the United Irish organisation. For years the two secret forces simply marched stealthily, side by side.

None of this drama, which culminated in Rowan's dramatic escape from gaol and flight to France in a tiny fishing boat, and Tone's departure for America in June 1795, found its way into Lord Edward's letters to his mother. By now, thinking both of the well-organised government agents opening mail in the post offices and of his mother's peace of mind, he chose to talk about only his domestic affairs. There was plenty to write about: Pamela's health, his hopes for the future, and his new house, a small detached villa in a perfect position in the town of Kildare.

'I do like a small place so much better than a large one,' Lord Edward had told his mother when he was considering a move to Kildare. Thomas Conolly had offered Lord Edward his own villa there, fully furnished and as a present. 'I don't think I shall take it: indeed I am determined not, it is too much to accept as a present. But I have some thoughts of borrowing it for the summer, trying if I like it, and if it will suit me, I will then take it off his hands, and pay him what it is worth,' Lord Edward explained to his mother, adding, 'The situation certainly is advantageous for me – six miles from Kilrush, across the Curragh, not too large and the country around pleasant.' But when he went to look at Conolly's lodge, Lord Edward found something that suited him even better, a small secluded house belonging to a Mr Hetherington, set in its own garden, yet open to the fields on the northern edge of the town. It stood on a circular walled rampart, and although the houses of Kildare town pressed up against it on the southern side, it was a secret place, elevated a little and surrounded by spreading old trees and shrubs. The house itself stood in the middle of this wooded plateau, reached by a narrow lane. It was stuccoed and painted white, with a gravel courtyard, a small detached kitchen building and a yard with stables for the horses which Lord Edward took on a sub-lease from a Mr Kilfoyle. To the side and round the front of the house was a lawn and the beginnings of a garden which Lord Edward immediately planned to improve and expand with flowers.

Lord Edward signed a lease for the house and moved in at

the beginning of June 1794 with Pamela, Tony and an idio-
syncratic medley of belongings which included two song
thrushes in cages, a new set of china sent by the Duchess of
Leinster, and a portrait of Thomas Paine to hang above the
parlour fireplace. There was not much room for more;
Kildare, like Lord Edward's wife, his wardrobe and his habit
of walking the streets, was a symbol of his way of life and
political beliefs; a rebuff to the grand country houses in
which his erstwhile acquaintances lived. 'It is the smallest
thing imaginable, and to numbers would have no beauty; but
there is a comfort and moderation in it that delights me,' he
wrote. 'In coming into the house, you find a small passage-
hall, very clean, the floor tiled; upon your left, a small room;
on the right, the staircase. In front, you come into the parlour, a good room, with a bay window looking into the garden, which is a small green plot surrounded by good trees . . .
the bay window covered with honeysuckle, and up to the
window some roses. Going upstairs you find another bay-
room, the honeysuckle almost up to it, and a little room the
same size as that below; this with a kitchen or servants' hall
below, is the whole house.' Lord Edward employed about
six servants: Tony and Sophie, probably a cook, a stable-
hand, and one or two local people who came from the town
of Kildare each day to clean the house and dig the garden
under Lord Edward's careful eye. At its core it was a close-
knit household. Besides waiting on and walking about with
his master, Tony danced with him, jaunting up and down
the parlour to the sound of Irish pipes.

Lord Edward was delighted by his little house, which he
was determined to make another Eden and another Frescati.
Even as he sat describing it for his mother, the planting was
beginning, with Pamela putting out old cottage garden
favourites that would flower through the summer. 'This,
dearest mother, is the spot as well as I can give it to you, but
it don't describe well. One must see it and feel it; it is all the
little peeps and ideas that go with it that make the beauty of

it to me. My dear wife dotes on it and becomes it. She is busy in her little American jacket planting sweet peas and mignonette. Her . . . work box, with the little one's caps, are on the table. I wish my dearest mother was here, and the scene to me would be complete . . . I have tired you by this long scrawl. I have not said half I feel, for it is one of those delightful days when one thinks and feels more than one can say or write.'

It was more for its site than its soil, though, that Lord Edward had taken the house. Its seclusion allowed visitors to come and go up the little lane in the shade of the elm trees without attracting notice, and its position, with fields to one side and the town of Kildare past an old castle to the other, meant that Lord Edward could walk out one way and talk to farmers tilling their land and stroll the other to confer with the small traders and shopkeepers in the town. Kildare, a bustling market centre astride one of the main routes between Dublin and the west of Ireland, was a town of great strategic importance. Immediately outside it lay the Curragh, an area of scrubby flatland which could serve as an assembly point for a rebel army before a march on the capital. To the north of the town lay the vast Bog of Allen, a waterlogged lowland of waving grasses and low damp shrubs criss-crossed by secret paths and the black scars of peat diggings. The Bog was inaccessible to outsiders like British troops who did not know how to find their way across the spongy land and who could easily be ambushed in the midst of its gloomy expanse. It was an ideal place for rebels to congregate, train, hide and appear from.

All around Kildare town and beyond the Bog of Allen was the County of Kildare itself, a centre of sedition that had concerned the government for some time. Its inhabitants were prosperous, well educated and used to opposition. For a long time it had been the power base of the Dukes of Leinster. Now it was becoming a centre of United Irish activity, an ideal place for Lord Edward to walk about and talk republicanism. He quickly made himself known there, advertising his politics by pointedly rejecting coal in favour of turf in his fireplace and by beginning to learn Gaelic. Under the cover of helping his brother recruit a new militia force, he began to discover who were loyal, who were indifferent and who were disaffected, potential recruits to the republican cause. 'We have been busy here about the militia. The people do not like it much – that is the common people and the farmers – and even though Leinster has it, they do not thoroughly come into it, which I am glad of, as it shows they begin not to be entirely led by names. I am sure if any person else had taken it, it could not have been raised at all . . . We are by no means so eager in this vile war as the people of England, and if it is not soon put a stop to in England I am in hopes that we shall take some strong measures against it here.'

Lord Edward's opinion of local recruiting was an exact echo of that voiced by George Cummins, an apothecary from the town of Kildare who quickly became one of his closest friends and political associates. Cummins, too, was actively campaigning for the United Irish cause. Using the language of Tom Paine, Cummins tried to recruit James Alexander, a rich young radical from Kilkenny who, as he put it later, 'secretly and very foolishly, God knows! admired the association'. 'The people of this kingdom are beginning to open their eyes to perceive their natural rights,' Cummins declared, 'and, if I mistake not, this very militia-business will ripen them for asserting those rights.'

Lord Edward and his modest household were soon attracting attention, becoming beacons of republicanism for people like Cummins and icons of danger for men of property. When he first arrived in Ireland Lord Edward's dress, his haircut, his habit of walking the streets, his choice of wife even, had often been regarded as merely modish, 'playing at revolution', as Matilda Tone scornfully said. But once he moved out of Leinster House to Kildare, hung up his portrait of Paine and began to walk about talking to ordinary people, his turf burning, Gaelic speaking and enthusiastic Irish dancing were recognised for what they were, political gestures to bring people towards him so that he could pass on his message and find out at first hand how far disaffection was spreading. They were gestures held out to all ordinary people, but particularly to the large numbers of rural, predominantly Catholic, Defenders; signals that his cosmopolitan, secularist politics could successfully unite with their popular religiosity. Unlike many United Irish leaders, Lord Edward had no disdain for the ordinary people of Ireland, and he had no fear of them either. Just as he had seen the Iroquois Indians leading an Edenic existence, so he planned for Ireland a new state where the Irish Adam and Eve, Catholic and Protestant, could worship God without interference from an irrelevant monarch or a wicked parliament. The revolution which he urged, as he walked the lanes and streets of Kildare with his energetic, springy step, might have to be paid for and led by the French, but it would be a popular revolution, rising up from the bogs and fields, the villages and cities of Ireland.

As Lord Edward became a popular figure he was gradually shunned by the aristocracy. With the season over, Pamela had few reasons to go to Dublin and in the summer of 1794 stayed in Kildare, sewing baby clothes, strolling out with Lord Edward in the afternoons and watching him indulge his love of cat-napping on the big parlour sofa in the evenings. Arthur O'Connor was often with them, talking politics and arguing about religion, fruitlessly trying to persuade Lord Edward out of his Anglican convictions.

During one of O'Connor's visits, he and Lord Edward went across the fields to the races at the Curragh. Leaving the stand and setting off for home in the evening, Lord Edward was accosted by a group of army officers who demanded that he take off his hibernian green necktie, which signalled his radical sympathies. In the account that went round Ascendancy drawing rooms, Lord Edward angrily refused, saying, 'Here I stand. Let any man among you, who dares, come forward and take it off,' and O'Connor backed him up, challenging any two of them to duels with Lord Edward and himself. The parties separated, but no message came to Kildare. Whispered round the dinner tables of Dublin, this story described Lord Edward as both hero and villain; his obstinate courage showed that he was still a gentleman, but the green necktie was an obvious sign that he had gone over to the people. Soon no amount of gentlemanly behaviour would convince his old acquaintances that Lord Edward was anything other than a traitor.

About a month before Pamela's baby was due, she and Lord Edward, with Tony, Sophie and a maid from Kildare, moved to Leinster House for the birth and lying in. The great house, with its dourly regular façade, long windows and cold, uncomfortable rooms, brought out all Lord Edward's dislike of Ascendancy grandeur; it was, moreover, his father's house, built to show all Dublin the Duke of Leinster's prominent position in Irish society. 'What a melancholy house it is,' he exclaimed to his mother. 'You can't conceive how much it appeared so when first we came from Kildare; but it is going off a little. A poor country house maid I brought with me cried for two days, and said she thought she was in a prison.'

Pamela was cheerful and fat. It was Lord Edward, already a father himself, who anticipated her labour with sober knowledge as well as optimism. 'She never thinks of what is to come, I believe, or if she does, it is with great courage. In short I never saw her, I think, in such good spirits; seeing her thus makes me so and I feel happy and look forward with good hope.' Towards the end of her pregnancy, Pamela abandoned her loose dress and American jacket for even more plebeian clothes. 'Pamela is like a ball,' Lady Sarah Napier reported, 'and she wears an Indian bed-gown Eddy calls it, which is no more than a maid's night bed-gown, and makes her look so large, so loose, so odd that I think a man would laugh at the immense size, and a cloak would not be amiss. But her looks are excellent . . . She intends to have no maid attend the child. In fact the *passion* with which she becomes a mother and nurse is an excellent passion for a young wife to take, and [even] if carried to extremes can do no harm.'

Pamela wrote long emotional letters to Lucy Fitzgerald in London and waited, certain that she would have 'un cher Petit Eddy, avec des grands yeux Bleus'. In the middle of October she did, although Lord Edward was not sure whose eyes the baby had, 'as he does not open them much'. Pamela was quite sure that Edward Fox Fitzgerald 'ressembles notre Edward'; he declared 'he has Pam's chin'. They were happy parents, Pamela saying, like mothers from time immemorial, 'il est le plus aimable petit enfant que je connais', and Lord Edward, thinking of his own mother as usual, writing, 'I wish I could show the baby to you all – dear mother, how you would love it! Nothing is so delightful as to see it in its dear mother's arms, with her sweet, pale, delicate face and the pretty looks she gives it.'

Little Eddy was fed by his mother and seemed none the worse for the daily baths in cold water that she gave him. By 17 November Lord Edward reported that 'Pam gets strong, the little fellow fat and saucy.' Little Eddy refused to settle in his cradle. He loved watching the flickering candle from the safety of his mother's arms and slept at night with his cheek 'on his mother's breast', snuggled down in his parents' bed. Soon he was demanding diversion too, as Lord Edward proudly reported on 25 November, 'The little fellow is delightful, improving every day, takes his walks, and, in short, is every thing we could wish; he must be taken great notice of, spoken to, and danced, otherwise he is not at all pleased.'

When Pamela was lying in at Leinster House, rumours reached Dublin that Lord Fitzwilliam – a disciple of Burke who had gone over to the government in the wake of the Terror and the war with France – was to be appointed Lord Lieutenant. Unlike most members of the Irish opposition, who believed that Fitzwilliam would dismiss the reactionary officials jostling in Dublin Castle and finally bring full emancipation to Catholics, Lord Edward showed no enthusiasm for the appointment. He was now so far committed to revolution and a republic that a liberal Lord Lieutenant seemed to him little better than a repressive one and might, if he succeeded in regaining Catholic loyalty to the Crown, be worse. In mid-November, when talk of Fitzwilliam's appointment had died down, Lord Edward wrote to his mother, 'there is no news here about our lord-lieutenant, with which people were occupied for so long a time. For one, I was very indifferent about it; and, if anything, am glad Lord Fitzwilliam does not come, as perhaps it may make our Opposition act with more spirit and determination.'

Rumours of Fitzwilliam's appointment did not stop Lord Edward's political campaigning. He was down in Kildare soon after his son was born, ostensibly to check on his house, probably to talk to fellow republicans. Explaining his movements to his mother at the end of November, he simply used what had become his routine substitute – an allegory almost – for news of his secret political dealings. 'My little place is much improved by a few things I have done, and by all my *planting* – by the by, I doubt if I told you of my flower garden – I got a great deal from Frescati. I have been at Kildare since Pam's lying-in and it looked delightful, though all the leaves were off the trees – but comfortable and snug. I think I shall pass a delightful winter there. I have got two fine large clumps of turf, which look both comfortable and pretty. I have paled in my little flower-garden before my hall door with a lath paling like the cottage, and stuck it full of roses, sweetbriar, honey-suckles and Spanish broom. I have got all my beds ready for my flowers, so you may guess how I long to be down to plant them. The little fellow will be a great addition to the party. I think when I am down there with Pam and child, of a blustery evening, with a good turf fire and a pleasant book – coming in after seeing my poultry put up, my garden settled, flower-beds and plants covered for fear of frost, the place looking comfortable and taken care of – I shall be as happy as possible; and sure I am I shall regret nothing but not being nearer my dearest mother and her not being of our party.'

Fitzwilliam's appointment was confirmed in December, leaving Lord Edward indifferent. But he was delighted by French military victories, believing that with every success Irish disaffection grew and French assistance for his revolutionary plans came closer. Just before the opening of the first parliament of Fitzwilliam's administration in January 1795, news arrived that the French had crushed the Dutch and forced the Prince of Orange to flee for England; there was one more republic in Europe and one more model of liberation for Lord Edward to study. On the opening day of parliament Lord Edward's revolutionary enthusiasm got the better of him; while arguing for peace, as Charles James Fox was doing in London, he let his real hopes slip out and, to the horror of his fellow MPs, praised the French in ringing tones. He found almost no support. Parliament reiterated its loyalty to the Crown and backed it up by voting two hundred thousand pounds for the British navy and providing for an expansion of both the regular army and the local Irish militias.

Lord Edward retreated to Kildare, to Pamela, Little Eddy and his turf fire. He did not have long to wait before politics turned his way. On 25 February, the Westminster government, lukewarm about Catholic emancipation and leant on by Dublin placemen who feared for their jobs, sinecures and influence if Catholics came into parliament, recalled Fitzwilliam to London. When he finally left on 25 March, Dublin dressed for a funeral. Shops were closed, shutters drawn and great crowds followed his coach to the quayside.

A week later, his successor, the stubborn and weak Lord Camden, arrived, with instructions to 'rally the Protestants in Ireland'. Riots broke out in the city, and angry crowds tried to overturn the carriages of politicians held responsible for Fitzwilliam's recall.

Catholics knew that the end of Fitzwilliam's administration was also the end of their hopes of emancipation. Their resentment and radicalism increased. Some turned to the secret organisation of the Defenders, others joined the United Irishmen and became active in its organisation. A new militancy, closer to Lord Edward's own, was in the air. At United Irish meetings, held in secret now and in an atmosphere of danger and suspense, revolution, not reform, was being planned. When at the end of 1795 the Defenders began to join the United Irish ranks, one unified movement was created big enough to make Ireland a republic and the Dublin government afraid.

While the Fitzwilliam administration was knitting up and unravelling hopes in Dublin, Lord Edward was in the country, talking to people and gathering information. In the spring of 1795, hearing that James Alexander, the young radical approached by the apothecary Mr Cummins two years earlier, was coming to Kildare, Lord Edward sent him a letter that was both a political invitation and a request for information about political sentiment in the counties south of Dublin. 'I received a most polite letter from his lordship,' Alexander wrote later, 'in which he informed me of his . . . acquaintance with Mr Cummins, and of an extremely polite character which that gentleman had given of me, as a very *curious* and intelligent man . . . This letter was so very flattering from a nobleman of whom I had no personal knowledge, that, had he not mentioned Cummins, I verily believe I should have innocently gratified his lordship to the utmost of my weak ability, and in the end to my own sorrow. But I was happy to bethink myself properly, and send an answer of refusal, fraught with sentiments of loyalty, and of warm attachment to the family of His Grace the Duke of Leinster.'

Lord Edward's tip-toeing towards Alexander had several connected intentions. Travelling around Kildare, ostensibly recruiting for the militia, he had realised that any dream he might have had about a popular rising – sparked off by the arrival of the French, but led by thousands of disaffected men with military experience – was hopeless. Even in Kildare, where hatred of Dublin and Westminster flourished in the back streets and grew luxuriantly in the fields, no more than a few United Irishmen were recruited from the militias. By 1795 Lord Edward was more than ever convinced that the rising would need French leadership as well as impetus. That spring he brought the rest of the United Irish leadership round to his point of view, and they jointly decided to send Wolfe Tone to Paris to ask for help. Lord Edward's revolutionary plan, discussed with Paine in a rhapsodic way at the end of 1792, had initially been one of a prolonged campaign of three months with an army of four thousand men. By 1795 his scheme was simpler. Landing somewhere on the south coast, the French force would sweep up through the south-western counties to Kildare, gathering local rebels all along the way; from Kildare the army would march into Dublin, close off the city, seize the Castle and imprison the government leaders. Later the sites of possible French landings changed from the south to the north and west, where the most disaffected groups might support them. But the shape of the plan stayed the same. Lord Edward did not plan for a long-drawn-out campaign of the sort he had encountered in America. He believed, on the contrary, that a swift and effective *coup d'état* could bypass most of the regular troops – who were scattered in barracks around the country, looking out to sea for ships or into towns and villages for pockets of disloyalty and violence – and head straight for the centre of power. Writing to James Alexander, Lord Edward was trying to plan the invaders' route, looking for points of rebelliousness which the invading army would join, mapping on the benighted country a constellation of sedition that would blaze, in a great arc, from the rocky southern coast to the resplendent gates of Dublin Castle itself. He hoped too that Alexander might join him in the cause.

By 1795 it was rare for Lord Edward to commit such proposals to the post. He had stopped writing about politics to his mother in England, and limited his correspondence with his brother the Duke of Leinster to family chat. Most of his recruiting was man to man, at festivals and handball matches, in the streets and fields of Kildare. The United Irishmen were progressively split in secret committees, each unknown to the others, that ascended in tiers like a wedding cake from the local societies at the bottom to the national executive at the top. Each local society, whose members paid a shilling to the treasurer at monthly meetings – or less if they were very poor – elected one delegate to a baronial committee which in its turn elected a committee for each county. County committees sent delegates to the four provincial committees, which at this early stage were not fully staffed, while final authority would rest with a national executive. With only single delegates shuttling between different tiers of the organisation, no member and no government informer could know the members of any more than two committees. Even if a whole committee was betrayed to the Castle, those below it could, so the theory went, easily elect delegates to remake it.

As the United Irish organisation spread in secret, acts of symbolic defiance, like flames bursting up from an underground fire, became more numerous and spectacular. In April 1795, when William Jackson was finally put on trial in Dublin, the United Irishmen were well prepared to turn the case, whatever its outcome, to their advantage. Jackson had had a gentle year in prison, receiving visitors and writing a book about Thomas Paine. One night, letting a friend out of the gaol, he found the turnkey asleep with the keys beside him on the table. He unlocked the prison gate, said goodnight to his visitor, relocked the door and went quietly back to his cell. Elderly and scrupulous, he posed a threat to the government chiefly as a magnet for publicity and sympathy. If the government hoped for a quick trial that would lead to a guilty verdict followed by an offering of clemency because of Jackson's age, the United Irishmen frustrated it. It hired the great opposition lawyer John Curran for the defence, thus ensuring courtroom drama and plenty of after-hours reading in coffee-houses and parlours. The case was serialised in magazines, celebrated in pamphlets and made much of in the *Northern Star*, the United Irish newspaper published in Belfast. Jackson was duly found guilty, and recommended to mercy. Sentencing was postponed for a week. When the day came, Jackson was brought up to court pale and twitching, with sweat running down his face. Passing his lawyers, he whispered, 'We have deceived the Senate', the last words of Jaffeir in Thomas Otway's play *Venice Preserv'd*, a conspirator against the state who kills himself before the Venetian government can reach him. While Jackson's lawyers were disputing the validity of his conviction, he fell down in convulsions and, to the horror of the court, died on the spot; earlier that morning his wife had brought him a cup of tea laced with arsenic and the dose seemed exactly calculated to kill him at the very moment when he might have learnt of the government's clemency.

Thus the Reverend William Jackson, a dissolute old Anglican, self-dramatising but memorably courageous, died a hero and rapidly became a martyr. To secularists and Dissenters Jackson was a man of reason with two decades of radical campaigning behind him. But his death and funeral, whose winding procession mimicked the stations of the cross, evoked for Catholics not just the defiance and sacrifice of Christ but also centuries of opposition to Protestant rule, and made the United Irish cause instantly comprehensible and attractive. So Jackson's became the first name in a new United Irish martyrology. Every state trial, every government reprisal and every sentence of death would add to it.

In the summer and autumn of 1795, as an economic crisis increased hostility to a government that was already unpopular, dissension spread rapidly in Ulster and Leinster, and conditions seemed ripe for the appearance of new martyrs. In the face of secret meetings, persistent and organised violence against landlords and magistrates, and the distribution of sophisticated propaganda, the government used the full strength of the law. But it was often hopeless. When, for instance, they convicted Laurence O'Connor, a schoolmaster from the town of Naas, of recruiting for the French cause, executed him in the gaol and set his head up on a pole in front of the building as a terrible example, they succeeded only in consecrating another martyr to the cause. Desperate attempts had been made to free O'Connor, and his death merely hardened the hearts of his followers and brought new recruits to the rebels' night-time cabals.

Walking out from his house into the town of Kildare and the farms around, Lord Edward saw his 'seditious county' ripe for rebellion. Although he was still not sworn in as a United Irishman – probably because he wanted to be able to tell his mother truthfully that he was not a member – he was now working closely with prominent United Irishmen in Kildare and Dublin. Although Arthur O'Connor remained his confidant and closest friend, he saw a good deal of Mathew Dowling, land agent to the Catholic Lord Cloncurry, and Cloncurry's son, Valentine Lawless, both of whom were active in the Dublin Society. Lord Edward was in Dublin frequently, to talk to United Irish leaders and, sometimes, to attend parliament, where in February 1796 he spoke out against an Insurrection Bill that proposed harsh punishments for a variety of seditious activities. At home in Kildare he continued to try to stir up those he met, offering

himself as an example of fraternity in practice. James
Alexander was told by his sister that spring that Lord
Edward 'danced among the rustics at bonfires, and in short
uniformly conducted himself among them with such uncom-
mon condescension, freedom and affability, that like
Absalom of old, he stole away the hearts of the people.'

By then Lord Edward's efforts at recruitment in Kildare
had convinced him that the time had come to put his plan of
a French-led rebellion into action. In Dublin he met Edward
Lewins and Richard McCormick, the local United Irish
leaders, along with Robert Simmons and George Tennant,
who were delegates from Belfast. He suggested that the
United Irishmen open negotiations with the French
Directory that would back up whatever they were unoffi-
cially being told. He offered to do the talking himself, saying
that under cover of attending the wedding of Pamela's
cousin in Hamburg and visiting Madame de Genlis, he could
approach an old Parisian acquaintance, Charles Reinhard,
who was now the French minister in the port.

Wolfe Tone had arrived in Paris from America two
months before with informal instructions to negotiate for
French help. In the absence of any unequivocal communication, the United Irishmen could not be sure of Tone's
whereabouts. But they reasoned that if he were in Paris, his
cleverness and sophistication could be complemented by
Lord Edward's eagerness and transparent loyalty. Besides, in
a capital where suspicion and concealment were rife, Tone
could vouch for Fitzgerald and Fitzgerald for Tone. Further-
more, Lord Edward would travel with the outrages of the
last year on his lips. He spoke flawless French and was far
more at home in Paris than the fastidious Tone, who had
been horrified by the debauched carnival of the Palais-Royal
and wandered through the Louvre alone, mournfully listing
masterpieces in his journal.

Lord Edward and his small party set off for London
towards the end of April. With him went Pamela, pregnant

again and enveloped in her billowing gown; little Eddy, running about, fascinated by horses and demanding entertainment; the French maid Sophie; and Tony, who, after over three years of hearing French spoken around him, could confidently interpret little Eddy's shouted commands and Pamela's effusive enthusiasm. At Harley Street the Duchess of Leinster was overjoyed to see her son and grandson but already apprehensive about Lord Edward's journey. She was certain that the visit to Madame de Genlis was a cover for her son's treasonable activities, and sure that his mission must be dangerous. Moreover, as a veteran of two dozen pregnancies herself, the Duchess knew that it was unusual for a woman to travel far a few weeks before her confinement. Pamela would not risk her health merely to see her mother or go to her cousin's wedding; her presence was necessary to make Lord Edward's journey look innocuous.

Despite his mother's anxiety, Lord Edward was in high spirits and eager to leave. In London he had found Arthur O'Connor ensconced in opposition drawing rooms and talking of buying a seat in the Westminster parliament, encouraged by a new admirer, the nervously intense radical Sir Francis Burdett. But it did not take Lord Edward long to persuade O'Connor to accompany him to Hamburg, ceding him first place in the expedition and happy to act as interpreter for his execrable French. Eager for adventure and ambitious for glory and notoriety, O'Connor agreed.

Leaving his friend to pack away the beginnings of his English political career, Lord Edward and Pamela set off, taking Tony but leaving little Eddy with the tearful Duchess of Leinster. The small party arrived in Hamburg in the middle of May 1796, just in time for Lord Edward to put his signature to the marriage contract between Pamela's cousin and Bellechasse schoolfriend Henriette de Sercey and a rich Hamburg banker, Johann-Conrad Mattieson. The wedding offered an explanation for his arrival, but few in Hamburg or London thought it sufficient.

Hamburg was a free port, open to people from all over Europe. Men and women unable to visit one another's countries because of passport embargoes brought about by the war with France could meet freely in Hamburg. Revolutionaries from Europe's monarchies could meet French officials there and plead for French aid for their insurrectionary causes. But Hamburg was also teeming with French royalists, some plotting to get back to Paris, others accepting exile and trying to repair their fortunes by spying for foreign governments. So it was Europe's spy capital too, dubbed by Archibald Hamilton Rowan an 'emporium of mischief'. Exiles and radicals inevitably acted as magnets for spies from their home countries, who stealthily pursued them, posing as allies. They opened postbags, learned about meetings, reported back to their employers and collected stipends and rewards. In London the spy-master William Wickham controlled a wide network right across Europe; a good deal of his information came from Hamburg. His spies, a motley collection of misfits whose venality was barely disguised by their constant reiteration of loyalty to King and country, were quick to notice new arrivals.

Lord Edward was soon marked out by many as a man on a secret mission. Some asserted that he was an Irish agent. Others believed that he was acting on behalf of the Orléans family and was therefore plotting to unseat the Directory and install an Orléanist government or even reinstate the royal family; Madame de Genlis, they claimed, was his *éminence grise*. Despite Lord Edward's well-known republicanism his connection with the remnants of the Bourbons made him an object of suspicion to French officials. Reinhard, the French minister in Hamburg, was not impressed when Lord Edward arrived at his door. Lord Edward's revolutionary fervour, his undiscriminating enthusiasm for the whole of the French Revolution, his lack of interest in political intrigue and his hopeful assessment that 150,000 men were ready to rise in Ireland if the French landed: all this convinced Reinhard that Lord Edward would be incapable of leading an insurrection even if he came with the imprimatur of the United Irishmen. Besides, he had arrived in Hamburg without any letters from United Irish leaders.

Taxed by Reinhard as to whether his mission was official, Lord Edward offered to go back to Ireland and return with letters to prove that he had the confidence of revolutionaries there. His fervour was courageous. If he suddenly left Hamburg, appeared in Dublin and swiftly left, the British government would be tempted to pick him up as he left Ireland; and if he was carrying letters addressed to the French Directory they would have enough to convict him of treason.

Reinhard dallied with Lord Edward, but doubted his story. He changed his mind abruptly when O'Connor arrived in Hamburg at the beginning of June. Bludgeoning his way through the French language, scattering half-finished sentences and mismatched words as he went, O'Connor repeated Lord Edward's arguments and battered them home with his Grub Street skills and all the force of his urgent ambition. Reinhard was quickly convinced, and now admitted Lord Edward's sincerity. He dashed off a cipher report to Paris that recommended that his government commit itself to invading Ireland.

The fraternal enthusiasm for liberty and equality that Lord Edward had found in Paris at the end of 1792, and the excesses of the Terror, had given way by the autumn of 1796 to a regime both more moderate and more fearful. Four Directors controlled the French government. They had allowed a resumption of trial by jury, the distribution of opposition newspapers and access for citizens at least to the margins of the great thicket of government bureaucracy. The waiting rooms of Carnot or Barras were thronged with tremulous citizen supplicants; but beyond the shining mahogany doors of the newly redecorated Palais de Luxembourg, the Directors were often found quarrelling about everything from the progress of the war to the minutiae of domestic affairs.

On one thing, though, the Directors were united: their hatred of Britain. Just as, across the Channel, the association between the country's ills and the baleful example of France was being firmly established in the national mind and Francophobia was fashionably acceptable, so in France Britain was equally cited as the fount of all the nation's problems. All the Directors agreed that Britain's defeat was necessary for the survival of the French republic and was perhaps possible now that France had signed an armistice with her other enemy, Austria. So although Lord Edward and O'Connor may not have known it, by the time they arrived in Hamburg the Directors were already considering ways of harassing their great island enemy on her own territory. Some ministers favoured landings in Wales or Cornwall to stir up provincial feelings against London. Others urged a full-scale invasion of Ireland that would swiftly bring Pitt to sue for peace and secure the preservation of France.

Wolfe Tone was trying hard to harness whatever plans the Directory was making to the United Irish cause. Tone had been gradually making progress with his meetings and memoranda in the spring of 1796, and at the moment when Lord Edward was painting a picture for Reinhard of an Ireland impatiently awaiting liberation by the French, Tone was beginning to believe that the Directory would accept his case. Although they were delivered without Lord Edward's emotional emphasis on fraternity, Tone's arguments were similar to those being put forward in Hamburg. He reiterated that a large part of Ireland was disaffected and that independence could only be secured with French help.

Although Lord Edward may have believed that France would act towards Ireland with a disinterested love of freedom equal to his own, the nature and price of French intervention were much on the minds of Tone and the Directory.

If the Irish people and a French army ousted the government from Dublin Castle, what kind of government would be installed, what kind of nation created? Tone understood that France's primary purpose in liberating Ireland was to make of the country a huge floating fortress from which it could undermine the government in London by fear, sedition and even invasion. Coincidentally, the French would be happy to help in the birth of a young republic. They were even prepared to consider the creation of a new monarchy if that was what the people of Ireland wanted, and hinted that O'Connor or Lord Edward might become titular chieftain.

Whatever O'Connor's monarchist ambitions, Lord Edward had no hankering after a crown. He was a republican by conviction, nursed a hearty dislike of living kings and was fond of quoting Charles Fox's recent assertion during a debate on the war with France that he had heard the phrases 'as rash as a king' and 'as great as a king' but had never yet heard 'as honest as a king'. None the less Lord Edward might have been willing to go along with and advertise a French proposal that he head a monarchy in Ireland. In the first place such a plan could appeal to a knowledge among his supporters of the long tradition of Geraldine opposition to the English Crown, to a hope that the Geraldines, as ancient rulers of a large part of Ireland, might once more come into their heritage. Still fresh in popular memory was the fate of Thomas Fitzgerald, tenth Earl of Kildare, who had renounced his allegiance to Henry VIII in 1534 and declared war on England and who, after the failure of his rebellion, was hung, drawn and quartered at Tyburn in 1537.

The second reason why Lord Edward might have been prepared to go along with the idea of an eventual monarchy in Ireland was that many Roman Catholic Defenders, whom he had been assiduously cultivating, had definite monarchist leanings. Among the Defenders, new French-inspired politics mixed with memories of the old Stuart cause and the hope that a rebellion might bring a Catholic king to Ireland.

Lord Edward, as an Anglican, was not an ideal successor to the last Stuart, his distant kinsman Bonnie Prince Charlie. But some Defenders, glorifying his Geraldine blood, might have overlooked his Anglicanism and invested in him their millenarian hopes for a great leader who would banish the Protestant English from Ireland once and for all. Gesturing to these Defenders' monarchism was a way of encouraging them into the United Irish movement.

Lord Edward and O'Connor might thus have been prepared to entertain French ideas of a puppet monarchy. But Wolfe Tone was uneasy about French influence in Ireland. He knew that France would demand a say in the country's government as long as French troops were stationed there, and that meant as long as England remained undefeated. But he was learning diplomacy and confined his fears to written memoranda that clung to a judicious and remote language.

Setting aside their worries and differences, all parties continued negotiations. Tone was unaware that Lord Edward and O'Connor were in Hamburg; they did not know how far Tone had got in his talks in Paris. The Directory tacked carefully between them, checking on their credentials and statements as much as it could. Lord Edward's offer to travel to Paris was rejected. With Tony looming by his side Lord Edward would immediately be recognised there, and the opposition press would soon be guessing aloud – and to its readers in London – about the purpose of his visit. But meetings could not go on in spy-ridden Hamburg. The Directory suggested Switzerland as a suitable place to talk. There were plenty of spies there too, as Lord Robert Fitzgerald had constantly complained when he had been in charge of the British embassy in Bern, two years before. But in the smaller towns close to the French border Lord Edward and O'Connor were at least unknown faces.

Lord Edward had no pretext for a journey to Switzerland, no excuse of family business with which to comfort his mother and provide distraction for the press. Moreover he was leaving in Hamburg not only his wife but his new daughter, a little Pamela a few weeks old. His absence from the Mattieson household was bound to be reported to London and probably to his mother worrying in Harley Street. He could not write to her to say where he was going. Hinting as to why was pointless: she already knew. So leaving a void to fill itself with rumour and anxiety, and leaving Tony and Pamela, he set off for Switzerland.

Immediately after they arrived in Basle, Lord Edward and O'Connor sent the Directory a memorandum that confidently set out once again the case for French invasion of Ireland. In a tone not of supplicants but of men with an asset to offer, they asserted that the United Irish organisation was spreading rapidly down from the north, that thousands of militiamen were secretly sworn into the conspiracy and that, apart from Protestant men of property, the whole country was in favour of revolution. Lack of arms and draconian laws made rising alone impossible, they concluded, so they had been entrusted with the task of 'asking the French government for help in effecting their separation from England'.

The Directory had given charge of the proposed invasion of Ireland to Lazare Hoche, a brilliant young general who had proved his Anglophobic zeal by helping to put down the British-inspired insurrection in the Vendée three years before. Hoche had heard about O'Connor and Lord Edward soon after he accepted the brief towards the end of June 1796. Before he began any detailed planning he diplomatically set about checking the credentials of the Directory's Irish informants. Lord Edward and O'Connor had already been asked about Tone. On 23 July Hoche found a way of introducing O'Connor and Lord Edward into a conversation with Tone, as Tone recorded in his diary. 'Hoche then asked me, "did I know Arthur O'Connor?" I replied, "I did, and that I entertained the highest opinion of his talents, principles, and patriotism" . . . "well," said he, "will he join us?"

I answered, "I hoped, as he was *foncièrement Irlandais*, that he undoubtedly would." Hoche then went on to say, "There is a lord in your country (I was a little surprised at this beginning, knowing, as I do, what stuff our Irish peers are made of), – he is son to a Duke; is he not a patriot?" I immediately recognised my friend Lord Edward Fitzgerald, and gave Hoche a very good account of him.'

Despite Tone's endorsement, Hoche decided to talk to O'Connor alone. He may have believed that Lord Edward's involvement could start rumours in Ireland that any Irish republic was somehow a cover for Orléanist ambitions in France; he may have felt it necessary only to deal with the more skilled negotiator; he may have been uneasy about Lord Edward's aristocratic lineage. Lord Edward did not demur. He had no ambitions to be a leader and he was happy to let O'Connor's persuasive volubility serve the cause. With high hopes that an agreement was imminent, and sure now that the French would commit themselves to the liberation of Ireland, he travelled back to Hamburg by public coach, going by way of Schaffhausen, Augsburg, Nuremberg and Brunswick, and making the long journey in ten days.

When he returned to the Mattiesons' house in Hamburg on 10 August, Lord Edward found his 'little Pam' and his large Pamela both much 'improved in their looks' and a stack of letters from his mother. Trying to cheer herself and Pamela up at the same time, the Duchess had eschewed politics in favour of domestic news and especially details of the health and happiness of 'little Eddy', whom she was already allowing herself to love. Eddy had brought a skin infection with him from Ireland, she reported, but had been isolated in the country and was now running about, healthy and cheerful.

After apologising for the 'piece of work my poor little itchy Edward has made' and exclaiming, 'what a début', Lord Edward in reply gave his mother a surreal and fantastic account of the negotiations with Barthelmy, the French government official in Basle. Unable to use gardening as a shorthand for his political activities, but anxious to reassure his mother without giving her any false hope, he fell back on Rousseau, a flag of republicanism to the Duchess if not to the British agents reading his letters in the post office. If Rousseau was not enough, his mention of walking was a sign to his mother that he was engaged in democratic activities; as she knew well, her son's penchant for pacing the streets was a signal that he spurned aristocratic distance and embraced the life of the pavement and the people. 'I had a very pleasant tour, am in raptures with Switzerland. I left my friend O'Connor in Switzerland taking another tour. There never were two persons who more thoroughly admired Switzerland than we did; we say it with the true Rousseau enthusiasm. He is as fond of Rousseau as I am so you may conceive how we enjoyed our journey. He entered completely into my way of travelling, which was walking most of the way, getting into a boat when we could, taking our dinner in some pretty spot etc, swimming when we could. In fact we agreed in everything, and if it had not been time to come home I should have been very sorry to leave him . . . I will tell you more when we meet . . . Kiss my dear boy. How I miss its dear face – Ever yr. aff. E. F.' While there was nothing here that could enable the British government to arrest him, Lord Edward's message to his mother was transparently and excitedly clear. 'We agreed in everything': a deal with the French had been as near as concluded even by the time he left Basle. Lord Edward was in high spirits. 'I will tell you more when we meet', he had concluded; but the Duchess of Leinster did not need to know anything else. Her anxiety rose and danced in time with his enthusiasm.

Arthur O'Connor finished negotiating with the French by the end of September. In the two months after he parted from Lord Edward in Basle, he travelled all the way across France to meet Hoche at Angers, not far from the General's headquarters at Rennes. O'Connor spent three weeks with Hoche and claimed later to have concluded a secret treaty that arranged for 15,000 soldiers and 80,000 guns to be sent to Ireland. The expedition was to be planned from Rennes and launched from Brest. Tone was soon on his way to Rennes from Paris to help preparations on the French side; the United Irishmen for their part were to alert their secret armies at home.

Lord Edward did not wait in Hamburg for O'Connor's return. Having arranged for all communications with Hoche to be sent to and from Ireland by way of the sympathetic Mattieson household (and possibly for arms to be bought and stored there too), he and Pamela left for the Duchess of Leinster's summer retreat in Ealing, west of London. Madame de Genlis, who had enjoyed being once again at the centre of revolutionary intrigue, was sorry to see them go, and recorded with relish, 'I parted from Pamela with great pain, especially at the thought that her husband was going to engage in perilous adventures'.

Lord Edward's party, besides himself and Pamela, was made up of his three-month-old daughter, who, he said, was 'always sleeping and never cries', Pamela's maid Sophie, a nursemaid, Julie, and Tony as usual. They stayed at Ealing for three weeks. Lord Edward was biding his time until O'Connor was ready to return to Dublin and they could begin preparations for the French invasion in earnest. But he also made a momentous decision: to leave little Eddy with the Duchess of Leinster. It was the kindest thing he ever did for his mother, the cruellest for his wife.

Lord Edward believed the French were coming. He knew that he might die in the uprising that would follow. Giving little Eddy to his mother was a way of assuaging the guilt he already felt at the misery she might have to bear on his account. Lord Edward loved his son but he had already surrendered one child because he thought it the right thing to do. Now he was ready to do the same again.

The Duchess of Leinster accepted this parting gift with greedy, desperate need. By the autumn of 1796 she probably knew the outline if not the details of Lord Edward's grand plan. Having failed to talk him out of his revolutionary fervour she awaited the future with miserable foreboding. 'My poor anxious mind is ever looking forward to some distress,' she confessed to Lucy on 8 October. Little Eddy made it better. Any guilt she felt about Pamela was soon overcome. The transaction, she knew, was between herself and her favourite son. Little Eddy was his father's love token; Pamela merely acquiesced in the plan.

Towards the end of September Lord Edward and Pamela left Ealing for Ireland. Two weeks after they had gone the Duchess wrote to her daughter Lady Lucy Fitzgerald, drowning her guilt in a torrent of words that none the less made it clear that she saw little Eddy as necessary compensation for the anxieties she anticipated. 'Our time was short,' she said of Lord Edward's visit, 'but we enjoyed it; I don't know how I could have borne all this but for their goodness in leaving their precious babe with me: was it not so good in them? They adore it and delight in all its pretty ways, and yet to leave it behind out of outright good nature and affection to me was a sacrifice indeed. It looks so pretty upon the Green Hill among the sheep under my window.

'His Papa and Mama will describe him to you, for they delighted in him, and I do think that their consideration for my comfort, their kindness and good nature on this occasion is really beyond what the most *exigeante* friendship cou'd ever have expected or looked for. In Edward nothing surprised me, dear Angel; he has always loved me in an uncommon degree since childhood, but in Pamela, dear thing, it is really a proof of the most amiable disposition to make such a sacrifice, and she has made me love her more than I can say. Pray make them sensible that it was well bestow'd, for I do dote on it and it would have broke my heart to have parted with it just at this time. The only drawback to my pleasure is the feel of having been selfish, which I hate, but I have moments of weakness and self-indulgence, and have suffered a great deal from disappointments and anxieties before I gave way to this temptation.'

Lord Edward was distressed to leave his mother and his son. All his thoughts about them and all his letters to his mother were henceforth overshadowed by a future that they both anticipated but never mentioned. Outwardly he remained resolute, as he reported to her from Chester on the way to catch the Dublin packet. 'I need not tell you my journey was a little melancholy, but I endeavoured to drive all distressing thoughts from me . . . I don't repent leaving Eddy as I am sure it is a comfort to my beloved Mother and I hate to think that by my own absence I have given her so much distress. But no more of this. Believe me, dearest Mother, you are truly lov'd and respected by me.'

Pamela too was as circumspect as her effusive style would allow her. She admitted that the sight of two-year-olds upset her but said that the thought of the Duchess's happiness comforted her. 'Je ne puis voir un enfant de l'âge de mon Eddy sans un battement de coeur, mais *bien vite* je pense à votre bonheur et je suis consolée.' Although she and Lord Edward had not formally handed little Eddy over for good, they had left him with the Duchess in the tacit understanding that they would not see him until after the French invasion of Ireland. But Pamela must have known too that if the worst came to the worst, the Duchess would cling to little Eddy with all the tenacity of her obsessive nature.

To take Pamela's mind off little Eddy and the future, and to give her a companion in the next few months while he was out and about planning for the invasion, Lord Edward had invited his sister Lady Lucy Fitzgerald to join them in Ireland. Bored with life in London and the decorous suburban retreats of Ealing, Norbury and Thames Ditton, she readily agreed. In the autumn of 1796 Lady Lucy was twenty-five. Like Lord Edward she had been educated into impulsive displays of feeling and enthusiasm and like him, too, she was obstinate and determined when opposed. But whereas Lord Edward always struck friends as mild mannered and gentle unless the sight of injustice got the better of him, Lady Lucy, granted few outlets for her sentiments other than marriage and family quarrels, was combative and angry. In the 1790s she was fighting off suitors who bored her and constantly quarrelling with her stepfather. Lady Lucy never accepted William Ogilvie, even though she could scarcely remember her own father and had been used to calling Ogilvie Papa since she was three years old. She resented Ogilvie's hold over her mother and chafed at his brusque discipline. While the Duchess chided her and tried to keep the peace, Lady Lucy fought running battles with her stepfather that always ended in her defeat. She never managed to detach her mother from Ogilvie and each new repulse left her angrier than ever. In lulls between hostilities truces were declared and the Duchess was, as she put it, left with 'a pleasant, happy feel'. One such peace broke out soon after Lady Lucy arrived in Ireland in October 1796. Ogilvie was on business there and the two temporarily agreed to an armistice after a long dispute, prompting the relieved Duchess to write, 'Oct. 29 – Another letter from dear Papa full of such tender and kind expressions about you as quite delighted me. You have no idea how his dear heart is relieved by this reconciliation. Keep it up, my Angel. He is an invaluable friend, believe me, and one who will stick to you thro' life, and in whose protection I shall feel so satisfied to leave you.'

Lady Lucy eventually gave up the unequal struggle with her mother and stepfather, married an admiral and settled into a long life as mistress of a grand country house. But for the moment she channelled all her rebellious energy into her brother's cause. The Duchess of Leinster was hoping against hope that Lucy might be able to talk Lord Edward into moderation after they arrived in Ireland. But Lucy confounded her mother and became as enthusiastic a revolutionary as her brother. She immediately took to wearing her auburn hair short and unpowdered in the democratic style, flaunted Parisian fashions at Ascendancy balls, danced jigs, sang French songs and joined her brother's cult of Thomas Paine. Fighting for democracy was far more absorbing than finding a husband; soon it was also to be tinged with an eroticism she had found lacking in even the most radical Whig drawing rooms in London.

When Lord Edward and Arthur O'Connor arrived back in Ireland at the beginning of October 1796 they found that the country had been in a state of unrest all summer. The Castle government was preparing to crush signs of disaffection with another round of legislation that would increase penalties for subversion, give more powers to magistrates and take rights away from those under suspicion. The Lord Lieutenant, Lord Camden, was fearful and weak. He constantly urged ministers in London to take his reports of sedition more seriously but they treated both them and him with equal, bored nonchalance.

But the letters coming in to Dublin Castle – both routine and extraordinary reports from magistrates, spies and informers – were beginning to tell an alarming story. Disturbances in the northern county of Armagh had spread through the north and into the south. Hundreds of Catholic cottiers and tenant farmers were forced from their homes and land and made into refugees who took tales of Protestant brutality with them as they fled to safer areas. Magistrates were ineffectual, blatantly sectarian and themselves made frightened by stories of United Irish reprisals. Many Protestants in these rural areas were spurred into joining the stridently loyalist Orange Order newly formed and proclaiming its Protestantism in naming itself after William of Orange, who had defeated Catholicism on Irish soil. On the other hand, as violence and rumour linked and bred one another, thousands of Catholic Defenders poured into the secret cells of the United Irishmen. Travellers in disaffected areas found the United Irishmen and their sympathisers openly and noisily celebrating French victories and talking confidently of invasion and liberation. Round the northern coasts lights twinkled in coves and bays at night as boats from France, and perhaps Hamburg, landed secret caches of arms. Rifles, shot, powder, swords and even cannon came ashore on the high tides and disappeared into woods and caves.

Contemplating these outbursts of violence, the United Irish leaders knew that their task was to condemn sectarianism and harness the energy of dissent into planning and training, holding the movement together until the day when the French flotilla would be seen sailing towards Lough Swilly or Galway Bay. But as fast as the United Irish organisation grew so did its mirror image, the government network of soldiers, militias, spies and informers. After a tour of the northern counties which convinced him that the alarmist reports coming into Dublin Castle were not inaccurate, Lord Camden moved quickly to crush the government's enemies. On 16 September the main leaders of the United Irishmen in Belfast were arrested, charged with high treason, brought to Dublin and incarcerated in Kilmainham gaol, where they were tormented with the tolling of the bell that announced each traitor's execution. In mid-October Camden recalled parliament and rushed through an act suspending habeas corpus.

Lord Edward thus arrived back in Dublin to a country that was tense and expectant. United Irishmen were lighting bonfires and demanding that passers-by stop and sing French songs; men of property, watching the sparks rise in the night air beyond their barred and shuttered windows, were afraid to sleep. 'The Protestants about me . . . are in a most horrid panic about those United people rising,' wrote one northern magistrate in August. 'They absolutely dare hardly go to bed at night . . . They tell me plainly, that they expect every night to be murdered.'

After leaving Lady Lucy at Carton, settling his family in Kildare and hurriedly celebrating his thirty-third birthday, Lord Edward threw himself into organising the rebellion. He came and went from the country, often staying in Dublin, where he put up at the Frederick Street Hotel to avoid the difficulties of meeting United Irish leaders at Leinster House. One of his first acts was, with O'Connor, formally to join the United Irishmen. As it grew, and as the government infiltrated it, the organisation was becoming more shadowy. The United Irish leaders wanted a demonstration of Lord Edward's loyalty and they wanted him as a talisman who would attract other members. He was, after all, an extraordinary recruit and he gave the whole movement a glamour and an instant pedigree of centuries of Geraldine resistance. Especially in Kildare and around Dublin his was a name to conjure with, and the United Irish leaders, whose propaganda was sophisticated and widespread, wanted to use it.

If Lord Edward and O'Connor wanted political influence within the United Irish organisation, they had to join now. Moreover, Lord Edward's scruples about his family were over. He could not and would not withdraw from any insurrection to spare his mother; he had silently told her so with his gift of little Eddy and he knew that the Duchess was slowly passing beyond anxiety into a resigned fortitude about the future. So in the autumn of 1796 Lord Edward and his friend took the United Irish oath and joined its secret world completely.

In response to the arrests in the north and in anticipation of a French landing, the United Irishmen were reorganising their society along military lines. Committee members became officers, ordinary members their footsoldiers. As one of the Society's trained officers with experience of battle – a man who therefore knew the ways of what would be the enemy – Lord Edward immediately became a pivotal figure, assuming far more responsibility in the Society than he had had before. He helped to plan both general strategy for the invasion and the drilling of local units – groups of artisans, farmers, apothecaries and tradesmen who had been trained to cut meat or paper rather than human flesh, more used to dressing wounds than inflicting them.

The new United Irish army was pitifully short of officers, arms and ammunition. But the most basic of its weapons, the pike, the men could manufacture easily themselves. Instead of talking rebellion in parlours and taverns they were now to go out at night and cut young ash trees for pike handles. In the villages sympathetic blacksmiths would beat out the sharp, curved heads in pauses between the making of horse-shoes and nails. Stealthily too the men began to drill at night, practising marching and turning in line and formation.

Expecting French and deserting militia officers to take command of this ramshackle army, Lord Edward recom-mended only the most basic training. Men should drill in small squads of fifteen or twenty, he said, and should perfect 'marching by the plummet', each group walking equal dis-tances in the same time, so that when they took command, the officers could move their troops with ease and confi-dence. At this stage he said, the men did not need arms, although he recommended lightweight rifles and may have designed a break-handled pike which came apart and could be slung across a soldier's back while he manoeuvred stealthily in confined spaces. But Lord Edward made it clear that getting guns was the business of the officers and not their men. Some arms (including those he was rumoured to have bought and stored in the Mattiesons' Hamburg ware-house) could be run ashore. Many others would land with the French. He disapproved of United men plundering arms, as they had begun to do throughout the country. Any arms that were in the hands of householders should be left there until the moment came to take them. Their owners were keeping them oiled and safe; removing them now would only produce alarm and reprisals.

Lord Edward's military enthusiasm and experience were respected by his United Irish colleagues, and there were few conflicts about the details of military strategy. There were differences, though, about the part which ordinary members should play in Ireland's liberation. Some leaders felt that the French, with their promise of fifteen thousand troops, should easily be able to push aside the scattered forces of the Crown if several thousand militiamen defected to their ranks. But Lord Edward was always in favour of a popular rising that would sweep the victorious French to Dublin. In his mind the French were merely lending the nascent republic a fraternal hand. He wanted the Irish people to free themselves and he was determined to believe that they desired that too.

When he arrived back in Dublin Lord Edward believed that the United Irishmen had about six months to organise their army. A letter he received from Reinhard in Hamburg expressing an eagerness to see him again in the spring seemed a simple enough coded confirmation of Hoche's intention to sail after the winter. While everyone waited, it was vital for them to maintain an air of quotidian unconcern, to perfect their strategies of duplicity so that the government left the swelling, secret army in peace. To this end Lord Edward took up family life in Kildare between tours of United Irish cells, and he encouraged Lady Lucy and Pamela to do the same. At Carton and Castletown he rubbed shoulders with the men whom he was planning shortly to set adrift in Dublin Bay, while they went to balls and assemblies given by officials who would sign his death warrant if the insurrection failed. 'I feel so happy to be at dear Castletown,' Lady Lucy wrote in her journal on 23 October.

'It reminds me of the days of my childhood. The Edwards came and the Castlereaghs.' Lord Castlereagh was related by marriage to the Conollys and by virtue of that could claim kinship with Lord Edward. Brilliant, charming and unstable, he was a rising star who was privy to much Castle business. He took an intense, personal interest in crushing sedition and a sadistic pleasure in maintaining friendships with his future victims. Charles Hamilton Teeling, one of the United Irish leaders in Belfast arrested in the swoop of 16 September, recorded that rather than leave his detention to officers of the police, Castlereagh, an intimate friend of the family, performed it himself. In the evening Castlereagh sat with the terrified prisoner in his cell and remarked with characteristic chilling self-absorption while Teeling ate his dinner, 'I have had much fatigue today.'

Lord Edward, who would have heard this story through the United Irish network, knew that Castlereagh was edgy and dangerous. Castlereagh must have been aware of government suspicions of Lord Edward. Both were waiting for the moment to strike. Meanwhile they observed the social niceties, greeting one another cordially and chatting for as long as manners demanded. Exactly the same ritual of friendship and suspicion was played out with Lord Clare, the Lord Chancellor, whom Lady Lucy and Lord Edward encountered at Carton in October. Lord Clare was a by-word for insolence and vanity in Dublin, universally regarded as a heartless placeman who had sacrificed talent to ambition without a qualm. But sentimentality lay thick under Lord Clare's unemotional manner. He was indulgent towards Lord Edward and in awe of his family; the sub-terfuge of the hunter may have come less easily to him than it did to Lord Castlereagh.

Despite this double life, which was lived out in less dramatic a form by every United Irishman, Lord Edward displayed few signs of strain in 1796. Life at Kildare, with its mixture of family gatherings, meetings with United Irishmen and symbolic gestures of hibernian solidarity and revolutionary commitment, continued as it had done for the last two years. Turf burned in the grate; Lord Edward drank whiskey stretched out on the big parlour sofa. Tony, Sophie, Julie and the young boy Terry came up from the servants' rooms in the basement to dance jigs to the accompaniment of Irish pipes and practise more formal dances when there were enough couples. 'Democrats' from Belfast, Dublin and Kildare came to dine and talk. In late November Arthur O'Connor arrived. Lady Lucy, already intoxicated by the democratic atmosphere, was quickly swept away by O'Connor's confidence and charm. He flirted with her over the construction of a pocket book on a cold wintry morning and he shocked her deliciously by declaring late at night that he did not believe in the immortality of the soul. 'Dec. 3. Edward went to bed early *in* the dancing-room where we sat, and Arthur, Pamela and I had a conversation which I *never* shall forget. I never heard anything of the kind before. I was very much amused and interested, lost in admiration of such superior talents, but not *convinced*, and grieved to tears at *such* a mind supposing itself *perishable*.' The next day Lord Edward and O'Connor set off for County Roscommon and the areas of the west through which the French might march if they landed at Galway. When they had gone Lady Lucy wrote in her diary, 'Ed. very angry with us for sitting up; he and Mr. O'Connor set off on a tour. Pamela and I very sorry. How I love this place.' But it was by now Arthur O'Connor as much as Kildare that made Lady Lucy's heart beat faster.

In the confined spaces of the house in Kildare danger bred love. The servants' hall was soon pulsing with the same emotions as the parlour above. While Lady Lucy thrilled to the republican violence of *Julius Caesar*, ably read by Arthur O'Connor in one sitting on 27 November, Tony was following his master's lead and flirting in French. Julie, little Pamela's nursemaid, was the object of his attentions and she was soon responding to him with more than the paper admissions of fascination with which Lady Lucy contented herself.

Lord Edward still had plenty of energy for life in Kildare and maintained his optimism about the arrival of the French. But he was running out of money. Pamela's annuity had been abruptly cut off with the duc d'Orléans's head, and his own income was too small to finance his household and his travels. The long trip to Hamburg and Switzerland had cost him a good deal and although his household was a modest one he still kept several horses and liked to entertain and go to the races. He may also have been buying arms for the United Irishmen on the continent, expecting to be reimbursed by the French or by a grateful young Irish nation. On 5 November he signed an agreement with Anne, Lady Cloncurry, which mortgaged his estate in Kilrush to her for two years and fifteen hundred pounds, the bulk of which was paid immediately. It may have been more than personal credit, because Lady Cloncurry was the mother of Valentine Lawless, an old friend of Lord Edward's who was now a prominent United Irishman, and she may herself have had United Irish sympathies.

Cash in hand, Lord Edward and O'Connor toured the west of Ireland. They came back to Kildare on 11 December only for the 'beloved quatuor', as Pamela and Lucy had taken to calling the foursome with O'Connor, to split up again on the 15th. Lord and Lady Castlereagh came from Castletown to collect Lady Lucy for the Christmas party. O'Connor and Lord Edward left for meetings in Dublin. Pamela and Tony stayed in Kildare, she to forward messages and information, he to act as valet and stay inconspicuously in the country. 'Here is Small who brings in my supper,' Pamela wrote to Lucy on 17 December.

From the snug opulence of the long gallery at Castletown, Lady Lucy watched drifts of snow pile up in the fields that stretched away beyond the lawn. Sitting by the cheerful fire, she heard news that was both unexpected and disastrous.

Lord Edward in 1796 by Hugh Douglas Hamilton;
there are several copies that emerged from Hamilton's
studio after Lord Edward's death with his red
necktie tactfully changed to white.

Elizabeth Linley and her sister Mary in 1772, by Gainsborough:
singer, star and muse.

Tony Small by John Roberts,
about 1786; a gentle exotic
and a good samaritan.

Pamela with little Pam by Mallary about 1800; her resplendent pulchritude
soon faded, destroyed by misery, alcohol and poverty.

'Christmas Day – Alarm of the French being off the coast of Ireland. Troops marching; all in consternation about the French. They have been trying to work into Bantry Bay.' As the Conollys and their Christmas guests panicked about the defenceless state of the country and waited hour by hour for news from Lord Castlereagh in Dublin Castle, Lady Lucy worried about Lord Edward, uncertain if he would go to meet the French and unable to confide in her aunt and uncle.

The arrival of a French fleet off the southern coast took both the United Irishmen and Castle officials completely by surprise. General Hoche, encouraged by reports of the inflamed state of Ireland, had assembled an invasion force with great secrecy and speed in Brittany. Even Wolfe Tone, who was to be aboard and had been promoted to adjutant-general in Hoche's army, had no idea of his destination. On 15 December, with Tone aboard the *Indomptable*, an eighty-gun warship, and Hoche on a fast-sailing frigate, the *Fraternité*, forty-three ships sailed out of the harbour at Brest. The day was clear and sunlit, and so were the hopes of the fourteen thousand soldiers aboard. In the ships' holds they had stowed forty thousand weapons: cannon, rifles, swords and small arms. With them they had packed five thousand uniforms captured by Hoche during his campaign in the Vendée. Now, in a deliberate symbolic gesture, these uniforms were being returned to Ireland, where they had been made for the Vendée rebels and paid for by the British government. In this new war they would be worn on republican, not royalist, backs.

Spirits were high. The soldiers, exhorted by Hoche and intoxicated by the certainty of victory, sang patriotic songs and looked forward to the army's heroic progress as it marched on Dublin, growing stronger and more powerful daily, liberating the benighted land as it routed the hated and ineffectual British troops.

The first night at sea ended this fraternal dream. One ship, the *Séduisant*, foundered straight away with the loss of fourteen hundred lives. Fog came down and the flotilla scattered as, one by one, the ships passed through a treacherously rocky channel leaving the Brittany coast and then, unable to see one another's lights, separated on the open sea. When the fog lifted, only seventeen ships were still together. The *Fraternité*, carrying Hoche and the detailed plan of campaign, was nowhere to be seen. Hoche and his naval commander were far out to the west of their route, alone in the Atlantic.

Without Hoche, the captains of the other ships lost courage and heart, sailing on listlessly, allowing the winds to blow them northwards. Eventually when two-thirds of the fleet had reassembled, the captains opened their instructions and found their destination; not Galway or the north, as the United Irishmen had indicated and they themselves expected, but Bantry Bay, carved into the rocky south-western tip of the island. Thinking that it was too dangerous to sail round the Irish coast in the winter, worried that the British might have reinforced defences in Galway and the north because of persistent rumours of invasion there, and believing that the local people would rise wherever he landed, Hoche had decided on Bantry, secluded and close to France. His secrecy had indeed been perfect. The British fleet in the Channel, learning that a flotilla had set out from Brest, set sail for Portugal in the belief that Lisbon was under threat. The United Irishmen were preparing for a peaceful Christmas, expecting the French in the north and in the spring. 'I have had no letters from Hamburg,' Pamela wrote to Lady Lucy at the beginning of January 1797, firmly indicating that Lord Edward had had no warning or hint from the French that they were to sail.

When the fleet of thirty-six ships arrived at the mouth of Bantry Bay, nothing moved but gusty winds and banks of grey storm clouds. No British patrols disturbed the ships' passage; no United Irishmen came down to the rocky shore to meet them. Looking landwards from their gale-sloped decks, as the wind banged into the stiff and frozen rigging above them, the French soldiers saw only desolation and emptiness, frosty grass and glassy rocks. The land seemed uninhabited and themselves unwished-for. Night and more storms sucked out their commanders' courage. Some ships stood off the shore, others were blown away. By the morning of 23 December only six-and-a-half thousand soldiers still faced the coast. On Christmas Day the remaining leaders finally decided to land their rump force the next morning. Wolfe Tone, walking cold and disconsolate on the gallery of the *Indomptable* that night, hugging his greatcoat around himself and wrapped in 'gloomy reflections', heard through the storm shouted orders for captains to cut their anchor cables and sail for France. Day broke to disaster. The *Immortalité*, now the flagship of the expedition, had vanished in the darkness. Other ships banged into one another in the choppy confines of the bay. One by one they gave up and left, slipping out to sea and safety. Tone watched in hopeless anger as his homeland melted into the mist and his dreams vanished into the perishing air; the *Indomptable* arrived back in Brest on New Year's Day. Hoche, already blaming his pusillanimous deputies, finally made it home on 12 January. The *Fraternité*, pushed out into the Atlantic by strong winds and a pursuing British man-of-war, had finally joined up with four other straggling vessels and arrived off the west of Ireland on 30 December. After cruising along the coast for several days, ignorant of the whereabouts of the larger fleet and losing hope and supplies as the hours went by, they turned for home on 5 January.

The French were stunned by the desolate quietude of Ireland. They had expected welcoming brigades of rebels, waving tricolors, marching in time to French songs and ready to put on uniforms and fight. Instead they saw nothing but the rocky coast where gulls mewed in the wind and snow covered the barren and deserted land. When they got back to Brittany the expedition's commanders spent more time showering recriminations upon one another than on planning a second expedition. Their vision of Ireland as a land fertile for revolution had been shattered. Hoche himself, angry and thwarted, transferred his energies to the landlocked Austrians and a pressing rival in the ranks of his own army, Napoleon Bonaparte.

The United Irishmen did not see the French failure as a defeat for their cause. On the contrary, they argued excitedly that having come once, the liberating fleet could and would come again. The government troops, scrambling out of Dublin on Christmas Day, had shown that they were not capable of defending the country, while the British navy had made no attempt to protect the coasts. If no one had risen when the French fleet was sighted, they argued, it was because the United Irish leaders had ordered their members to stay absolutely quiet until the invading army had landed.

Lady Lucy's fears for Lord Edward had been unnecessary, as she recorded with relief in her diary. 'Dec. 28 – Dear Eddy came over from Kildare. I never saw him with such pleasure. Heaven protect him.' Lord Edward was in high spirits. The day after he went to Carton he travelled to Dublin and then Belfast and the north, bound for conferences with O'Connor and the northern leaders. He left Pamela making copies of the *Marseillaise*, the *Carmagnole*, the *Ça ira* and *Le Réveil du peuple*, all songs that underground bands might sing under their breath as they drilled at night. All over the country United Irish representatives were reporting a flood of new recruits for the cause and an air of fevered expectation. Rumours of invasion had been right and now rebellion seemed possible. On 5 January 1797 Lord Edward wrote, summoning Pamela and Lady Lucy to join him, pretending, as he had done to his mother when he went to Switzerland, that they would go through the countryside as tourists. 'You and Pam are to set off. I will not take any excuse – no wisdom – no prudence – no reflection – no reason – no what will be said – in short, no nonsense. Your wise brother E. F. High for the Giant's Causeway in all the horrors of winter!'

But they did not go. The arrival of the French had sobered Lady Lucy and now her family began to frighten her. 'Jan. 2 – I was not well and spent most of the day upstairs. Still in alarms about the family . . . Aunt Sarah took me apart to talk of very unpleasant subjects: made me low; indeed I am wretchedly so.' Pamela too was anxious. 'To tell you the truth I fear to look at the future,' she wrote to Lady Lucy after Lord Edward had left her. 'I see the future, the heavy future, but covered with a thick veil. Kind nature has thus veiled it to help us endure life. For our existence would be wretched if we had no hope. You see how sure I feel of your love, my dear friend, since I am letting my pen write all that my heart feels. I know all that passes in your heart; I know that you feel all these troubles as I do; but sensitive souls always think *en noir*.' When Pamela came over to Castletown she and Lady Lucy fortified themselves with singing what she referred to as '*the song*', and rousing talk of Belfast. But after listening to Sarah Napier's relay of government suspicions she alerted Lord Edward to the rumours about him by writing, 'all that Aunt Sarah has said about this journey is incredible,' and decided not to make matters worse by joining him. 'Pamela is for prudence and no Giant's Causeway,' Lady Lucy noted. A few days later Lord Charles Fitzgerald repeated Sarah Napier's warnings. Lord Charles had gone over to the government some years before. He was close to Dublin Castle and his report was far more likely to reflect government feeling about Lord Edward than the sources of the Foxite Napiers. Lord Charles came to Leinster House, where Lucy had gone in the New Year, 'and frightened me about Edward, saying that Lord Camden had information against him and that he must leave the country. I am constantly distracted with these kind of things. Edward is at Belfast which is the cause of all this.'

Several members of the family now took steps to dissociate themselves from Lord Edward's activities. By mutual agreement he and the Duke of Leinster no longer met, although he was allowed into Leinster House by the back door when Lady Lucy was staying there. Lord Charles Fitzgerald loudly expressed his loyalty to the government; Lord Robert, now *chargé d'affaires* in Copenhagen, maintained a judicious silence and could justifiably claim a long-standing loyalty to Westminster and an ignorance of Irish politics. William Ogilvie was prepared to meet Lord Edward but refused to see him in company with Arthur O'Connor.

The Duchess of Leinster was at first unruffled by the thickening crowd of rumours from Dublin. When news of the French in Bantry Bay reached London, she assured Lady Lucy, 'I am quite stout about this business; thank God no horrors have as yet seiz'd my mind about it,' and concluded when the last of the fleet had sailed away, 'It is very shocking to think that so many lives have been lost in this attempt. God send it may discourage any future one of the same nature. Be as easy as you can make yourself about me, for indeed I am wonderfully well and surprised at myself. I don't listen to any of the stories, and your dear Papa continues, I see, to have it talked about as little as possible before me.'

When Lord Edward had come back from Hamburg the Duchess had tried to persuade him to give up his political idealism. But she was unable to dent what she called his 'enthusiasm' and only succeeded in making him miserable. 'To work upon those feelings only makes him wretched; but does not remove the prejudice.' She knew the depths of her son's obstinacy and did not try again, deciding instead to trust in her benevolent God, who, she said, always had 'some gracious good end in view, tho' hidden from our eyes', and to immerse herself in little Eddy.

The Duchess weathered the bleak winter of 1796 well. But her fortitude gave way when she started to get alarming letters from her sisters and children in January 1797, telling her about government suspicions of her son. She was then 'very wretched some days,' she told Lady Lucy. She allowed herself to be calmed by a letter from Lord Edward, but from then on lived in a state of anxiety which she resolutely conquered by her devotion to little Eddy and her determination to create a new picture of her beloved son in her own mind. She still followed Lord Edward around in her imagination, just as he did her, thinking of him at Frescati in February with 'the spring flowers peeping out every day, the birds and the little green buds swelling in the hedges'. But she was carefully laying on top of her extravagant love a new image. Lord Edward was growing in her mind into a martyr, a saviour of his country whose virtue would be recognised by history even if his actions were condemned by law. In this way she could excuse what many were now openly saying was his treachery and prepare herself for possible disaster. She already had little Eddy and now she began to collect other tokens that might in time become relics. When Lady Lucy sent a lock of Lord Edward's hair, the Duchess replied, 'Yes, that dear lock so lately growing on Eddy's precious head is a very acceptable present. I have it in my bosom, after dear little Eddy had kissed it a thousand times. "Papa's hair, Eddy's own Papa's hair!" I really think he understands it all, pretty love.' Despite her half-humorous, half-desperate idea that little Eddy sympathised with her distress, the Duchess was not overcome by feeling. She was a survivor, who might inveigh against the coldness of reason but nevertheless would put it to good use in extremity. She put reason to the service of endurance, preparing herself for crisis and building a new vision of her son that could survive even his death.

When he formally joined the United Irishmen, Lord Edward had acknowledged to himself that he was dedicating himself to the cause and that secrecy and danger might mean he lost his family. But he never stopped thinking about his mother, loving her and trying to alleviate her anxiety without giving her false hopes. Perhaps knowing that she was

beginning to collect memories and objects to remind herself
of him, he had himself painted in the winter of 1796 by the
respected portraitist Hugh Douglas Hamilton. He ordered
an innocuous three-quarter length, from which he stares
with mild-mannered cheerfulness beyond the viewer, his
grey-green eyes fringed by long lashes and roofed by sturdy
black brows. Although he necessarily wore his hair democ-
ratically short, he avoided his customary hibernian green
cravat (although he did compromise on one which was a
sanguinary scarlet), and made sure there were no symbols –
no pipes or harps, weapons, manifestos or flags – that might
be interpreted as revolutionary. He presented himself to
posterity as an unassuming gentleman, alone, and in a studio:
an image for his family to remember him by, nothing else.
Even so, when it was later copied several times for members
of Lord Edward's family, Hamilton or his assistants saw fit
to replace the red cravat with one of blameless white and to
leave out completely the swatch of scarlet cloth that in the
original had hung behind the figure and served as a rhyme
for the red encircling necktie.

When writing to his mother Lord Edward tried as hard as
he could to stick to the old comforts of the family and the
garden. 'Let me talk of little Edward,' he wrote at the beginning of 1797. 'I hear he is charming, *the dog*; think of its liking to play cards and win. What idea has it of winning that
can give it pleasure. Pray don't let it win often. Teach it not
to mind success . . . Aunt Sarah says it is not so obstinate as
its Papa: so much the better.' As for baby Pamela, now nine
months old, he wrote, 'it grows like Edward in its actions
and ways, knocks its head on the ground, tears its cap, cries,
"ah! ah!", looking at one in the face and watching one's
countenance.' Lord Edward had just arrived in Frescati to lie
low for a few weeks. The house was empty, spurned by its
hoped-for tenant, so he was also able to write comfortingly,
'I can't tell you how pleased I was to see this place again. I
have always a thousand delightful feels about it . . . In a

moment one goes over the years; every shrub, every turn, every peep of the house has a little history with it. The weather is delightful and the place looks beautiful. The trees are all so grown that there are a thousand pretty sheltered spots, which near the sea, and at this season, is very pleasant.'

But politics kept breaking into his mood and his narrative. He could no longer conceal his anger, and went on, 'the birds sing, the flowers blow and the whole scene . . . makes me for moments *forget* the *world* and all the villainy and tyranny going on in it. Every day the violent measures of our Irish tyrants increase, and every day throughout the country they lose strength and make enemies, while they in the true spirit and ignorance of despots [take] revenge on individuals, as if the movements or indignation of a whole people depended on men not causes.'

Lord Edward's insistence that seizing on individuals was useless in the face of a mass movement impelled by ideas was heartfelt and revealing. Arthur O'Connor had been arrested in his company a few nights before and Lord Edward was still staggered and disturbed. 'I never saw Eddy so unhappy,' Lady Lucy wrote in her diary the day after O'Connor was taken to gaol. Without O'Connor's confidence and easy way with words Lord Edward felt exposed and intermittently despondent. Together they had represented a north-south axis within the United movement, supported by the most popular elements of the Society, the ordinary footsoldiers Lord Edward had taken such pains to recruit in Kildare. With O'Connor in gaol Lord Edward might have to argue the French case alone in the face of a growing desire from other leaders for an immediate and more local rising.

O'Connor was picked up for writing an inflammatory address, *To the Free Electors of the County of Antrim*. The charge against him was high treason, its purpose to signal unequivocally to the newly confident United Irishmen that the government would not hesitate in moving against their leaders when the time was ripe. O'Connor was locked in the Bermingham Tower of Dublin Castle and stayed there until August. Although he was alone, he had his dog, his own servant to wait on him and a supply of books, and his quarters were far more salubrious than the gloomy cells of Kilmainham, Newgate and Bridewell gaols where other United leaders were immured. O'Connor was treated like a gentleman and his gaolers turned a blind eye to the parade of well-wishers under his window and the well-worked flirtations he sent to Lady Lucy Fitzgerald pencilled in the flyleaves and margins of his books. On 14 February he wrote in a copy of James Thomson's *Seasons*, 'I saw my dear beloved friend from my grated prison: alas! she looked pale, she grieves for her friend. Do not then, dear friends, add to his misery by letting it prey upon your warm generous hearts. I can bear my own sufferings without a sigh, but the sight of you, my ever dear, dear friends, brings torrents from my eyes. Against oppression's galling hand my heart is adamant, but to you, my friends, it melts softer than the softest. Let persecution do its worst, we will yet meet, and cruel absence shall but enhance the joys of meeting.'

Just as he set Lady Lucy's heart beating without any declaration of love, so O'Connor set out in his address to rouse the Irish people without any direct mention of a republic or a revolution. O'Connor and the United Irish lawyers were confident that the government could never convict him of treason and that his imprisonment without trial could only add to the glamorous aura that was now beginning to surround the movement.

On Lady Lucy Fitzgerald the effect of O'Connor's imprisonment was immediate. 'Saw poor dear Arthur at the window of his prison,' she wrote on 12 February. 'He look'd very melancholy. We kiss'd our hands to each other.' With her kiss went her new commitment to the cause and to the pulsating atmosphere of danger and excitement that

O'Connor's imprisonment quickly fostered. From then on Lady Lucy stopped listening to the warning voices of her family. She became an unwavering supporter of the United Irish cause, self-consciously practising her new role as 'citoyenne' and recording Lord Edward's 'democratic' activities in her diary. 'Mar. 15 – Pamela and I walked a good deal. I *cleaned* the house. . . Mar. 17 – St Patrick's Day. Edward dined in town with some citizens . . . Mar. 24 – Edward went to town and did not return until the middle of the night . . . Apl. 18 – went to town for a ball at Lady Clare's. I had my hair turn'd close up, was reckon'd democratic, and was not danced with.'

By now Lord Edward was not only a marked man, but also a hero to every rebellious youth in Dublin. The poet Tom Moore, just starting out on a long career of writing patriotic and popular 'melodies', saw him walking down Grafton Street early in 1797 and thirty years later remembered that 'on being told who he was as he passed, I ran anxiously after him, desirous of another look at one whose name had, from my school days, been associated in my mind with all that was noble, patriotic and chivalrous. Though I saw him but this once, his peculiar dress, the elastic lightness of his step . . . and the soft expression given to his eyes by their long dark lashes, are as present and familiar to my memory as if I had intimately known him.'

Lord Edward's fame and popularity brought recruits to the United movement, but he himself had long passed from living his legend into being a committed and active revolutionary, less interested in chivalry than in accomplishing his aims as quickly and efficiently as possible. Violence was at the heart of his solution and always had been since 1792. Lord Edward was, with the Sheares brothers, the first to put forward a practical plan to achieve equality by violent means. He never moved significantly from this plan, and unlike the Sheares, he knew from active service as a soldier exactly what it would involve. Although the violence he advocated would be controlled and as short-lived as possible – a rising, a *coup d'état*, banishment without retribution of the Castle officials and then a National Convention to determine the form of the new republic – it was violence none the less, and the military campaign at the centre of the plan would be surrounded by casual murder, reprisals, looting, burning, executions and torture on both sides. There was nothing noble about this, it was the plan of a practical political revolutionary, a man impelled by abstract principles of equality and fraternity, but a man of violence all the same. Still less was Lord Edward's day-to-day life chivalrous; it was a round of meetings and journeys, plans and dispatches, worrying, tiring and dangerous. All the time he had to face the possibility that the rebellion would fail, that he would die a traitor's death, ruin his family and destroy the happiness of his mother.

As he travelled through the country in the spring of 1797, Lord Edward could see already these two faces of revolution. The United Irishmen were full of confidence. The organisation was growing rapidly, fuelled by hopes of a new invasion and by widely distributed, skilful propaganda that ranged from the stirring rhetorical sophistication of O'Connor's address to the hastily printed, easily concealed sheets of French marching songs and patriotic ballads. The *Northern Star* was distributed free throughout the north, and once even tossed from the galleries of the theatres in Dublin, its cream half-folio sheets floating down on to the decorous and outraged occupants of the stalls and the rowdy crowd in the pit like wide-winged birds gliding to earth. Secret United Irish cells proliferated across the country in a vegetable growth, each one sprouting another as soon as it was full, spreading out underground in a dense, concealed mass. Hordes of arms were piling up in barns and caves, subscriptions to the movement coming in. Hopes and expectations had never been higher. But betrayal and violence were spawned, too. As the Society grew, so did the squalid network of paid informers, the severity of magistrates and the fears of landowners. Some men took the government's money from simple greed; many others nursed grudges against the United Irishmen or fears that their prosperity would be wrecked in a revolution.

Francis Higgins, proprietor of the government newspaper the *Freeman's Journal*, was less a spy than a spy-master, running a successful network of middle-level informers. He made a good living out of Dublin Castle, declaring his loyalty frequently, but was a businessman at heart. Some of the best informers, like some of those whom they betrayed, were infatuated with conspiracy and excited by treason. Leonard McNally, a barrister who often acted for United Irish prisoners, lived for years on the dangerous edge of things, defending some United Irishmen in court, betraying others to Dublin Castle. Men like Samuel Turner, a trusted member of the Belfast executive committee, who was turned by the government in 1797, or Samuel Sproule, a landowner who volunteered to join the Society to become an informer after United Irishmen raided his home, were intoxicated by their importance and their closeness to danger. Turner was recklessly brave and able to act superbly the part of a rebel while feeding his employers with exaggerated accounts of the plots and horrors he was discovering. Sproule was more costive and careful, maintaining, 'from principle, and to serve my country, I do think it my duty to counteract these hellish plots formed to ruin the kingdom and butcher innocent people'. But both men were infatuated with their roles, writing excited and sometimes overwrought letters to government officials that made it clear that neither money nor duty were sufficient motive for their activities; like some of those they were betraying, they were enthralled by the unexpected power of their double lives and their opportunities for voyeuristically enjoying their own cruelty.

Suspicion and betrayal bred terror. Summary justice was given to those suspected of betraying the cause; men were beaten, their houses burned, their families threatened. Mistakes were made that contributed to the wave of sectarian violence that was lashing through the country from north to south. Ireland was a country of young men; its population had nearly doubled since the mid century. Thousands without employment left for service in the British armed forces, some willingly, some pressed in the ports or sent from the gaols. Many others were competing for land and homes. Insecurity stirred the cauldron of dissent; under-employment gave young men time to worry, plot and fight. Magistrates, fearful of roving armed bands, alternately meted out long sentences and called on Dublin Castle to bring in more statutes and more soldiers. Finally, on 13 March 1797 the province of Ulster was proclaimed under the Insurrection Act, giving the control of violence into the hands of an ill-disciplined army and its ferocious commander, General Lake. Terror and repression henceforth danced grimly together.

In anticipation of the formal proclamation of Ulster, General Lake began disarming it on 3 March. He interpreted his informal brief from the Lord Lieutenant with licence and gusto, sending his soldiers to search houses, farms and whole villages for arms, allowing burnings, beatings and the occasional murder of those who refused to hand over their weapons and those who had none to bring forward. In their turn the United Irishmen ambushed parties of soldiers, raided houses in pre-emptive strikes for arms and tried persistently to infiltrate the militias and bring them over to their side.

Lake chafed at his instructions, wanting not just *de facto* but also *de jure* powers to push through his rough justice. 'These villains do most undoubtedly meditate a rising and that very shortly,' he wrote to the Home Secretary in London, adding, 'I cannot help wishing that we had full powers to destroy their homes, or to try some of them by our law, if they did not bring in their arms . . . Nothing but terror will keep them in order.' Lake's tactics were mostly brutal and simple, but he was capable of occasionally organising chilling symbolic events. On 14 May four members of the Monaghan militia camped outside Belfast were charged with being United Irishmen. When they refused to confess the names of other members in their regiment, they were condemned to death. They were immediately marched through the streets of Belfast to the encampment at Blaris Moor, where they were forced to stand by their waiting coffins and were then shot in front of massed ranks of militiamen who had assembled in silence and the pouring rain to watch them die.

Such acts may have terrified the watching soldiers, but they immediately elevated the dead men into martyrs. A few days after the executions ballads telling of their heroism were being passed out under smocks and greatcoats on the streets of Belfast, while in the militia camps handbills were distributed which used the best rhetoric United Irish journalists could command to transmute the grim physicality of the event into a story of glorious sacrifice. Government executions brought revulsion and recruits simultaneously, frightening some and stiffening the rebelliousness of others.

Despite the new recruits, the spring and summer of 1797 were times of crisis for the United Irish movement. No news of a French fleet came with the spring, and as the weeks passed, many United leaders began to criticise their ally. Some argued that French intentions towards Ireland would always be colonial rather than fraternal and that the United Irishmen should rise and create a republic alone. Lord Edward still desperately wanted a French-led revolution. He hung on to his belief in the Directory's fraternal altruism and he was convinced that French military help was vital for a quick, successful campaign. In February a secret committee, of which he was a member, had sent a new agent, Edward Lewins, to the Mattiesons in Hamburg, to urge the French to come quickly. Pamela wrote to her cousin

Henriette telling her to expect a visitor, and Lewins arrived with one of her dresses in his luggage by way of introduction. But March and April went by without any response from France, even though Lake was discovering arms by the thousand and the situation in the north was becoming difficult for the United leaders to control. Afraid that a rebellion might begin spontaneously, fearful that something had gone wrong in Hamburg, and anxious that his policy should prevail, Lord Edward immediately offered to travel to London, confirm Lewins's official status to Jagerhorn, the French agent there, and press again the case for intervention.

When he had gone to Hamburg the year before, Lord Edward had used as an explanation the need to accompany a woman abroad. Now he did the same thing, announcing that Lady Lucy Fitzgerald had to go home to London and that he was taking her there. Lady Lucy did not explain the reason for her hurried departure to her diary, writing only, 'May 21 – Came to town: saw Edward who proposed to take me over to England immediately. I consented, but with a heavy heart. I long to see Mama, but don't like leaving Ireland just now.' They set out two nights later, drifting out of Dublin Bay and watching the stars twinkle in the clear, velvety sky, sitting talking on the deck of the packet until four in the morning.

The Duchess of Leinster was overjoyed to see her favourite son again. Before she knew he was coming to London she had written to Lady Lucy that she was prepared for the worst, calling it 'the Evil': 'nothing can happen without the permission of God, and we must trust in His providence which will avert the Evil if best for us, or support us under it if it is to happen. I find my mind much less weak than I thought it would be. Tell my Eddy so and press him to your heart for me.' Thus she had already hardened her heart against future sorrow, and she fortified herself by going over and over past happiness with little Eddy, repeating the familiar stories with him in a litany of comfort. 'My little Eddy is lovelier than ever,' she told Lucy. 'He says: "sit by me, Grandmama, and tell me stories about Papa, Mama and little Pam and Tony and Sophie at Ealing." Then he stops and seems to recollect everything that passed there, and if I omit one circumstance sets me right as how Papa used to make him ride on a good stupid bishop's horse, then on a wicked horse that went fast, how "pretty little Mama took him in her arms" and danced pretty dances upon the green with him, how he used to play in her bed with *poor* little Pam, how Tony took him to Mrs Fisher's garden, and so on by the hour will he sit and talk about them.'

It was Lord Edward whose mood was volatile. He was forthright and tough with Jagerhorn, vouching for Lewins's probity, demanding French help soon and saying that those in favour of an immediate rising could not be restrained beyond the end of June. But inwardly he was beginning to be despondent, worried about the splits in the United Irish movement, sceptical about the prospects for a successful spontaneous rising and above all losing confidence in the French. He had never envisaged himself as a military leader; he always imagined a military campaign led by a French general in which he himself would play a subsidiary and local role. He had, too, cheerfully left negotiations with the French and detailed planning of a future government to the lawyers and journalists in the movement who were more articulate than himself. Even now he was prepared to act with the majority; if most leaders wanted an immediate rising he would acquiesce and plan for it. Privately, though, he was still hoping and working for French intervention.

For their part, French agents had no good news to pass on to Ireland. General Hoche was busy pursuing his rivalry with Napoleon on France's western borders. The Directory was distracted and the people longed for peace. Ireland no longer seemed a great island barracks from which to harass Britain, more a jagged speck at the edge of the government's vision. The Directors might be willing to lend it rhetoric, but they were now dubious about troops and money. In June peace negotiations began with London; by the summer, Hoche was obviously dying of consumption; a plan to send Dutch ships and troops to Ireland languished and faded away. Ireland dropped over the horizon and out of sight.

Sensing that practical schemes had dried up, many United Irish leaders, especially those in the rebellious north, were now pushing for an immediate uprising. A meeting in Dublin in June broke up in acrimony; another in July ended in an agreement to keep everything calm for the moment. But soon afterwards warrants went out for the arrest of a clutch of senior Ulster leaders. Many fled abroad; others began to disagree about policy, splitting along Catholic-Protestant lines. Even as lawlessness spread throughout the country the United Irish movement, especially in the north, seemed to be arguing itself to a standstill, organising for a rebellion but unable to agree on its form or timing.

In all this uncertainty Lord Edward longed for O'Connor, who was still in gaol. In his friend's absence he picked up his old friendship with his Kildare neighbour, Valentine Lawless. The cheerful dancing and whiskey-drinking of the winter before had given way to nights of tension, expecting visits and alarms in the darkness. When there were no meetings or secret drill, they whiled away the evening hours with discussions on religion and the political situation. Like O'Connor, Lawless was unable to argue Lord Edward out of his Anglicanism, although his teasing was, he admitted, 'manifestly productive of much pain to his affectionate heart'. But Lord Edward did allow Lawless to write an address to his constituents in Kildare, explaining why he would not be seeking re-election after the summer dissolution of parliament. In the daytime they were often busy, pointedly attending trials of suspected United Irishmen to whom Lord Cloncurry's land agent, the Catholic lawyer Mathew Dowling, frequently offered his services. Dowling was a committed United Irishman and his able cross-examination of witnesses and haranguing of juries prompted one alarmed magistrate to call him 'the executive officer of sedition and rebellion'. His performances, together with the presence of Lord Edward and Valentine Lawless were often enough to sway juries towards acquittals and to convince magistrates that sedition in Kildare was more deep-rooted and well organised than elsewhere in the south. Lord Edward and Lawless went to trials to show their personal support for accused men, many of whom they knew well. But they also went to gesture to those who disagreed with them from inside the United movement that their commitment was to the rank and file, to the ordinary footsoldiers of revolution. Like his turf-burning, his street-walking and his attendance at country festivals, Lord Edward's haunting of courtrooms was a way of renewing and advertising his populism.

In August, Arthur O'Connor was released from his confinement in Dublin Castle, let out on bail put up, and probably borrowed, by Lord Edward. As soon as O'Connor emerged, he, Lord Edward and Lawless joined with other United leaders in starting a new propaganda sheet, *The Press*, to succeed the defunct *Northern Star*. O'Connor was its editor and Lawless its principal backer. One of the other shareholders was Leonard McNally, the suave Dublin lawyer and government informer who was supplying Dublin Castle with a stream of letters in which gossip and accurate reporting of United Irish activities were gleefully and indiscriminately mixed.

By means of such men Dublin and Westminster were compiling a damning dossier on Lord Edward. McNally claimed that he was a convinced and unashamed advocate of regicide. There were reports that he was at once planning a diversionary uprising to cover a French invasion of England and that, with O'Connor, he was contemplating an immediate rising with or without French help. Samuel Turner, the Belfast leader who had gone over to the government, confirmed Lord Edward's new militancy in letters from Hamburg.

Turner was a self-dramatising spy who loved to lecture his handlers in London. He chose the name 'Richardson' as his alias, hinting that his reports would be as imaginative as that writer's epistolary novels; and he demanded from his employers a similarly literary sense of style, advising Lord Downshire on 1 December 1797, 'It will be requisite for your Lordship to lay aside every emblem of *noblesse* and adopt the style of an Irish *sans-culotte*, for fear of accidents.' He negotiated a pension of three hundred pounds a year in return for his services and enjoyed flaunting his extravagance and mercenary status, demanding 'a cool five hundred' when his money ran out.

In the autumn of 1797 Turner established himself as a trusted guest at the Mattiesons' house in Hamburg, where he had already stayed as a United Irish emissary before he changed sides. He watched the pattern of letters in and out of the house and was able to pass much useful information on to London by raiding the postbag. He suspected that among the family news that passed between Ireland, London and Hamburg was coded information from Lord Edward to the Directory. 'All letters from Lady Lucy Fitzgerald ought to be inspected; she, Mrs M. of this place and Pamela carry on a correspondence,' he warned Downshire sternly in October. But he was evasive about Lord Edward, perhaps unwilling to betray him from the Mattiesons' house. In October he presented Lord Edward as a firebrand, ready to lead a rising without the French. A little while later he sent Dublin Castle a letter from Jagerhorn to Reinhard, the French minister, which he had fished out of the Mattiesons' postbag and copied; in it Jagerhorn reported Lord Edward as declaring, 'without foreign succour the Patriots in Ireland must either see their country enslaved by its oppressors or by a hopeless effort fall gloriously in asserting her cause', and demanding arms, ammunition and officers of artillery from the French. Later still, Turner said Lord Edward 'was a tool merely, and being an active enterprising man and a man of spirit and name he was made use of by the more cunning and wicked.'

Even if his Whitehall masters could have risked it, Turner refused to act as a witness against his former associates, and by going to Hamburg he had in fact cleverly contrived to seem whirled in the maelstrom while actually gliding to safety. For 'Mr Richardson' supplied plenty of damning information, but was adamant about keeping himself quietly on the sidelines. Hamburg was no longer the crossing point for all communication between Dublin and Paris. Reinhard, who had been Lord Edward's contact there, had been pushed out of office in July. And the United Irishmen now had a whole group of exiled spokesmen in Paris. Besides, with French interest in an invasion dropping daily, the most exacting and useful place for a double agent like Turner to be was Ireland itself. But one set of betrayals was enough for him.

Notwithstanding a paucity of hard evidence, the Lord Lieutenant, Camden, convinced that O'Connor and Lord Edward were now the leading militants in the republican movement, considered picking them up. On 2 December he wrote to the Home Secretary in London, 'The intelligence with which we are now furnished would, if certain people could be brought forward, be sufficient to bring the conspiracy to light, defeat its ill consequences, and make a salutary impression on the minds of the people.' But Turner stayed in his Hamburg haven and in his absence Camden could not risk imprisoning such well-connected men without trial. He had suffered at the hands of O'Connor's lawyers once, and he was unwilling to be made a fool of again. 'Under the impression of the disadvantage of taking up persons without bringing them to trial,' as he put it, he dropped the plan. But Lord Edward was still a marked man. He was tailed in the street. All letters to and from Kildare were opened. Tony was carefully watched, an easy marker for his master's movements; Pamela was more than ever an object of suspicion.

Watchers were themselves followed. The United Irishmen had their own informers to deploy against the Castle, converts and infiltrators in the offices and homes of the highest government officials. Mr Cross, well known as a bookseller and unsuspected as a United Irishman, calling on a favoured client with the latest titles from London or Paris, might just have time to riffle through the post on the hall table as he waited. A carpenter in Dublin Castle, walking the corridors with his chisel and saw, could report on who hurried by him: there was Francis Higgins, who ran the *Freeman's Journal* to see Secretary Cooke; here, and everywhere, was Lord Castlereagh; there was General Abercrombie, the angry new Commander-in-Chief of the army. In the countryside, a faithful valet, standing at his master's shoulder at dinner and helping him off with his clothes at night, became, as silence fell, a pikeman and a United spy, noting visitors, gossip, moods. Riding to town, the coachman, phlegmatically slapping the steaming necks of his horses, caught the conversations that came from behind him and took them to his brothers in the movement. Anyone might be an informer, anyone a spy.

Trust, in this climate, became the most valuable element of friendship. Confidence shrank in everyone but the oldest and steadiest companions. Lord Edward could no longer talk to his beloved aunt Louisa Conolly; her husband had become a loyal Castle man and her fear and rigid sense of duty had sent her into the arms of her kinsman, Castlereagh. He could no longer write honestly to his mother because his trust was too great a burden for her to bear. His brother the Duke of Leinster was unreliable, sympathetic one day, horrified the next. Pamela, Arthur O'Connor and his particular friends in the United movement: these marked the new circumference of his confidence. Anyone beyond that boundary might be a danger to the movement and to his life. There were few hours of peaceful sleep on the sofa at Kildare any longer; but he did still feel safe there, lulled by the knowledge of the secret army beyond the drive and by Tony's solid steadfastness within.

At the end of November Lord Edward had recruited a newcomer to the upper echelons of the United organisation in Kildare, a new companion for his circle of trusted confidants. He was a tall, flamboyant Catholic called Thomas Reynolds, who, at twenty-six, was eight years Lord Edward's junior. The son of a wealthy silk manufacturer, Reynolds had grown up to luxury and fine prospects. But when he was just setting out on adult life his father's business failed, ruined by the introduction of cottons. This disaster destroyed Reynolds's expectations of prosperity. He turned his feelings of anger and rebellion into political activity. As a nineteen-year-old he joined the long-established Catholic Committee, which campaigned for the abolition of the penal laws. In early 1797 he became a United Irishman. He was energetic and resentful, full of grudges against all forms of authority. He worked hard for the overthrow of the government, rising quickly up the organisation to become treasurer of the Kildare baronial committee, attending meetings in the dark back rooms of the old Brazen Head Tavern in Bridge Street and at the Struggler's, round the corner in Cook Street. But all the time he was also striving to pay off his dead father's debts and re-establish himself as a man of property. He married, moved out of the sleazy Liberties into a house in Park Street, and soon after joining the United Irishmen signed a lease with the Duke of Leinster for the old Geraldine stronghold, Kilkea Castle, which, for an annual cost of £482 would bring him £1500 a year from its estate.

Respectability cooled Reynolds's ardour for reform, and he later claimed to have resigned his membership in the United Irishmen that summer. But when, in November, he met Lord Edward on the broad grey steps of the Four

Courts, where Dublin's legal business was carried out, he did not shrink from the acquaintance. Lord Edward, knowing of Reynolds's involvement in the movement and aware of his obligation to the Fitzgerald family after the granting of the Kilkea lease, asked for a private talk. The next day he came to Reynolds's house. Impressed by what a Castle official would later describe as Reynolds's 'passion' and 'imprudence', Lord Edward suggested that his host become a colonel in the United Irish army, responsible for the troops that would assemble around his estate. Reynolds replied that 'he did not think the United Men could stand in battle before the King's troops.' Lord Edward, still eager to convince everyone that the French would set sail soon, insisted that 'the actual battles would be left to foreign troops' and the United Irishmen who joined the invading army, but that the job of the 'multitude' would be like that of the American colonists in the War of Independence: 'to harass the escorts of ammunition, cut off detachments and foraging parties, and in fine, to make the King's troops feel themselves in every respect in a foreign country'. Perhaps thinking that the United men would protect his new castle if there were a rebellion and that he lost nothing if there were not, Reynolds agreed to take the post. When he later changed his mind and directed all his vehemence towards his own protection, this position of authority would prove highly destructive for the movement. Lord Edward had made a mistake; Reynolds was not someone he should ever have let into his circle of trusted companions.

That Lord Edward still put his faith in the French was evident. That he thought an expedition was still planned was shown in his eagerness to pull the shadowy United army into some kind of shape, with regiments, colonels, minor officers and a commander. But while he tried to bring coherence to the mass of the members, the leaders themselves were splitting into factions, unable to agree on when and how to rise. O'Connor was becoming more militant and ambitious for leadership; others were growing more cautious. Reports came in to the Castle that O'Connor and Lord Edward wanted to promote an immediate revolution and assist a French invasion of England by spreading rumours among Catholics that the Protestant Orangemen were going to attack their chapels as they assembled for Christmas Mass. Such a use of the growing sectarian divisions both within and beyond the movement would have been anathema to Lord Edward; the last thing he wanted was an uprising that might assume the character of a religious as well as a civil war.

But he was still intermittently dreaming of a rising that would demonstrate to the French the value of an invasion of Ireland, and convince them finally to set sail. On 19 December he wrote to his mother saying he thought the French might land in England and added that he was thinking of sending Pamela and little Pam to Hamburg. But he now believed the French would not come until the spring, for he confidently told his mother it was quite safe for William Ogilvie to travel to Ireland that winter. 'I do think if Ogilvie could contrive to come over for a month it would do no harm. I have nothing to tell my dear Mother from this place. The papers show you the state we are in. Wretched bad it is. Things take such a violent turn. I have sometimes thought of sending my Pam to her Mother to have her out of the way. Do not mention this to anybody as it is yet only a cursory thought and anyhow it would not be in the course of a couple of months . . . I should not be surprised if the French attempt an invasion in England. I do not see how they can be prevented if the war goes on. The country has got into a critical situation, and by all I hear is likely to remain so, for I see no sign of a change of those men who have brought it to this state. But I won't talk of politics for they only torment one . . . Bless [you] my darling mother . . . your affectionate and loving son Edward.'

Lord Edward's uncertainty glinted uneasily behind the

cover of opacity that he threw over everything in his letters. He spent the winter in a state of frozen indecision, a hesitant partner in O'Connor's strident militancy, unwilling to suspend plans for the arrival of the French. The militants and moderates in the United leadership were now openly at loggerheads. Their situation was perhaps unprecedented and certainly perplexing. Returns from members showed that the movement commanded the allegiance of almost two hundred thousand men spurred to hatred of Dublin Castle and Westminster by economic and political grievances. This mass was still working as one movement, but it threatened at any moment to split along religious lines, which would mean that despite the common struggle against their rulers, the people might begin fighting among themselves in a separate dispute, one that had political origins and ramifications but could easily degenerate into a straightforward battle between Catholics and Protestants.

The United leaders were also aware that with a few exceptions, of which Lord Edward was the most glamorous and charismatic, they had failed to capture the minds of Ireland's rulers. The leaders of the army still answered to London; the judiciary and Members of Parliament remained loyal to Dublin and the English connection. So this revolution, if it came, would be unlike any other. Although many United leaders had believed that it could arise from the political defection of the ruling élite, like the Glorious Revolution in England, their wishes had not been fulfilled. It was unlikely to be precipitated by a loss of confidence within the regime like that which, with economic hardship, had brought on the recent revolution in France. Again there were no signs that Ireland could sustain a long-drawn-out war supported by men of property like the American Revolution. This Irish revolution, if it were to succeed without outside help, must involve an unprecedented organisation of ordinary people, the transformation of a Bastille-storming rabble into an army capable of seizing Dublin in days and showing itself to be so strong that men of property would support it for their own safety as well as from conviction of its justice. With this task before them it was no wonder that many United leaders lost heart, and not surprising that men like Lord Edward, who had military experience, looked continually and longingly towards France. They doubted the capacities of their citizen army and believed that it needed outside leadership and arms to sustain any sort of campaign.

Walking around the lanes of Kildare and along the back streets of Dublin, Lord Edward sensed a desperation among ordinary United Irishmen for forthright leadership and a rebellion soon. But in the drawing rooms of Carton and Castletown he could find no inclination to join in. On the contrary: signs of disaffection around her, and particularly among her own servants, finally induced Louisa Conolly, moderate in politics and charitable to her tenants, to join her husband on the Castle side. As Lord Edward drilled his secret army, who looked to him as evidence that the aristocracy might join the rebels, he felt the force of the case for an immediate rising. But when he remembered his family, the Foxite Napiers, the wavering Duke of Leinster, the increasingly Pittite and Castle-led Conollys and his confirmed Tory brother Lord Charles Fitzgerald, he was thrown back on the necessity for French help. 'One sees the mischief, but not the remedy,' he wrote candidly to his mother. Faced with an unprecedented situation Lord Edward did not know what to do.

Most other United Irish leaders shared his uncertainty. Arthur O'Connor, however, was confident in his militancy, according to informers. He quarrelled with his more anxious colleagues and, said the spies, argued with Lord Edward for a decisive action. He lost the dispute and in December 1797 made an angry exit from the country. He left behind an inflammatory letter to his supporters, which announced that he was going to France, made it clear that he expected to be vilified by the remaining leaders and concluded in the highest revolutionary rhetoric, 'In contempt of calumny, UNITED with you in brotherly love and affection, and in the glorious cause of reform, I will ever remain your faithful friend and fellow-citizen'. With that O'Connor packed his trunk, sliding among his clothes and books several hundred pounds that would finance his journey and slipping into his razor case a cipher with which to encode letters to Lord Edward. Then he left for London, where he spent several weeks caballing with a delighted Francis Burdett, seeing Lady Lucy Fitzgerald and Valentine Lawless, who had fled to England a few weeks before, and planning his journey to Paris.

O'Connor's intention of heading for France was inconsistent with his declared belief in an indigenous Irish rebellion. If he did not believe in or want French help, why head for Paris? Perhaps the Castle spies misrepresented his case. Perhaps Lord Edward, desperate for one last, direct embassy, persuaded him to go; perhaps O'Connor was cleverly getting out of the way. Whatever the case, his seditious letter had made it impossible for him to come back. If they had an agreed policy, Lord Edward would now have to argue it alone. The knowledge made him first more despondent, and then more persuasive. O'Connor's abrupt departure was the first in a series of events that turned Lord Edward into the leader he had never thought he would be.

REVOLUTIONARY AND CONSPIRATOR

'Fatal Year', Dublin, 1798

For Tony loss and loneliness came inexorably. Edginess, fear and mistrust clouded the clear water of Lord Edward's disposition. Anxiety conquered his habitual optimism, and frenetic activity overtook his old air of relaxed energy. He stopped thinking about Tony and was entirely caught up in secret meetings and plans. He moved constantly from place to place, now in Kildare, now down at Black Rock, now riding for days about the countryside. Their old companionship was destroyed. Lord Edward, to whom Tony had given his trust and his love, was no longer giving anything back; he was absorbed in his secret life, sunk in his worries, absent. When he left the house a group of silent men condensed from the shadows; some walked by his side, glancing constantly down alleys and lanes; some went ahead; others followed unseen at a distance. To remain at liberty, Lord Edward travelled like a prisoner. Tony could not go with him; he was confined in Kildare or Dublin, a house-bound free man. All Tony's old loneliness, his life before Lord Edward, returned, as if America had come to Ireland.

Lord Edward was slipping away from his mother too, becoming insubstantial, silent, unwriting. His letters had always been full of his character; in their plain language and open display of feeling they had carried him to her. But after he left for Hamburg in 1796 his letters had become vague; he was disappearing behind the language he used, making off under cover of allegory and imprecision. From the beginning of 1798 he fell silent, leaving his mother only with memories, relics and bits of paper. Understanding that the language he had used in better days contained him, the Duchess would later treasure his letters as part of himself, labelling the last bundle she had received 'precious remains'.

Unlike Tony, who had trustingly placed all his love in Lord Edward's heart, the Duchess had other people to lean on. She had Ogilvie, her many children and a great galaxy of grandchildren, legitimate and illegitimate, who swirled around her, some in England, some in Ireland, some scattered bronze and brown in colonial outposts across the globe. Above all she had little Eddy, one bit of Lord Edward whom she was determined would never leave her or betray her love. She knew exactly why she loved him so, explaining later, 'transferring to the [child] of my beloved son that anxious tenderness which filled my bosom so many years for his happiness and welfare, I fondly hoped, in this occupation, to find some relief for my afflicted heart.'

The Duchess knew her son was gone. Tony knew he was going. Only Pamela believed that she was with him, his help-mate and, as Francis Burdett had called her, 'his dangerous little wife'. At the beginning of 1798 Pamela still knew what her husband was doing and where he was. When he went away she eased herself towards the end of another pregnancy and received his letters and visitors. She had lived through one revolution and did not flinch from a second. Despite her anxieties she drew a veil over the future and carried on.

Lord Edward was making plans for war. A military committee was formed and he was at its head. The committee was to provide planning and senior officers for the United army.

With or without the French, Lord Edward would be the Irish army's commander. In February he drew up an order sheet for the adjutant-generals who would serve under him in each county and whose job it now was to coordinate training and send as much information as they could to help him plan whatever military campaign the situation demanded.

Lord Edward wanted a complete picture of each county. He needed to know where there were woods that would 'afford shelter to troops without tents', he demanded information on where men 'could conveniently find fuel, straw and forage', where there were bogs to hide in, towns to stay in, flour mills to find food. He also wanted to know if there were government troops stationed in the counties and if 'the enemy', as he now habitually called both the British army and officials of Dublin Castle, moved about or was stockpiling weapons.

The latest letters Lord Edward had sent from France talked of a possible sailing in April, so he gave special instructions to commanders in coastal areas. As soon as they saw friendly ships they must send word to Dublin, gather their troops together and march to meet the French, 'each man to be provided with at least three days subsistence, and to bring all they can of cars, draft horses, horses harnessed, and horses to mount cavalry, with three or four days forage'. Horses were essential to Lord Edward's plans because the French, who would be bringing ammunition and cannon, would sail without them.

Even as he drew up these instructions Lord Edward was falling into frantic despair. Weeks went by without any definite commitments from France. Arthur O'Connor dallied in London, seemingly unaware of the need for speed. Reluctantly, Lord Edward made up his mind to the necessity for a domestic rising. The country was in a state of smothered, disorganised rebellion, with constant sectarian fighting and brutal reprisals by government troops. Many United Irishmen seemed prepared to rise, encouraged by their own propaganda to believe that with or without foreign help they would soon be able to rid themselves of the Castle government. Women who were sympathetic to the movement were said to be going through towns and villages singing seditious songs of the sort that Pamela had been assiduously copying in Kildare. Castle officials were becoming obsessed with rooting out sworn United Irishmen and circulated memoranda that translated their secret sign language. On approaching, one man was supposed to clasp his hands, at which his fellow, if a member, would put his right hand on his left hip and say, 'Be steady', to which the first man would reply in a whisper, 'I am determined to free my country or die. Liberty! Liberty!' This fascination with secrecy was self-fulfilling. Any discovery proved that there was a vast seditious force at hand; no discovery showed how effective it was in keeping quiet.

Determined now to build on this confidence and excitement among the rank and file, and fearful that if he did not the government would jump first, Lord Edward arranged early in February to meet the moderate Catholic United leader William MacNeven in the Shakespeare Gallery in Exchequer Street. There, a hundred yards or so from where Lord Castlereagh and Secretary Cooke planned their incarceration, MacNeven and Lord Edward walked round pretending to look at the pictures like a couple of country gentlemen up in town for the day. As they moved between the famous scenes – Fuseli's two terrifying paintings of the regicidal traitor Macbeth might have given them pause for thought – Lord Edward pressed his new determination on the cautious doctor, a man he had himself recruited into the movement. He had decided on a rising of the people now, he explained, because 'their impatience was no longer to be restrained'. His tours of the countryside had convinced him that the time was ripe and he told MacNeven that he could secure the capital without a pitched battle. The United men in Dublin could easily overwhelm the garrisons in the most important buildings – the Castle itself, the Customs House, Trinity College and the banks. The armies outside the city, of which he himself would have the overall command, could quickly set up road blocks and cordon it off. This would prevent the government troops encamped around the capital, particularly the militia at Loughlinstown, near Bray, from rescuing officials. Once they saw Dublin in rebel hands, government troops might surrender or defect. If they did not, the advancing armies could deal with them as they marched into the city.

MacNeven tried to dissuade Lord Edward from this scheme, although he admitted to having come up with no alternative. But he said that he knew it was fruitless to argue because, 'once his lordship had made his mind up on a point, he was little influenced by the counsel of any man'. They parted with no agreement, which left Lord Edward free to continue his planning.

He was now drawing up instructions for the rank and file in Dublin, those who would have to hold the city while the armies from outside marched in. Since this paper was written for mass distribution and was bound to be found floating on gusts of wind in Dublin's back alleys or in the pockets of men searched as suspects, Lord Edward prefaced it with a disclaimer that made its contents appear hypothetical rather than openly treasonable. 'If ever any unfortunate cause should put our city . . . into the possession of a cruel and tyrannical enemy,' he wrote, 'our conduct then should be regulated in a manner best calculated for obtaining victory.'

The 'apparent strength' of the enemy, Lord Edward declared, should not intimidate the poorly armed and inadequately trained United troops. Once in the city, even in the wide streets of the new suburbs south of the river, the very size of the British force would become an unmanoeuvrable liability, while the soldiers' slow-loading rifles could be overcome by a lowered forest of ten-foot pikes. Lord Edward recommended that the pikemen charge any government troops assembled on the streets. The first line of soldiers – some sixty at the most – would fire and then have to retire; while the second line waited to come into position the pikemen could come forward, running at 'a smart trot' and wreaking havoc with their light weapons. If the second line of troops could be punctured, panic would follow and the King's force would be transformed into a terrified mob that could be 'easily disposed of'.

While the pikemen were engaging knots of troops in the city streets – and it would be a very bloody and costly battle, Lord Edward knew, but forbore to say – other men could hem in the government forces by pulling up paving stones and building barricades every thirty yards or so along the streets, like Parisian *sans-culottes*. Their wives and daughters, 'without imitating the women of Paris', as Lord Edward put it with heavy irony, would torment the army from their windows and roof-tops, hurling down 'showers of bricks, coping stones etc' which they had carried upstairs 'in their aprons'. Thus even without French help, the people of Dublin would have their own French Revolution.

Organising for war became Lord Edward's life. All through January and February he travelled about, exhorting, persuading and attending local meetings. Samuel Neilson, one of the Belfast leaders, who had recently been released from Kilmainham and who shared Lord Edward's view that the mood of the people must be honoured with a rising soon, was often with him. Neilson was capable and energetic and he soon attracted the attention of spies. One reported that he was 'constantly riding to different parts of County Dublin, west, north, south, etc, delivering instructions' and that 'the lower orders much admire him'.

The provincial committee of Leinster, of which Lord Edward was treasurer, now needed a more consistently available member than he could be. Remembering the passion and zeal of Thomas Reynolds, Lord Edward asked him to take over his post. Reynolds allowed himself to be persuaded. But after his election he began to have doubts. He had prospered in the three months since Lord Edward had seen him last, renovating the old castle at Kilkea into a house fit for a country gentleman, buying more land at Castle Jordan just over the Kildare border in County Westmeath, and moving into a new house in Cumberland Street only a few minutes' walk away from Leinster House and Trinity College. But his plans for business and propriety were entirely dependent upon the rents he was receiving from the Kilkea and Castle Jordan lands. Kilkea was in the heart of Kildare, in the southern epicentre of sedition. If the United men rose, his estates might be spoiled and his tenants unable or unwilling to pay rents for lands where crops had been commandeered or ruined. For a couple of weeks Reynolds waited. Towards the end of February he went down to Black Rock with a fellow United man, Mr McCann. McCann was Pamela's apothecary; he often attended her because she was in the last stages of her pregnancy and had visited frequently because she had a 'gathering' in her breast, which kept her at home. McCann often carried messages between United leaders who were lying low. He was a familiar figure on the streets of Dublin and could always claim, even at the dead of night, that he was visiting a patient.

At Frescati Lord Edward gave Reynolds a paper to pass on to the Leinster provincial. It showed the latest returns and the resolutions of the last meeting of the national executive, a five-man committee on which Lord Edward sat which had control of the whole movement. Headed 'National Committee 26th Feb. 1798', the paper described a huge shadowy army of two hundred and eighty thousand men sworn into the movement all across the country – a hundred and ten thousand in Ulster alone; a hundred thousand matching them in the south in Munster; forty-five thousand in Dublin and the surrounding counties. The committee minutes showed that down the eastern side of Ireland the mood was belligerent and militant, and was contained only by the request of the executive 'to bear the shackles of tyranny a little longer, until the whole kingdom shall be in such a state of organisation as will, by their joint co-operation, effect without loss their desirable point, which is hourly drawing to a crisis.'

Lord Edward breached the Society's own etiquette of secrecy when he gave Reynolds this paper. Information and personnel were never meant to travel down the hierarchy, only up. One member alone of the Leinster provincial was supposed to know who belonged in the Leinster executive, and none of them should have been aware of the names of the men who sat on the national committee. Even if, in the upper echelons, men had more than one role, and if many of those in Reynolds's position knew who ran the entire organisation, information should not have been passed down to them, especially not on paper.

But Lord Edward had admitted Reynolds into his circle of trust. He wanted to galvanise the Leinster provincial and he trusted Reynolds to give them information that would stir them to expect a rising soon. But Reynolds was horrified by what he read. He determined in the next twenty-four hours to protect his new-found respectability and wealth at all costs. Riding down to Castle Jordan with a fellow specula-tor, Mr Cope, he put a finger out towards the officials at Dublin Castle, where he knew Cope had good contacts. He hinted that he had some distant knowledge of a treasonable conspiracy and said that he knew of a man who could reveal everything to the government.

Instantly aware that this third party was Reynolds him-self, Cope went straight to Secretary Cooke at the Castle. The government had for some time been looking in vain for a traitor from within the higher ranks of the United move-ment. Hitherto their catches had been small fry operating at local levels and, apart from the suave and slippery McNally, they had been forced to use spies rather than turncoats to find out about the United leaders in Dublin. Cooke was excited, and according to Cope, reacted to the news by say-ing, 'You *must* get him to come forward; stop at nothing – £100,000 – anything.'

A hundred thousand pounds was a vast fortune, enough to put Reynolds immediately into the ranks of the richest men in Ireland. It would have been unwise for Reynolds to accept, even if the authorities really had been willing to pay. He was already an object of suspicion within the United movement; a huge increase in his obvious wealth would have seemed to confirm the mistrust with which he was regarded. Cope, who was himself a moneymaker, clearly thought the sum too much. He went to Reynolds and negotiated a fee of five thousand pounds and the promise of a thousand a year for life. If he could come up with information that would lead to important arrests, Reynolds could live like a country gentleman without ever having to work again.

Reynolds knew some of the men on the national execu-tive, mentioning to the Castle the names of Dr MacNeven, the cautious Catholic who had urged Lord Edward not to sanction a domestic rising, and two well-known barristers, William Sampson and Thomas Emmet. He was unwilling to be the direct instrument of Lord Edward's arrest, but he handed over the papers that Lord Edward had given him at Black Rock. Written in Lord Edward's hand, these were cer-tainly enough to justify his arrest and probably enough to send him to the gallows. Reynolds also found out that the next meeting of the Leinster provincial committee was to be held on 12 March at the house of Oliver Bond, the wealthy woollen draper whom Lady Lucy Fitzgerald had admiringly described when he visited Frescati as 'one of the handsomest and most delightful men to all appearance that ever was'. Reynolds gave all this information to Cope, along with the password that would allow the magistrate entry to Bond's house.

Reynolds could easily have told Cope where Lord Edward could be found, but he did not. Some residual feeling of deference and loyalty to the Fitzgerald family, even distaste, held him back from betraying a man who so transparently trusted him. The evening before the provincial was to meet at Bond's, he went round to see Lord Edward at Leinster House. He found him in an agitated and anxious mood. In the last week, Lord Edward had learned that Arthur O'Connor had been arrested at Margate. With him was another United Irishman, Father James Coigly. They had been bound for France, and along with money to finance the trip and perhaps to buy arms, they carried official memorials from Dublin to the Directory that could convict both themselves and Lord Edward of treason. Soon afterwards the offices of O'Connor's old newspaper, *The Press*, were raided. Lord Edward happened to be in the *Press* office with another senior United man, William Sampson, when the magistrates walked in. He was rattled by the raid, distressed that the magistrate allowed accompanying troops to wreck the house where the paper was printed, and he offered the family living there a temporary home in Kildare if they needed it.

Lord Edward's mood lifted a little when word came through from London that O'Connor's servant had coolly managed to destroy the most incriminating documents, shovelling them into the privy while magistrates searched the room next door. They found the cipher O'Connor and Lord Edward had agreed to use in their correspondence, in which Dublin Bay was glamorously to be described as 'Honduras Bay', Bantry Bay became 'Chesapeake', a musket was rendered innocuous as 'a nail', a cannon became 'a jar' and Lord Edward himself was to be referred to by his grandmother's name of O'Brien. Lord Edward thought the cipher useless as evidence of a conspiracy, and jokingly told a friend that O'Connor had 'nothing *odd* with him but 1200 guineas'. But although O'Connor was clever enough to look after himself, his arrest was a disaster for Lord Edward. It had destroyed the chance of a decisive mission to France and it meant that his friend was now securely behind bars.

Arriving at Leinster House on 11 March, Reynolds added fear to Lord Edward's anxiety. He dropped enough hints to make Lord Edward believe that the government intended to arrest him straightaway. He wished he could go to France, he burst out to Reynolds. He had had very little information from Paris, but he was intimate with the Foreign Minister, Talleyrand-Périgord, and if he could only get there he was sure that he could get him to agree to an immediate invasion. All Lord Edward's dampened-down hopes came out; a few fast frigates, loaded with trained officers, could land at Wexford, he said. The country would rise and the rebels could hold out until more French ships arrived with desperately needed ammunition.

Reynolds was careful not to hint that Bond's house was to be raided. Had he done so, Lord Edward could have called McCann and put word out that the meeting should be cancelled. Reynolds left Lord Edward fearful for himself, not for others. Lord Edward spent the night – perhaps at Leinster House, perhaps hidden near by – suspecting nothing.

Punctually at ten the next morning the meeting of the Leinster provincial began at Oliver Bond's house in Bridge Street. Reynolds had excused himself by writing, in time-honoured fashion, that his wife was 'taken very ill'. Shortly after ten Major Swan, a Dublin magistrate, arrived with several constables in uniform and a long warrant which listed the names of all those expected at the meeting and as many members of the executive committee as Reynolds knew. Giving the password, 'Is Ivers of Carlow come?', Swan was ushered into the house. His constables noisily followed him, pushing past the servant and alerting the assembled United Irishmen. When Swan flung open the door to the meeting room he found the men he had expected, but could see, smouldering in the grate, the papers that had been spread out before them. Those that were dragged from the flames were unimportant details of the last meeting. But Swan had got his prisoners. Thirteen members of the provincial committee were arrested then and there; MacNeven and Thomas Emmet, both members of the executive, were picked up soon afterwards. Two others, realising that warrants were out for them, fled the country. Of the five-man executive only Lord Edward remained free and in Dublin. Of him there was no sign. Like other members of the executive, he was waiting eagerly for the outcome of the meeting at Bond's, hoping that it would confirm the desire of senior officials to sanction an immediate rising. But he had never planned to go himself. On the morning of the meeting, Lord Edward was probably still thinking about Reynolds's warnings of the night before. He had no idea what was happening there. But he was now the effective leader of the movement, the man who would decide whether the United Irishmen would go to war and when.

Once they had rounded up the men at Bond's the magistrates interrogated them. According to United Irish protocol they said nothing. George Cummins, the apothecary from Kildare Town who had been Lord Edward's intimate companion there for nearly four years, calmly denied all connections with and knowledge of the United Irishmen. The exasperated magistrate concluded his report of the examination by writing, 'Being obstinate in denying everything he was committed.' The government got no information from the men of the Leinster provincial. They had scored a propaganda coup, they had several more important leaders behind bars, but they had not succeeded in halting any rebellion.

Immediately after the arrests at Bond's the Castle sent out two search parties with warrants for Lord Edward's arrest. One went to Frescati, found nothing, and returned to Dublin with a sheaf of unimportant papers from the drawing room. The other, led by Sheriff Oliver Carleton, went round to Leinster House. The moment the butler let the sheriff in, Tony, who had never lost his nose for danger, realised what they had come for. Running quietly out of the hall he found Lord Edward, hurried him through the house, across the stable yard at the back and out into Merrion Street, where he trusted Lord Edward would disappear down the streets and alleys that led to the river. Tony could not go with him, so Lord Edward made his way to safety alone.

Carleton was sent up to the room where Pamela was convalescing from her illness. Opening the door he saw her desperately feeding sheets of paper from a drawer into the fire. Carleton gathered up the last few pages and then turned his attention to a leather writing case on a table. Reluctantly Pamela opened it for him. Inside she saw letters from O'Connor and Coigly and a plan for the capture of Dublin, showing the most suitable points of attack and defence. Realising that the plan at least would compromise her husband even if it were not in his writing, she lost the last of her composure, and as the sheriff reported to the Castle, 'threw herself upon her knees and clasped those of Mr Carleton, begging for it to be returned to her and appealing to his feelings as a Husband and as a Parent to permit her to destroy it'. Pamela's terror made Carleton more thorough. He spent an hour and a half combing the house. He took away everything that might be suspicious, returning to Pamela only a bundle of letters from the Duchess of Leinster 'which did not appear of any consequence'.

By now the government had enough written evidence to convict Lord Edward of treason, but no idea where he was. Lord Edward had vanished. Like a miraculous vision, he was sighted now in Dublin, now out of town in Kildare, now in Wexford. Everywhere his supporters longed for him to be, he appeared, materialising out of the spring clouds and vanishing again without trace. He haunted the imagination of supporters and enemies alike, and he became in the ensuing months a mythical figure, going about, it was said, disguised as a gipsy fortune-teller, as a pedlar, as a doctor, as a woman, as a postilion, and, like Christ, as a shepherd, invisibly guarding his faithful flock.

His family were desperate to know Lord Edward's hiding places, but did not want to be told and have to carry the treasonable burden. Many of them were overcome by superstition and the suggestions of Lord Edward's new otherworldliness. Three days after the arrests at Bond's Louisa Conolly went to Pamela at Leinster House and charged her 'not to name his name', as if invoking him might make him appear before them. Pamela was 'not to give a *soul* a hint of where he was, if she knew it, and to stay at Leinster House, seeing everybody that called and keep[ing] strict silence.' 'To which,' wrote Sarah Napier shortly, 'Pamela agreed.'

One man who did know where Lord Edward was hiding was Reynolds. Two days after the arrests at Bond's the unsuspecting apothecary McCann came to him with a message from Lord Edward asking him to come to Aungier Street, where he was staying at the house of his friend Dr Kennedy. Reynolds went twice, and found Lord Edward large as life and concerned not with divinely inspired visitation but with down-to-earth details of planning the revolution. On his second visit, Lord Edward, trustingly believing that Reynolds had escaped arrest from sheer good luck, gave him, as the only surviving member of the provincial committee, an address to the members of the county committee. It asked them to fill up the vacancies created by the arrests, telling them to be in good spirits and assuring them that he was ready to lead them out when the day came.

Reynolds himself went to ground in Kilkea Castle as soon as he had delivered Lord Edward's message. But the Kildare members were as active as Lord Edward had hoped. Word went out to other committees that only four days after the arrests, the Leinster provincial 'had recovered from the shock'; new men had been elected to fill the gaps and morale was high. Two days later a handbill was circulating, essentially a printed version of the paper Lord Edward had given to Reynolds. The sheet declared confidently, 'The Organisation of the capital is perfect', and ordered the rank and file to remain calm and to resist sectarian divisions, concluding, 'Be firm, Irishmen, but be cool and cautious; be patient yet awhile; trust to no unauthorised communications; and above all we warn you, again and again we warn you, against doing the work of your tyrants, by *premature*, by *partial*, or *divided* exertion.'

Soon another broadsheet appeared on walls and tree trunks, addressed to all United 'Friends'. It claimed that 'half a million heroes' were biding their time until a second French expedition should arrive; 'they only wait the second coming, to commence the millennium of freedom.' Lord Edward was addressed in the most stirring rhetoric of which the United journalists were capable; he was the avenging angel, the 'noble minded youth', the focus of all hopes. 'Oh! may the genius of Liberty, ever faithful to its votaries, guard your steps,' the paper finished, 'may the new Harp of Erin vibrate its thrilling sounds through the land, to call you forth, and hail you with the angelic cry of the deliverer of our country.'

Despite the fact that Lord Edward had now become the cynosure of all United aspirations and the most wanted man in Ireland, he was not alone at the top. In the days after the arrests at Bond's the national executive was quickly reconstituted. The Belfast journalist Samuel Neilson, the surgeon William Lawless and the two Sheares brothers, both lawyers, came in to fill the places of those who had been arrested or who had fled. All were men who would sanction a domestic rising, but that they still hoped for French help was evident from their talk of a second coming. The Sheareses had been with Lord Edward in Paris in 1792; they had been members of the Jacobin Club and were both committed regicides. Because of the way the arrests had fallen and perhaps because cautious leaders were no longer prepared to serve on the national committee, the earliest advocates of violence were now in charge of the United organisation, and Lord

Edward himself became in the eyes of government and members alike the movement's figurehead and chief.

To have the burden of command thrust upon him was unwelcome to Lord Edward and further unsettled his jangling mind. He had never regarded himself as a leader, as he had told his mother long before from Canada. Command came to him now partly because he was the only man left with sufficient military experience even to attempt to lead an army, partly because the rank and file bestowed it upon him.

The officials of the Castle were well aware of Lord Edward's magic. Although a number of leaders were still at large, he was the man they wanted. They wanted him dead, or if not dead, out of the country. Lord Edward captured but alive would be the worst outcome; his gaol would become a place of pilgrimage and a site of repeated rescue attempts; legends would grow and wind themselves around his person. The most ruthless officials, especially Cooke and Castlereagh, recognised Lord Edward's increasingly mythic status and wanted to prove his ordinary corporeality with his capture, conviction and execution. Others, more deferential to Lord Edward's family and more sentimental about his noble birth, hoped to persuade him to flee to America or France. Lord Clare, the Chancellor, was reported to have said, 'Will no one urge Lord Edward to fly – I pledge myself that every port in the country shall be left open to him.' Louisa Conolly, told by Lord Castlereagh, 'You may rely on the earnest wishes of government to do all they can for Lord Edward,' believed that he was hinting that the Castle would connive in his escape. But Sarah Napier, whose hatred of Castlereagh was increasing by the day, saw it as at best an expression that the government would be just, at worst an attempt to fool her trusting and credulous sister.

Lord Edward's disappearance immediately became a drama which involved not just Pamela – who sat, heavily pregnant, its still and knowing centre – but the whole extended family: the Duchess of Leinster, her children and husband in England, Lord Edward's aunts in Castletown and Celbridge, the hapless Duke of Leinster and Lord Edward's brothers Henry and Charles. Sarah Napier kept herself busy in the first few weeks by writing a diary for her husband, who was lying in bed with a fever. Louisa Conolly went back and forth between Castletown and Dublin Castle. In London Lady Lucy worked for the release of Arthur O'Connor and waited anxiously for news of her brother, well aware that by the time any reassuring snippet reached her he might be captured or dead. On 25 March Louisa Conolly drove the length of Celbridge High Street from the Castletown gates to Sarah Napier's square grey house, and gave her sister a letter from Mr Ogilvie, saying, 'My poor sister was supported by her confidence in Edward not deserving *any thing* by word or deed'. The Duchess did not say her son was innocent; merely that he had said or done nothing that could get him convicted. A few days later a letter arrived from the Duchess herself, as majestic and commanding as anything she had ever written, offering her sisters advice and reassuring them of her strength of mind. 'I know my dearest sisters will wish to have a line from myself,' she wrote. 'Thank God I have nothing to fear for my dear, beloved Eddy. I am not in the least nervous, my health very good and you know, my dear sisters, how mercifully I have ever been supported in trying occasions. If my later days are destined to be unquiet ones let me be thankful for the share of happiness I have enjoyed in my long life and trust in God to give me strength to weather the storms that may attend the future.' In private, though, the Duchess conceded that relying on God was not enough, and she begged her husband to try and extract her son from Ireland before it was too late. On 14 April Ogilvie set off for Dublin, to try and find Lord Edward and convince him, for his mother's sake, to leave the country.

Pamela was the only member of the family who had reliable reports from Lord Edward. After the raid on Leinster

House she moved to Denzille Street just north of Merrion Square, 'to have a quiet home of her own to lie-in', as she put it to Sarah Napier. The United men who guarded Lord Edward came and went with news of him, and within a few days had brought him in disguise to see her. While his men watched the house, Lord Edward sat with Pamela in the drawing room, cuddling little Pam, who had been carried from her bed for him to hold and kiss. Coming into the room Sophie, the maid, found both husband and wife in tears.

'Reports say that Edward was seen in a post-chaise with his brother Charles at Newry, but it is false,' Sarah Napier noted on 24 March. 'Others, that he is at Leinster or Carton – all false, I believe.' Rumours proliferated about Lord Edward's hiding places. Some believed that he had fled to America; others that he had been spirited away to France. In fact he never left Dublin. After lying low in Aungier Street for a few days, he was taken to the house of a Mrs Dillon at Porto Bello by the Grand Canal on the southern outskirts of the city. Porto Bello was a cluster of houses off the road to the village of Rathmines; Dublin petered out there in muddy tracks, ditches and cottages. The canal, occasionally busy with sooty coal barges by day, was deserted at night. The place had an air of damp dereliction that would be uninviting to nervous government patrols, and Mrs Dillon's house, on a lane off the Dublin road, could be surrounded by hidden watchers who noticed strangers and checked on the credentials of visitors. Mrs Dillon's was a good place to hide, close to town yet eerily remote.

Lord Edward's mood at Mrs Dillon's swung wildly between lighthearted optimism and inactive despair. At times he seemed reckless about his safety, leaving his boots outside the door with his name clearly written all down the inside. When he had nothing to do in the evenings, he walked restlessly by the canal, careless about who might see him, seeming to trust in the reverence with which he was held by ordinary people who might meet him as he trudged along. Often he took a companion, Mrs Dillon's daughter, a girl of twelve or thirteen who in her old age was proud to hint that Lord Edward did more than amuse her by jumping noisily into the half-submerged hulks that lined the nearby canal basin.

When he was confined to the house he sat gazing at Mrs Dillon's garden from his upstairs room. It reminded him of all the gardens he had cultivated – at Frescati and Aubigny, in Nova Scotia and Kildare, and he could not resist the lure of being a gardener again. With Mrs Dillon's daughter as Eve to his Adam, he set about turning over a large bed of lilies that were growing at the garden's end. She remembered their digging and pulling as a prank, a bit of naughtiness to catch her mother's anxious eye. For Lord Edward merriment was tinged with purpose; tilling the soil, with all its accretions of meaning, calmed him. It brought back his happy childhood, it summoned the memory of his mother and it rooted him again in his revolutionary task. The lilies, with their green leaves and orange flowers, would blossom like a living flag of the Ireland that would one day flourish. Lord Edward's gardening was a confirmation and reprise of everything his life had been. In that muddy suburb by dank waters where rats swam and rotten hulks sank to the riverbed, Lord Edward tilled his Eden and dug his republic.

But he was not always optimistic or cheerful. He had heard nothing from the French and as April came, he felt that they had abandoned him. Dublin Castle, on the other hand, had begun to act with decision. Spurred on by the arrests at Bond's, the government had ordered General Abercrombie on 14 March to begin disarming the counties around Dublin. Abercrombie, already losing confidence in Camden and his ministers, proceeded slowly and relatively mildly, drawing the ire of the Lord Lieutenant and confirming his own determination to resign. At the end of March he left the country. Camden appointed the draconian General

Lake to succeed him and on 30 March declared the whole country to be in a state of rebellion. Lake was given a free rein to impose martial law, which he did with gusto, quartering troops on villages and burning down houses whose owners were suspected of sedition. New forms of torture were invented by imaginatively cruel soldiers. Picketing, when men were strapped against a wooden tripod and flogged, became commonplace. 'Croppies', who had signalled their politics by cutting their hair short, were easy targets. Soldiers burned away the symbol of their beliefs by 'pitch-capping', sticking a paper or linen cap to the victim's head with burning tar, and leaving the man to torture himself by pulling off cap and hair together. In the red haze of pain that came with the burning, men confessed to all sorts of crimes and readily condemned their neighbours to save themselves. Simpler forms of barbarity were used too. Soldiers sliced off ears, raped women and split families apart. They destroyed possessions, burned homes and marched off with cattle and poultry. Brutality and intimidation worked. Great piles of pikes and small arms were collected and scores of confessions were recorded.

When Lord Edward left Dublin – making good use of the theatrical skills he had developed at Frescati to perfect his various disguises – he saw the results of the army's campaign of terror; both zealous United men and their huge body of inactive supporters were at one and the same time surrendering their arms and losing their confidence. There was no time to lose if there were ever to be a rebellion. The United Irishmen persisted with their plans despite the disarming. On 19 April the reconstituted Leinster provincial committee put out a secret handbill telling members to prepare for war, and giving instructions for the storage of bullet moulds and powder. It recommended that one man in each company learn to sound the bugle calls and suggested that every company have a green flag two feet square to hang defiantly from the end of pikes as the United footsoldiers advanced at the raised gun-barrels of the enemy.

The government too was getting ready for confrontation. More and more informers were coming forward with information and hopes of reward. Two of the most active in Dublin were Samuel Sproule, who reported constantly on United Irish meetings in the city, and Francis Magan, a new recruit to the Castle cause who provided the Castle with a stream of information that kept flowing just as long as money went the other way. Magan was a nervous, solitary man, well known to many United Irish leaders and trusted with their plans for invasion and knowledge of their meeting and hiding places. He had trained as a barrister but needed no lessons in the art of informing after he had been brought on to the Castle payroll by Francis Higgins in December 1797. Higgins was delighted with his new catch. 'M. wants money and I am sure will serve your intention,' he told Secretary Cooke at the beginning of January 1798. Magan was canny and tenacious, demanding advance payment for his knowledge and becoming ominously silent if he did not get it. At the beginning of March, he came to Higgins, hinted that he had some good information, but refused to divulge it because, he said, he had not been paid a hundred pounds that the government had promised. 'For God's sake send it, and don't let me appear in so awkward a situation,' Higgins pleaded with Cooke. But the government seemed insufficiently appreciative and a week later Higgins wrote again. 'M. became quite offended that I did not send w[ha]t was proposed. He has not communicated anything to me for ten days past, tho I know he must have much information to give.' Cooke made sure Magan got his fee and the reporting resumed.

Most of Magan's goods were secondhand, titbits given to him in conversation with confiding United leaders. He could not give the government what they really wanted, accurate details of Lord Edward's movements that could lead to his arrest. Magan knew the value of that information; like every other spy in Dublin, he now concentrated on trying to get it. On 22 April he wrote to Cooke hinting that he was getting close, dangling the prospect of triumph and repeating unctuously his desire to serve his country. 'I have *all along* had in contemplation to put you in possession of some act that would essentially serve the Government as well as the country, and it may not be very long till such is effected. At present perhaps you may not know that Lord Edward lurks about town and its vicinity; he was with Ne[i]lson a few days ago in the custody of a patrol in the neighbourhood of Lucan, but not being known and assuming other names they were not detained for any length of time.'

What Magan was repeating was one of the stories that were circulating in Dublin of Lord Edward's many manifestations in the capital and in the surrounding country. It was said that Lord Edward and Neilson were reconnoitring the approaches to Dublin from Kildare one night when they were stopped by government soldiers patrolling through the dark. Lord Edward, heavily disguised, pretended to be a doctor on the way to succour a dying patient, and the two were allowed on their way. Like the story of Lord Edward appearing with the smock and crook of a shepherd, this tale had a mythic ring, whatever its relation to any event. The image of Lord Edward as deliverer of his mortally sick country was a potent symbol with which to revive the flagging hopes of ordinary United Irishmen.

Magan, though, had no better knowledge of Lord Edward's whereabouts than the officials he wrote to. Lord Edward had disappeared; the authorities flooded Dublin with patrols and soldiers, but to no avail. But they did succeed in alarming Lord Edward's protectors. After he had been in Porto Bello for about a month, Mrs Dillon's maid watched in horror as a detachment of soldiers filed down the canal a few yards away, while at the same time Lord Edward, looking out of his upper window, noticed that a police officer was scrutinising the house from the street. It was time to move on. A new hide-out was found for him in the house of a feather merchant called Nicholas Murphy in Thomas Street. Lord Edward was taken there in another disguise; he was not a doctor this time, but a countryman, complete with old-fashioned pig-tailed wig and an all-embracing greatcoat.

Lord Edward stayed about two weeks at Murphy's, but he was now moving about constantly in his efforts to evade soldiers and spies. Besides Murphy he stayed with Mr Cormick and Mr Moore, who both lived in the same street, slipping from one house to another at night, heavily guarded and dressed differently each time.

It was in Thomas Street that William Ogilvie caught up with him at the end of April. On arriving in Dublin, Ogilvie visited Lord Clare, anxious to hear at first hand the assurance that Lord Edward would be allowed to leave the country if he abandoned the United movement. Clare did not hesitate, saying that if Ogilvie could persuade Lord Edward to leave Ireland with him, 'the ports shall be thrown open to you, and no hindrance whatever offered'. Pamela pointed Ogilvie in the direction of Thomas Street and Ogilvie found his stepson there, in the middle of a meeting. Lord Edward came out of the room and sat with Ogilvie for some time. But to Ogilvie's desperate entreaties that he give up the conspiracy, he only replied, 'I am too deeply pledged to these men to be able to withdraw with honour.' Miss Moore, coming unexpectedly across them, watched as Lord Edward took a ring from his finger and pressed it into Ogilvie's palm. Ogilvie wept openly while he held Lord Edward's hands, then turned and walked out of the house.

Despite the danger, Lord Edward continued to meet his United Irish colleagues and to go out at night, partly to calm his restlessness, partly to reassure his supporters that he was still in town and preparing for rebellion. Soon after he arrived in Thomas Street he decided, with all his old recklessness, to visit Pamela. He arrived without warning, in the evening and in a long dress and cloak. Pamela was so shocked to see him, she later said, that she went into labour that night. A few hours after Lord Edward had left, her second daughter, Lucy, was born, healthy but two months premature. She started life inauspiciously in hired lodgings, to a mother distraught and a father on the run.

Samuel Neilson, kept informed by Lord Edward's body-guards, always knew where he was hiding. Neilson visited Lord Edward in Thomas Street and talked him out of his gloom and panicky nervousness. 'The moment Neilson made his appearance Lord Edward appeared like a new man,' Moore's daughter remembered. 'His features brightened up and he spoke with all his natural vivacity.' Lord Edward lived now in an inverted world. By day he tried to sleep; at night the secret committees met as they had done for months and argued inconclusively. Neilson, Lord Edward and the other members of the national executive refused to name a date for the rebellion to start, even when pressed to do so by delegates from more lowly committees. They were still waiting for the French.

When a letter finally came from Paris at the beginning of May, it contained the worst possible news. 'I have just received a letter from L., who had made applications to the trustees for the advance of £5000 upon your estates, which they refused, saying they would make no payment short of the entire, and that they would not be able to effect that for four months,' it ran. A French expedition with five thousand troops could not set off until August. This time there was no misunderstanding. The French did indeed sail in August, far too late and with far too few men to do much more than land, skirmish and surrender. Wolfe Tone, who went with them, walked on Irish soil once more, was arrested and committed suicide with insouciant inefficiency and immense courage in his Dublin cell.

Once the Directory had sent this unequivocal communication, it remained only for the national committee to decide when and how to rise. Even in their new isolation they still found ways to disagree; Neilson and Lord Edward wanted the rebels to follow the plans already drawn up for a rising in Dublin, supported by the marching in of United armies from outside. The Sheares brothers and the surgeon William Lawless argued that it must involve disaffected militiamen from the Loughlinstown camp. The executive split, leaving Neilson and Lord Edward to pursue their plan alone.

Both the government and United Irishmen round the country now expected a conflict. 'I shall not lament the attempt at insurrection. It will enable us to act with effect,' Camden wrote to the Home Secretary in London. Rebellion would justify repression and would pave the way to the abolition of the Irish legislature and its merging with Westminster, a plan mooted for years in both London and Dublin.

None the less, the authorities were still determined to capture Lord Edward. Castle officials, just like the United Irish rank and file, had come to believe all the propaganda about Lord Edward's ferocity, glamour and special status. Their own press tried lamely to make him a less attractive figurehead. *Faulkner's Dublin Journal*, a government paper edited by John Gifford, and charged with the task of spreading a reassuring veneer of loyalism over the chaos in the country, asserted in its issue of 3 May that Lord Edward, 'used to mix with and participate in the breakfasts and the dinners of the meanest peasantry in the country . . . that he used to hold the plough in order to obtain the confidence (for the purpose of abusing it) of the unsuspecting and ignorant tillers of the land'. Such uneasy abuse only increased Lord Edward's mythic potency and did nothing to quell the fears of loyal subjects.

A week later Dublin Castle issued a proclamation for Lord Edward's capture. Printed sheets went up all over Dublin offering a thousand pounds for information that would lead to his arrest. If government officials hoped that such a huge sum would bring one of Lord Edward's guards to them, they were wrong. United Irishmen secretly pulled down the proclamation, trampling it in the dusty gutters. No one betrayed Lord Edward, and soon afterwards he set the date for the rebellion for 23 May.

Francis Magan had been trying as hard as any other informer to deliver Lord Edward to the Castle. He often knew where United leaders met, but he did not know where Lord Edward was concealed or the routes he took between hiding places. The information he passed through Higgins to Cooke was not precise enough to allow the government to move. Lord Edward's guards were very careful with him; any sign of a soldier's red coat or of the magistrates and their burly henchmen warned them from bringing him on to the street. Meetings were cancelled at the slightest hint of danger. With a date now fixed for rebellion, they had to protect Lord Edward at all costs; without him, only the most desperate and committed men would come out to fight. In March and even in April he had been reckless about his own safety. Now he allowed himself to be disguised, hidden and moved every day. He made no second attempt to visit Pamela to take a peep at his tiny baby daughter or cradle little Pamela in his arms.

Lord Edward moved back to Mrs Dillon's in Porto Bello in the first week of May. But on the 13th he returned to Thomas Street to make final preparations for the rising. In his last letter to his mother he had told her that he was thinking of sending his wife to her mother in Hamburg. Now he sent Pamela word that she should go and that she should take Tony, Julie and the two little girls with her. If Pamela did not know that the rising was imminent, he was telling her now. Pamela was still in her month-long confinement and needed a good reason to break with custom and travel before it was over, especially since three-week-old Lucy would be going with her. She did not want to leave the country, but dutifully applied to Castlereagh for a passport, explaining that an illness of Madame de Genlis called her to Hamburg. Castlereagh happily seized the chance to humiliate her. Instead of granting a passport as a result of her request, he issued one as an order, threatening to have her arrested as a spy if she did not leave Ireland in ten days. Castlereagh chose Louisa Conolly as his message-bearer, as she explained to William Ogilvie on 19 May, 'In compassion to her sex and regard for the family, I have been fixed upon for the communication of the sad tidings, and at the same time to tell her, that she had permission to withdraw from this country, unmolested, provided it was within ten days.' Pamela did not see any compassion in Castlereagh's injunction. 'Lady Egality complains dreadfully about Lord Castlereagh ordering a short passport,' Francis Higgins reported to the Castle, keen to show that, through Magan, he was privy to all the United Irish gossip.

By the middle of May Lord Edward's preparations were almost complete, although he was fatalistic about the rebellion's prospects and still unsure about the strength of the army he would command. A plan for the beginning of the rising had now been agreed. On the night of 23 May, Dublin would rise according to the scheme he had worked out in February. At the same time the mail coaches leaving the city would be stopped. When they did not arrive in the towns outside the capital a few hours later, the armies in the countryside would begin their march into the city, overwhelming government garrisons on the way. He himself would be smuggled to his heartland of Kildare to lead the army into the capital. When the mail coaches that fanned out from Dublin failed to arrive at their destinations, the armies of more distant counties would rise up, and the rebellion would spread out in a great, unstoppable wave across the country, till the whole land from Dublin to Cork, from Cork to Galway and from Galway to Belfast had staked its claim to freedom.

Remembering the costumes that Jacques-Louis David had

designed for officials in revolutionary France, Lord Edward had had his own commander's uniform made and brought to him where he was hiding in Thomas Street. It was a spectacular outfit. Revolutionary scarlet braiding adorned the front of the hibernian green jacket and the seams of the matching breeches. A green cape would swirl from Lord Edward's shoulders as he led his army into battle, while the suit was topped off with a cap of liberty that was green on the brim, scarlet on the crown and decorated with a long side-hanging tassel. For good measure Lord Edward had also commissioned what his amazed host described as 'two dresses – one a long-skirted coat, vest and pantaloons; the other a short jacket that came round quite close, and braided in front'. These two suits were perhaps designed to be worn at the National Convention that would be called as soon as the messy military phase of the revolution was over. One was in the close-fitting style then fashionable, with military trimmings. The other, though, with its loose trousers and long coat was more fanciful and in its closeness to Tony's exotic outfit was perhaps intended as a symbol of the nation's rebirth into innocent goodness.

It only remained to sit out the last few days. Despite the floggings and burnings in the countryside and the undertow of fevered preparations for war in the city, an atmosphere of bizarre carnival had settled over Dublin. The weather was beautiful, clear and unexpectedly hot, and the town was excited by a sensational trial in the House of Lords, where the Earl of Kingston was accused of the murder of his pregnant daughter's seducer. It was a case with all the necessary ingredients of a satisfying scandal: a family feud, since the deceased was related to his victim and his killer; marital scandal, since he was already married, and theatricality, since Kingston arrived at court in deep mourning dress, honouring the relative he had himself killed. Dublin was ready to be diverted; such a case only came round once in a generation, and it offered delights enough to distract both those who attended the trial and those who read about it in the press from the horror that was pressing in on them from outside the city. To some desperate members of the Dublin United Irish committees, the trial seemed a golden opportunity to announce in the bloodiest way possible the start of the rebellion. At a meeting on 17 May, the idea was floated of an attack on the courtroom. The Lord Chancellor and the assembled Irish peerage would be wiped out in one spectacular assault, and the city and counties around would rise in acclaim. But the plan was not adopted. Fearing massive casualties as the United force hacked its way through the soldiers in College Green, the committee fell back on Lord Edward's original plan to converge on the Castle.

Magan, though, was not to be put off by any ephemeral excitement. He continued to hint that he could bring Lord Edward in; failing to do so, he accused the Castle of dragging its feet. But his communication of 15 May was no more exact than his reports of the previous few weeks. 'Lord Edward skulks from house to house, has watches and spies, armed, who give an account of any danger being near,' Higgins relayed. Magan was no nearer his prey.

Then everything changed. A friendly carpenter working in Dublin Castle overheard Cooke say that the Yellow Lion, Moore's pub in Thomas Street, where Lord Edward was staying, was going to be searched. He hurried over to Thomas Street and gave his news. A terrified Moore decided to leave the city then and there and told his daughter to find a new lodging for their revered but burdensome guest. Moore had already made arrangements for Lord Edward to move along to Murphy's house in the same street, and probably expected that his daughter would simply walk him round there. But, thinking perhaps that the soldiers turning over her father's house might be tempted to extend their searches down the street, Miss Moore remembered Magan, an old acquaintance of the family well known to sympathise with the United cause. She went trustingly round to Magan's house on Usher's Island by the Liffey and asked if he would conceal Lord Edward there. Agog that the prize should thus fall into his hands, Magan agreed, showing enough anxiety and sympathy to convince Miss Moore that Lord Edward would be safe with him. When she left, Magan summoned Higgins to write to Cooke.

Magan was careful; he did not want Lord Edward discovered in his house. 'He therefore puts himself on your honour not to admit of any person to come and search his house,' Higgins wrote, 'but to place Watches after dark this night near the end of Watling St., or two houses up in that street from Usher's Island and towards the Queen's Bridge, and a third in Island St., the rear of the Stables near Watling St. and which leads up towards Thomas St. and Dirty Lane; and at one of these three places they will find Lord Edward, disguised – he wears a wig, or may be otherwise metamorphosed, attended by one or two, but followed by several armed banditti with new daggers. He intends to give battle if not suddenly seized.'

Usher's Island ran along the Liffey near the large brewery belonging to the Guinness family. From his drawing-room windows Magan and his sister could watch the lighters laden with grain and barrels beat their way to the quayside just up-river, where they glided up to the slime-covered wall and unloaded on to the bustling wharf above. Other neighbours were more desirable than the brewery. Lord Moira lived a few doors away, and it happened that Pamela, her children, Tony and the maids were all staying there when Miss Moore asked Magan for help. Lord Edward would once again be hiding within shouting distance of his wife.

Usher's Island was bounded to the west by Watling Street and to the east by what afterwards became Bridgefoot Street. Magan's long, messy garden, where he was in the habit of indiscriminately throwing the cinders from his fires, ended in a stable block opening into Island Street, which ran from east to west between Bridgefoot and Watling Streets.

Magan lived at number 20 Usher's Island, at the Watling Street end. His back door could be reached from Island Street, his front by walking along Usher's Island from Watling Street or Bridgefoot Street. His directions for the watches were precise: his house must be covered all round. Major Sirr, Dublin's town-major, or chief of police, carried out Magan's instructions to the letter. With his deputies Major Swan and Captain Ryan in attendance, he posted uniformed soldiers at each of the three approaches to Magan's house.

Mr McCabe, Lord Edward's agent who guarded him, was well aware that Usher's Island could be easily isolated, so he divided his body-guards into three groups to take Lord Edward there. The first would go up Watling Street, the second up Bridgefoot Street, while the last, in which Lord Edward himself was concealed, would follow once the way had been found clear.

In the evening of 18 May, about ten o'clock, McCabe's two parties came stealthily up towards Usher's Island and ran straight into the waiting soldiers in Watling Street and Bridgefoot Street. Lord Edward's body-guards drew their swords; Sirr was thrown to the ground in the scuffle. But knowing that Lord Edward was just behind and wanting to get him off the street as quickly as possible, his guards retreated, one letting off a pistol at Sirr, but missing. As they ran back down Watling Street, Sirr scrambled to his feet and hurried through Island Street past the stables where Magan waited for his victim and into Bridgefoot Street. There he found a similar struggle going on. McCabe himself was captured, but, putting on a broad Scottish accent, convinced the Major that he was an innocent muslin manufacturer out for an evening stroll, and was released. By the time Sirr's party came to search the surrounding streets, Lord Edward had disappeared. Magan had lost his prey and his reward, and he could only close his stable door and spend the night in regret that the inefficiency of Sirr and his soldiers had cost him so much in secret gold and solitary glory.

It was now nearly eleven at night. Left on the street with their precious charge, Miss Moore and Lord Edward's bodyguards knew they had to get him to safety before search parties swamped the district. They hurried back to Thomas Street and knocked at the door of Murphy's house, number 135. Reluctantly Murphy let them in. Lord Edward was looking unwell and told Murphy he had a heavy cold. But he seemed quite calm, and went upstairs to the back attic room Murphy had prepared for him, carrying a glass of whey with sherry in it and planning to sleep.

Lord Edward appeared at breakfast the next morning looking better. A few doors down, in the Yellow Lion, Miss Moore had also recovered from the shock of the night before. Just before eleven she sent a maid along the street with a bundle containing Lord Edward's uniform and other costumes, which astonished Murphy when he opened it. Francis Magan called on Miss Moore sometime in the day, anxiously enquiring what had happened, saying he had waited for them in vain until after midnight. Miss Moore explained that they had been stopped but told Magan that Lord Edward was now quite safe, down Thomas Street with Mr Murphy.

Soon afterwards a detachment of soldiers arrived at the Yellow Lion and began a systematic search, rooting through cupboards with the disdainful tips of their bayonets, turning out chests and puncturing barrels of beer. Miss Moore let them wreck the house, miserable for her family, but relieved that Lord Edward was safe. It was Murphy, hearing the commotion from down the street, who was terrified. He hurriedly moved Lord Edward up the stairs out of his attic room and on to the top of his warehouse, concealing him as best he could in one of the valleys between the peaked roofs.

Lord Edward lay up there for several hours, looking up at the blue sky and listening to the muffled sounds from below;

the unusual metallic clatter of the soldiers as they progressed
along the street mixed with the everyday rumble of carts and
carriages. He could not see what Murphy saw: Major Swan
and a party of yeomen walking menacingly towards the
house. At four o'clock he came down to dinner. Samuel
Neilson arrived and stayed to eat. They drank only a little of
Murphy's wine and the conversation flitted desultorily from
subject to subject. After all the months of planning and waiting there was nothing much to say; the time for patriotic
songs and fine declarations of intent was over. Lord Edward
was subdued and weary, listening to his friend through the
haze of his cold, imprisoned by muzziness and fever;
besides, fear crowded out conversation. After dinner
Neilson left and Lord Edward went upstairs to lie down.

At seven o'clock Murphy went to Lord Edward's attic to
ask him to come down to tea. Lord Edward was lying in bed
reading a comforting Frescati favourite, Le Sage's *Gil Blas*, a
happy picaresque comedy of a soldier's adventures that
reminded him of his childhood and soothed with its famili-
arity. As Murphy stood there, Major Swan burst in. He saw
Lord Edward in bed and yelled out, half in triumph, half in
shock, 'You are my prisoner.'

Grabbing the black-handled dagger which he always carried, Lord Edward sprang off the bed and struck Swan
across the hand. Captain Ryan heard Swan shouting. He ran
up the stairs, seized Lord Edward round the waist and
pinned him back against the bed. Lord Edward resisted as he
had always said he would, trying to break free from Ryan's
grasp and escape up the stairs on to the roof. He stabbed
Ryan in a frenzy of rage, overwhelmed by the desire to be
free and the desperate knowledge that unless he could get
away all his years of dreaming and planning would be
reduced to nothing and that the rebellion, doomed to failure
and pointless bloodshed, would go on without him. But the
more he cut at Ryan, the more Ryan hung on, slumping
down to the floor with his arms clasped around Lord

Edward's legs and blood pouring from his ruptured intestines. Lord Edward started to drag the bleeding burden towards the staircase, pushing Ryan down with his hands, hitting out at him and pulling him across the floor at the same time. Swan stumbled over to help Ryan, but at that moment Sirr ran into the room and calmly aiming his pistols, shot Lord Edward twice in the right shoulder, making him drop his dagger. Lord Edward staggered for a moment under the force of the shots but, recovering his balance, went on trying to pull the two men across the floor. Several soldiers then rushed in, battered Lord Edward down to the floor with their muskets, cut him across the neck to force him to let go of Ryan, and overpowered him. Blood from Lord Edward's neck and shoulder dripped on to the wooden boards and mingled with the bright viscous pool from Captain Ryan's stomach.

As Ryan moaned and Lord Edward shouted in rage they were carried one after the other down the stairs to the street, where two hundred soldiers had been hastily collected to prevent a riot and get the prisoner safely away. Ryan was taken to a surgeon's house nearby, Lord Edward put into a closed sedan chair surrounded by soldiers and carried to Dublin Castle. Francis Magan, listening to the commotion from Usher's Island, or perhaps in the gathering, angry crowd, could now reflect that he had fulfilled his claim to be able to deliver up the most wanted man in Ireland. The fact that luck rather than knowledge had brought about Lord Edward's capture would do nothing to lessen his righteous enjoyment of the thousand pounds' reward or the pension that would follow it annually for the next thirty years.

By the time he reached the Castle, Lord Edward was calm, though not yet resigned to failure or imprisonment. Hearing that he was sitting in the office of the Secretary at War, a nervous Lord Camden sent round Mr Watson, his private secretary, to assure Lord Edward that 'every possible attention' would be shown to him. Watson found Lord Edward lying across a couple of chairs while the Surgeon General, George Stewart, dressed the wound in his right shoulder where the two balls from Sirr's pistols had entered his arm. There was no talk of operating to remove them, and the wound was pronounced slight. The atmosphere in the room was strained, with all the officials trying to show at one and the same time the deference required in the presence of the brother of Ireland's premier peer and the severity that must be displayed to a man violently apprehended on a charge of treason. Watson, noting that Lord Edward's face was 'pallid but serene', did not hesitate to put the nobleman before the traitor. None of the assembled officials made an attempt to restrain him when he went up to Lord Edward and spoke quietly into his ear; they too were overcome by Lord Edward's presence, confused that the legend was, after all, one of them, a Protestant, a gentleman and only thirty-four years old. Watson whispered that he had orders to inform Pamela of his arrest and asked Lord Edward if he had any message for her or if he could do anything else for him. Lord Edward replied, 'No, no, thank you, nothing, nothing,' and then added, 'only break it to her gently.'

Watson hurried through the dark city to Denzille Street but found that Pamela had gone to a party at Moira House and the only people to tell were 'two of her female attendants'. Tony, left in the house with Sophie and Julie, must have learned then that his master was no longer free. Lord Edward was at the mercy of his captors just as Tony had been at the mercy of his owner when he was a slave. They could torture him, execute him or let him die, and there was nothing that Tony could do about it.

The magistrates had fewer scruples about Lord Edward's exalted status and mythic reputation than the Castle officials. Arguing that because he had wounded Ryan he might face a charge of murder as well as treason, they took him at once to Newgate gaol and locked him in a room with a thickly barred window that looked out towards the street. Aware that attempts would be made to rescue him, even from within the gaol, an armed guard stood, weapon at the ready, by Lord Edward's bed. The first night, Thomas Russell, an old United friend already in gaol, was allowed to stay with him. But afterwards Lord Edward was alone except for his guards and doctors.

News of Lord Edward's capture was taken across the city by knots of United Irishmen running between houses, shops, warehouses and chapels. Francis Higgins reported to the Castle that a number of butchers from the meat market in Patrick Street and others from the notoriously seditious neighbourhood of the Liberties grabbed their pikes and set out, determined to rescue Lord Edward from Murphy's house. 'But finding the prisoner had been removed they desisted, and the more hastily as some persons told them a squadron of horse was on their way up Castle Street to meet them.' Angry crowds rampaged through the streets, so thick that Higgins's messenger could not force his way through. By the next morning, with Lord Edward in gaol, the city seemed deserted and calm, and the anger of the crowd had turned to dejection. But Samuel Neilson, now left in charge, refused to be downcast, declaring unequivocally that the rebellion would go ahead on 23 May as they had planned. Its first act would be to liberate Lord Edward from Newgate and put him at the head of the army. Messages went out to the countryside that 23 May was still the day to rise.

The government signalled its triumph by demolishing and burning the houses in Thomas Street where Lord Edward had been staying and redoubling its efforts at disarming in the countryside. Lord Castlereagh told the spy-master William Wickham on 20 May that Lord Edward's arrest had had 'a considerable effect upon the rebels within the metrop-olis', and that the United Irishmen in the country, 'although in some districts inclined to a desperate effort, are in many subdued and are delivering up their pikes in great quantities'. But as much as demoralisation, it was the burnings that were bringing the weapons in. Sending William Ogilvie the news of Lord Edward's arrest the next day, Lady Louisa Conolly added that, 'Maynooth, Kilcock, Leixlip and Celbridge have had part of a Scotch regiment quartered at each place, living upon free quarters and every day threatening to burn the towns.' Horrified by the discovery of treachery among her own servants and by the thought of disloyalty among her husband's tenants, Lady Louisa was now a reluctant supporter of Dublin Castle, and added, 'I have spent days in entreaties and threats, to give up the horrid pikes. Some houses burned at Kilcock yesterday produced the effect. Maynooth held out yesterday, though some houses were burnt and some people punished. This morning the people of Leixlip are bringing in their arms. Celbridge as yet holds out though five houses are now burning.'

News of Lord Edward's arrest was immediately sent to the family in London by both Lady Louisa Conolly and George Napier. It was kept from Pamela until the morning of 20 May, but she took it better than the family expected. Pamela had known that a rising was imminent and she must have prepared herself for the possibility of her husband's death. But her request to see him was, like all others, refused, and the government officials replied to it with an order that she leave the country within three days, using the passport they had already issued.

In his closely guarded cell, Lord Edward had no idea what was happening to his family or what was taking place in the city. When he was told that his wounds were not serious he said, 'I am sorry for it.' He seemed resigned to his imprisonment. But his supporters outside were desperate to free him. Samuel Neilson quickly formed a plan for his escape which the informer Sproule reported to the Castle on 20 May: '30 the most desperate men this evening or tomorrow to attack Newgate in the following manner, each armed with a dagger and a case of pistols – 2 that know Newgate and Fitzgerald's room very well are to get in under some pretence. When they are in, they want to come out, and when the door is opened for them 14 rush in to assist them in seizing or stabbing the guard. 3 of them outside to seize *each* sentinel – they count on all this being done in five minutes. A horse ready for Fitzgerald to mount and make off – each one willing to be sacrificed provided he escapes.'

Sproule's information was only partially accurate. Neilson soon abandoned the idea of an all-out attack on the gaol. Knowing that Lord Edward's room was at the front of the building, he decided to get him out by running a ladder up to his window, prising open the metal grating, pulling him down the ladder and rushing him away. Moreover, worried that Lord Edward might be re-arrested, Neilson decided that his liberation should coincide with the beginning of the rebellion. On 23 May, the day set for the rising, Neilson met his fifteen Dublin colonels, produced a map of the city and assigned a post to each. As they gathered their men together from houses and taverns and silently took over the city, he would be rescuing Lord Edward.

When the meeting broke up, Neilson's colonels disappeared into the warm night, while he went to reconnoitre the gaol in Green Street and to check the height of Lord Edward's window from the ground. But Neilson was a journalist, not a mathematician. As he stood in front of the gaol, slowly counting the stone blocks up to Lord Edward's room, he was spotted by Gregg the gaoler, who knew him well from his last stay in the prison. Hardly able to believe his eyes, the astonished Gregg sent his guards out from the prison porch, scooped up Neilson and locked him in the building. Any chance that the rebellion would have a leader ended with this disastrous failure.

Dublin was now flooded with soldiers. Hearing from one of their informers that the rising was to start at ten o'clock, Castle officials sent the yeomanry out on to the streets. Red-coated soldiers sealed off bridges, set up checkpoints on approach roads and occupied the open space of Smithfield market, where the rebel army was expected to congregate. None the less the rebels were gathering; dressed in makeshift uniforms, armed with pikes and muskets and carrying their flags of hibernian green, they came together in twos and threes, coalescing into bands and companies, concealed in warehouses, behind doorways and in the dark centres of the deserted parks and squares. They stopped the departing mail coaches by the post office, and only waited now for the signal to charge out, overwhelm the yeomanry, make for the government buildings and proclaim the republic.

But no word came to them. With Lord Edward still unknowing in his cell and Neilson snatched unresisting inside the gaol itself, there was no one left to give the signal to rise. As they peered from their hiding places at the armed and watching companies of government soldiers, the rebels' confidence drained away with the hours and finally gave out. The Dublin army of the United Irishmen melted away as it had grown, bit by bit, and its members retreated back into their hiding places and ordinary lives, leaving their weapons behind them. When another hot day began, the rising sun shone on piles of abandoned muskets and pikes in the lanes and alleys leading to Smithfield, and in Dublin Castle relieved officials congratulated themselves on their timely prevention of carnage.

But in the surrounding countryside a bloody tragedy was beginning. When the mail coaches failed to arrive from Dublin the United Irishmen in the counties ringing the city rose as they had planned. By dawn on 24 May they had occupied roads, river crossings and hilltop lookouts in a great crescent about twenty miles beyond its boundaries. Then they waited for Lord Edward, the shepherd of his flock, the doctor to his sick country, to appear. But no miracle could spring Lord Edward from Newgate and he did not come. In some places the leaderless rebellion went ahead; in others the rebels left their weapons in ditches or by bridges and went home. The risings were local and uncoordinated, flaring up sporadically throughout the summer, punished everywhere by burnings, torture and sectarian killing. Only in Wexford, where twenty thousand rebels marched into the town and proclaimed a republic, was there a tangible sense that political ideals were overriding economic and sectarian grievances, and that rebellion was punished by wholesale slaughter. By the time it was over, thirty thousand subjects of George III had been killed. The vast majority had been trying to cast off the monarchy, filled with hatred of its representatives; the rest trying to protect their property or the connection of Ireland to the Crown. Officials in Dublin attempted to justify the army's brutality by pointing to the strength, determination and organisation of the rebels. 'I understand,' wrote Lord Castlereagh to Thomas Pelham when the worst of the fighting was over in June, 'that you are inclined to hold the insurrection cheap. Rely upon it, there never was in any country so formidable an effort on the part of the people.' But the thirty thousand dead were only the first victims of the rebellion; thousands more were to die after it. What followed was a disaster that bound Britain and Ireland in an endless and bloody embrace: the Act of Union and the dissolution of the Irish parliament in 1801. With the union also came the end of Ireland's brief Enlightenment. In the next century the fires of sectarianism would burn ever brighter until the United Irish dream of a secular, ecumenical and democratic republic would be reduced to bitter dust.

Early in the morning of 25 May Pamela set off for London, helped aboard the Holyhead packet by Louisa Conolly and Sarah Napier. With her went her two daughters, two maids, Tony, Julie and their little child, Moirico, and a parson, Mr Murphy, sent by Lord Moira to give the party a semblance of propriety and a less fugitive air. By 27 May, when the melancholy group reached Llangollen, a stream of travellers had already brought the news of Lord Edward's arrest down the Holyhead road. The landlady of The Hand, meeting the famous 'Ladies of Llangollen' on their way to church, said she '*suspected* Lady E. Fitzgerald was in her house'. Sarah Ponsonby and Eleanor Butler had entertained Pamela six years before when she had visited them with Madame de Genlis; now curiosity, disguised as politeness, got the better of their fear of Jacobins. 'We could not bear the idea of avoiding her in such a situation, therefore sent word that if the Lady was, as we believed, an acquaintance of ours . . . we were within call,' Sarah Ponsonby told a friend. Pamela came, but when she offered to stay for the day, the Ladies were horrified. 'We persuaded her principally for her own sake and a little for [our] own to proceed as fast and as incognito as possible for London.'

Long before Pamela reached London the Duke of Portland had sent a short note to William Ogilvie reporting Lord Edward's arrest and telling him that 'Mr Ryan's wound is considered to be mortal'. As much as the charge of treason it was the charge of murder hanging over Lord Edward that concerned the family. There was no time to lose in begging their powerful relatives and acquaintances to postpone his trial, using all their aristocratic and political contacts on behalf of a man whose life for a decade had been bent on spurning just such abuses of birth and privilege. First Lord Henry Fitzgerald, then the Duchess herself decided to set off for Ireland to canvass Lord Camden and Lord Clare directly. The Duchess, not having been told of Lord Edward's wounds, and determined only to think of the immediate and practical future, spent the time before she set off feverishly writing letters to anyone who might be able to influence the Prime Minister, the King or the Irish government. But her contacts were all on the wrong side. Charles James Fox, who had just come back from the spectacular acquittal of Arthur O'Connor at Maidstone, was now a positive liability. The Prince of Wales had no influence with his father, although he wrote a letter to Camden for the

Duchess to carry with her to Ireland and wept openly when he saw her distress. Sheridan, as an Irishman as well as an opposition figure, was worse than Fox, and the Duchess's other relatives, like Lord Holland, were equally impotent. They filled the house in Harley Street with concern but could offer no influence, only advice. Only her brother the Duke of Richmond had the ear of William Pitt and any hope of getting to the King. So although she knew the relations between Richmond and her son had been shaky ever since Lord Edward came back from Canada in 1790, she appealed abjectly to him. Richmond yielded as far as his dignity and lack of sympathy with Lord Edward would allow, saying of the Duchess to Lord Henry, 'her fortitude adds a respect and dignity to her sufferings that I think no heart can resist'. He saw Pitt, put the case to him for a postponement of any trial until after the end of martial law, and sent a letter to Camden with Pitt's approval which argued that Lord Edward could not receive a fair trial while a rebellion was going on and ended by appealing to their mutual loyalty to the Prime Minister: 'I have been with Mr Pitt today, to whom I have stated these arguments. He heard them with that feeling we know him to possess, and it is by his advice that I submit them to your Lordship.'

None of these appeals were likely to move Camden or his officials, who were adamant that Lord Edward should receive no visitors and no special treatment. They set the date of his trial for 11 June and waited to see whether Ryan would recover from his wounds. On 29 May the Duchess was at last told by Ogilvie that Lord Edward had been shot and that he had badly wounded Captain Ryan in the struggle. Refusing to be crushed by the fear that her favourite son might die, the Duchess declared that she would go to him in his prison, redoubled her efforts to get his trial put off and made plans to set out as soon as possible and to take little Eddy with her.

Lady Lucy Fitzgerald, who could guess better than the

other members of the family what was happening in Ireland, was allowed to do nothing. Pamela gave her some hope when she arrived on 30 May by declaring her belief that Lord Edward would be freed. 'The United Men have risen,' Lucy noted in her diary, 'and in their success she sees his salvation.' Lucy tried to remember Lord Edward's own advice to her and 'my promises to him to be stout when *the time came*', but she was still terrified, far less hopeful than Pamela that Lord Edward would be saved by his supporters or spared trial by the authorities. Told by Mr Ogilvie that she would be immediately put back on the boat if she tried to go to Ireland, she could only wait miserably in London, 'distrusting all' and 'watching the motions of the insurrection', as she put it in her diary.

The house at Harley Street was crowded with opposition politicians offering sympathy and advice, and disordered with packing. Pamela and Tony alone were not preparing to set off up the road to Parkgate; Tony was powerless to do anything to help his master; Pamela had been given a passport for only a week, and was expected to leave for Hamburg as soon as she could. In the end, Lord Henry was the first to go, leaving London for Dublin on 27 May and noting anxiously and with misplaced concern in his pocket book on the way, 'Has he got fruit? Does he want linen?'

Lord Edward did not know that his brother had arrived. Every day he was visited by George Stewart, the Surgeon General for Ireland, and by Dr Lindsay, a physician paid for by the family. Samuel Stone, a captain from the Derry Militia, stood guard constantly over him, stopping any visitors and keeping out the news. Lord Edward's wounds did not heal, and he was in constant pain from his neck and shoulder. But he seemed to get no worse, remaining calm, resigned or even indifferent to his fate, eating and sleeping better as the days passed. The unusually hot weather continued, making it more likely that infection would breed in his wounds. An operation to extract the balls from Sirr's pistols was vital. But Stewart dithered, saying that the heat made surgery impossible and that the inflammation of the wound, which was weeping and oozing pus, was not dangerous. A baggy swelling in Lord Edward's armpit he pronounced to be the balls working their way down his arm, but insisted at the same time that they might be forced spontaneously from the wound. Lady Louisa Conolly, trusting to Lindsay's probity and connection with the family and clinging on to scraps of good news that she could pass on to her sister, saw no contradiction in these reports. 'Lindsay cannot pronounce him out of danger until the balls are extracted, which is not yet the case, though the discharge one day was so great as to make him expect it,' she wrote to William Ogilvie.

Lady Louisa tried not to think ahead, forcing herself to concentrate on practical matters. But she was tormented by thoughts of her sister. 'Oh good God, what is to become of her?' she asked Ogilvie. 'Her wish to come over I also expected, and it is so natural that I think it must be the best for her, and yet I *dare not* advise.' Although Lady Louisa may have reiterated her belief to Ogilvie that Lord Edward's 'heart could never be brought to the guilt imputed to him', her contacts in the Castle, particularly Lord Castlereagh, painted a gloomy picture of her nephew's prospects even if he did recover.

Lord Edward was not getting better; the festering wound was beginning to spread its poison round his body. Without an operation it was almost inevitable that a flesh wound would become infected and septicaemia set in; it was thus the doctor's professional duty to take the risk of getting the balls out. If the doctor operated Lord Edward might die as a result of an infection he introduced; if he did not operate he was more than likely to die anyway. Stewart turned his face away. No word had come down from Camden that the Castle would rather see Lord Edward die than brought to trial, but a sense that this was so hung in the air and imperceptibly guided his decisions. For Camden especially, the thought of the Duchess of Leinster weeping before a jury, of appeals from royal princes and appearances by brilliant opposition figures like Fox and Sheridan, was terrifying, and he probably doubted that any jury would pronounce Lord Edward guilty. Far better to do nothing than have to face the misery and wrath of the entire extended Leinster family and a sympathetic courtroom. Acting on this silence from the Castle, Stewart did no more than check Lord Edward's wound each day and Lindsay repeated his diagnosis that it had a 'favourable appearance'.

But Stewart knew that septicaemia was an invisible killer, coursing round the body through the veins, bringing shaking and delirium, then paralysis and death. He was well acquainted with its symptoms and sufficiently alarmed at the spasms that had already occasionally racked Lord Edward's body to suggest that he make a will. On 26 May, a week after his arrest, he did so, with the help of Mr Leeson, a lawyer who worked as the Duke of Leinster's agent. Forbidden to see his client, Mr Leeson sat outside Newgate in his carriage, while Lord Edward's attendants went up and down the stairs with the drafts. Lord Edward was painstaking about the form of his will; it was the last statement of his values and the only means he might have left of bequeathing his beliefs to posterity.

Although he must have known that there was little chance that his wishes would be honoured, Lord Edward made a will that was republican through and through. Alone in his Newgate cell, with an armed guard at his bedside, with no friends to talk to and unable to send any messages to his supporters, Lord Edward used this opportunity to proclaim to the world that he had not wavered in captivity. 'I, Lord Edward Fitzgerald, do make this as my last Will and Testament, hereby revoking all others: that is to say, I leave all estates, of whatever sort, to my wife, Lady Pamela Fitzgerald, as a mark of my esteem, love, and confidence in her, for and during her natural life, and on her death to descend, share and share alike, to my children or the survivors of them; she maintaining and educating the children according to her discretion; and I constitute her the executrice of this my last Will and Testament.' Lord Edward signed the document in the presence of his surgeons and his guard.

Leaving everything to Pamela was conventional enough; it was leaving his property to be divided equally among his children that was unusual. In removing the privilege from his son and treating little Pam and Lucy in exactly the same way as little Eddy, Lord Edward was being true to the dislike he had long professed of the almost universal system of primogeniture, of leaving everything to the first-born son and of treating him as of greater importance than his siblings. Lord Edward's injunction that his children share his estate was a twofold radicalism: it declared that the first born was no more deserving than the others, and it declared that boys were no more deserving than girls. But it was also a political statement, a way of proclaiming, at a time when he had no other, that his politics were intact. Various parliamentary Acts of Succession had enshrined the principle of hereditary right in law, laying down the basis upon which the crown was inherited. Primogeniture was, as Paine declared, the legal basis for the monarchy; remove it and the legal justification for the monarchy was gone. Lord Edward's own rejection of primogeniture was a declaration of his republican as well as of his radical principles. His will was thus not only his last testament in the ordinary sense but also his last testimony to the principles that had guided all his public actions, all his private behaviour and all his feelings for the last ten years.

Lord Henry arrived at Leinster House on 31 May. Before he left London he had applied to the Home Secretary for permission to see his brother. Portland replied to his desperate entreaty with frosty denial, writing, 'as Lord Edward is not under confinement in consequence of a warrant issued by me, I have not the power of complying with your request.' Once in Dublin Lord Henry tried again, going to see Lord Camden personally and offering, if a visit was refused, to share his brother's cell. 'How dreadful the idea that I shall not be allowed to see him,' he wrote to William Ogilvie. But Lord Camden was implacable; he had already twice refused Lady Louisa Conolly and now he extended the prohibition to Lord Henry.

But worse news met Lord Henry than Lord Camden's coldness. Captain Ryan had died the night before he arrived, and his death would add a charge of murder to the charge of treason already levelled at Lord Edward. 'How will the death of Ryan affect him?' Lord Henry asked his diary and added, looking forward to his brother's trial, 'What informers are supposed to be against him?'

In Newgate, Lord Edward was still guarded and solitary. He knew of neither the death of Ryan nor the arrival of his brother. His health had gradually deteriorated after he had made his will, though Stewart still denied the need for an operation. But, in acknowledgement of Lord Edward's dangerous condition, Stone was removed on 2 June and a young Dublin surgeon, Armstrong Garnett, took his place. Garnett was a careful man, and slightly overawed by his unexpected assignment, although when asked by Lord Edward if he had not better things to do, he replied gravely 'that my most important occupation was the attendance on the sick, and that I trusted his Lordship would have no reason to complain of any want of care or vigilance'. To forestall any criticism of his work and professional skills, and feeling too that he was caught up in a momentous event, Garnett kept a running diary of what passed in Newgate.

Garnett's medical eyes saw immediately that Lord Edward was very ill. 'His countenance showed a great degree of wildness mixed with that kind of expression that accompanies pain.' Lord Edward was saying goodbye to Captain Stone as Garnett came into the room, thanking him for his attention and expressing sorrow that he had to leave. Garnett arranged his clothes and books in the room next door and then came back to examine his patient; he found that his tongue was furred over and his pulse weak and erratic. But Lord Edward said he was in no pain and agreed to lie down and try to sleep.

The grim silence in Lord Edward's cell was in stark contrast to the commotion in the rest of the gaol. Prisoners who were not in solitary confinement crowded the corridors and stairs, and outside the gates soldiers were massing. In the late afternoon Garnett looked out of Lord Edward's window into the street below and saw several corps of yeomanry drawn up in front of the prison. From the crowd of onlookers words floated up which roused Lord Edward to anger and agitation. 'Damn all the croppies,' said someone, 'I wish all croppies were hanged,' said another. Garnett closed Lord Edward's windows and went to his own room, from where, by craning his head and peering diagonally through the barred main gate, he could see the open space in front of the prison. A break in the tumult and the looks on the faces of the soldiers facing the gaol confirmed Garnett's suspicions that a condemned man was about to be hanged and that the yeomen were listening to his last address. Garnett could not see the gallows, which was set up against the gaol wall, but he heard one of the sergeants say, leaning nonchalantly on his halberd, that the man was going to his death 'a bad soldier', and then he heard the crash as the trap door was opened beneath the man's feet and he fell to his death.

Before he arrived in Newgate Garnett had been terrified at the thought that he might have to witness one of the executions that were taking place there every day; but he had no time to dwell on his own horror because an attendant ran from Lord Edward's room anxiously calling for him.

Garnett rushed in to find Lord Edward violently agitated, his tongue thrust forward between his teeth and his jaws locked. His whole body was convulsed and rigid, and although Garnett was able to stop him biting his tongue by forcing a spatula covered with linen into his mouth, it was half an hour before the spasms subsided and Lord Edward was able to open his mouth and speak. Then he complained that his wounds were painful, that he could not stop his jaw dropping open or his tongue sticking out.

Just as these symptoms were subsiding, noise from outside broke in again. The executed soldier had been a United Irishman called Clinch who had confessed his treason in his last address. The crowd were now watching his body swinging from the gallows in the evening light. First the words came up, 'Cut him down, cut him down'; then someone tried to reach the body and a soldier shouted out, 'Don't touch him, damn you, don't touch him,' and a shot was fired. The scuffling and commotion below his window distressed Lord Edward again. Remembering his common cause with the dead man, he cried out loudly, 'God look down on those who suffer! God preserve me and have mercy on me and on those that act with me.'

From now on Lord Edward's behaviour veered uncontrollably between an angry violence and the gentleness and fine manners which had for years seemed two of his defining characteristics. At seven o'clock he told Garnett that he wanted to sleep, and when Garnett said that he would sit by his bed, thanked him and seemed pleased. But almost immediately he sat up in bed and said he wanted to walk about. Garnett replied that he should stay in bed and rest, hinting at the 'ill consequences to his health that would follow' if he got up. This remark seemed to release Lord Edward from self-restraint. He replied furiously that he did not want to live, that he was 'happy in the persuasion that he was dying for his country', 'that God would receive him for having contributed to the freedom of his country'. He rounded on Garnett for trying to make him rest, saying 'that it was cruel in me to resist his dying when he chose it'.

Gradually Lord Edward became violent as well as restless, trying repeatedly to get out of bed and shouting loudly, 'Dear Ireland! I die for you! My country, *you will be free!*' Garnett and the prison guard forced him down on to the bed, but he fought back, shouting at the same time, 'Damn you! Why don't you let me die! I want to die! You are a tyrant! If I had a knife I would kill myself.'

The infection that had spread through Lord Edward's body now darkened his mind. He became delirious and uncontrollable, wild with poison and with pain. For over an hour he raged at Garnett and the world, exclaiming, 'Damn you! Damn you! God damn you!' and throwing himself about the room. His shouts drew a crowd to the prison gates and all the prisoners who could walk about the gaol assembled on the staircase to his room, horrified witnesses to his suffering.

Among them was Mathew Dowling, Lord Cloncurry's land agent and Lord Edward's old United Irish friend, with whom he had attended trials of United suspects in the summer of 1797. Dowling thought that the appearance of someone he knew would calm Lord Edward, and he begged Garnett to be allowed into his room. Desperate now for any remedy, and anxious that he might himself be accused of inflicting wounds on his charge, Garnett agreed, noting in his diary, 'the best method of guarding against such a report, I conceived to consist in admitting the most particular of his friends that was within reach, to be witness to his real state'.

Dowling was shocked at Lord Edward's condition. His old friend seemed neither to know him nor to take any notice of him, lashing out at him and shouting, 'Damn you! Damn you!', just as he had to Garnett. Consumed with sadness and horror, Dowling gave up and went away. But he did not abandon Lord Edward's cause; he had good contacts in the gaol and set about organising a group of United men to stay close to Lord Edward's room and to watch over him.

Lord Edward had a difficult night. Exhausted by his own violence he agreed to take forty drops of laudanum but was unable to sleep. His mind was rambling now, moving disjointedly from one subject to another, unable to settle for long. But even so he talked about what he valued most. First he mentioned a Presbyterian minister, Dr Samuel Barber, who allowed his chapel in Rathfriland, County Down, to be used alternately by Presbyterians and Roman Catholics, and asked if he might be brought to see him. Then he thought of those he had longed to help. When Garnett came into his room at six-thirty in the morning, Lord Edward said with great earnestness, 'Would to God I had thirty thousand guineas this morning! they would make thirty thousand happy men.' Garnett answered in his grave way, 'Your Lordship would distribute them generously,' and Lord Edward replied, thinking equally of benevolence and recruiting, 'A guinea would do a great deal with a poor man,' and added, 'and nothing can be done without money.'

In the middle of the morning Lord Edward remembered his family. He had some idea that Lord Henry was in the country and with pathetic humility appealed to Garnett to be allowed to see him. 'While I sat by his bedside he observed to me, "I have a brother Henry that I dote on; I wish greatly to see him, but that I suppose cannot be allowed." After a short pause he said, "I have a brother Leinster for whom I have a high respect. He might depend on everything I did."'

Garnett had come to feel an overwhelming compassion for his patient, and he could no longer bear to be the instrument of a regime so cruel that it was allowing a man to die alone in gaol while his desperate family was forbidden to see him. Although Lord Edward did not know it, Garnett had already broken the government's rules and got a message to Lord Henry Fitzgerald at eleven o'clock that morning. John Leeson, sent by Lord Henry for information, returned with the news that Garnett thought Lord Edward very ill and 'there was no reasonable hope of his recovery'. A few hours later Lord Henry got another message smuggled out of Newgate by a distraught Mathew Dowling. 'My Lord,' Dowling wrote, 'I take the liberty of writing to inform you that your brother, Lord Edward, is most dangerously ill – in fact dying – he was delirious some time last night. Surely, my lord, some attention ought to be paid to him. I know you'll pardon this application . . . Past 2. Seeing you, or any friend he has confidence in, would, I think, be more conducive to his recovery than 50 surgeons. I saw him a few moments last night – but he did not know me – we'll watch over him as well as is in our power.'

Before he got Dowling's note, Lord Henry had already written to Lord Clare to ask again for permission to go to his brother. But Clare's reply was unyielding. 'My Dear Lord. I am sorry to tell you, that it will be impossible, for the present, to comply with your wishes; and if I could explain to you the grounds of this restriction, even you would hardly be induced to condemn it as unnecessarily harsh.' Lord Henry was in no mood to concede the justice of Lord Clare's case. After he had got Dowling's letter, he applied yet again, noting in his pocket book, 'wrote Chancellor a pressing letter to see E.'. This time Clare admitted that Lord Edward was very ill, but maintained his injunction, citing the gravity of the rebellion and hinting that Lord Camden, not he, forbade the visit. 'My Dear Lord. Be assured that it is not in my power to procure admission for you to Lord Edward. You will readily believe that Lord Camden's situation is critical in the extreme. The extent and enormity of the treason which has occasioned so many arrests make it essentially necessary, for the preservation of the State, that access should be denied to the friends of all the persons now confined for treason. Judge, then, my dear lord, the situation in which Lord Camden will be placed, if this rule is dispensed with in one instance.'

In his cell, Lord Edward was now calm and weak. Garnett read him the account of the crucifixion from St John's Gospel, and 'he listened with the utmost attention'. After Garnett had felt his pulse, Lord Edward asked simply 'how long I thought it would last', and then said that 'he was pre-pared for *death*, if the translation to a state of external hap-piness could be called death; that he confided in the mercy of God and the *purity of his own intentions*; that he had been zealous for the freedom of his country.' He ate a few straw-berries and cherries that Lord Henry, in his concern that his brother should have fruit, had sent over, and observed that they came 'from dear Carton', as if he had forgotten his own dislike of the house and remembered only his happy child-hood. Gradually he became restless again, imploring Garnett to allow him to get up and walk about and then saying angrily that it was 'very cruel' of him to forbid it. Mortified, Garnett answered, 'My lord, you must be persuaded that your health and safety are at stake and that my only motive can be a desire to contribute to them.' Seeing Garnett's unhappiness, Lord Edward stretched out his hand to him and said, 'I give you a great deal of trouble, Sir,' and then said he would stay in bed and try to sleep.

Throughout the long afternoon Lord Edward alternated between a calm acceptance of his state and a frenetic desire to move about. He ate little, as if he understood that he did not need nourishment now, only the courage to face death. He allowed his body and mind to part in their own way, only hanging on to the belief that his dying was a part of his country's struggle to be born. When Garnett mentioned his service in America, Lord Edward replied that 'he hoped *God would forgive him*,' and a little while later started addressing an imaginary crowd of people, talking 'of principles and *being up*'. But he was getting weaker and more gentle now. His sight was failing, distorting and blacking out people and objects around him. As evening came on he began to think that Garnett was way above him near the ceiling, and asked politely, 'Can they hear you from where you are?' Garnett had the presence of mind to answer that they could, and Lord Edward said with relief, 'Well then, stay up as you are there.'

By this time Lord Henry and Lady Louisa Conolly were frantic with fear and misery. Taking her adopted daughter Emily Napier with her, Lady Louisa set out for the vice-regal lodge in Phoenix Park to confront Lord Camden with his cruelty. Leaving Emily in the carriage, she ran in to the house, only to emerge a few minutes later 'in a most dreadful state of agitation,' as Emily put it, 'saying as she leant back in the carriage, "order them to drive me home. I have knelt at his feet and the brute has refused to let me see my dying Edward."' But they did not turn back to Castletown. Knowing that as chief legal authority in the country Lord Clare had the power to override government decisions and aware that he was a softer and stronger man at heart than Lord Camden, Lady Louisa decided on one last appeal. In the fading light they drove round to Ely Place, where Lord Clare was finishing his dinner. When he saw Lady Louisa's distress, Lord Clare's resolution crumbled. He gave permission for the visit, said he would come to the gaol to make sure she was let in, and still holding his napkin, sat down in into the carriage beside her. They hurried to Leinster House, where Emily ran across the stone forecourt calling out for her cousin. Lord Henry, too, squeezed into the carriage and they set off for Newgate. Just after ten Lady Louisa and Lord Henry, with the Lord Chancellor following behind, walked into Lord Edward's room and saw him lying on the narrow bed, guarded by a standing soldier and comforted by Dr Garnett sitting beside him.

Dr Garnett noticed that Lord Edward was already in another world. When his brother and aunt came up to his bedside, he looked through them, his mind wandering, his vision imprecise. But after Garnett had told him that Lady Louisa and Lord Henry were with him, Lord Edward held his arms up in the candle-light and embraced them, calling Lady Louisa his 'dear aunt' and saying heartbreakingly, 'my brother' to Lord Henry. Lord Clare was overcome. He stumbled into Garnett's room next door, where, at last forgetting that he was an official of the government, he wept openly and unashamedly into his crisp white table napkin.

Lord Edward seemed intermittently to know his aunt and brother and tried to listen to them. But mostly he was rambling and absent, living through the rebellion in his head. 'He talked while they were with him of battles between the insurgents in the north and some regiments of militia. He particularly named the Fermanagh Militia, and talked of a battle at Armagh that lasted two days,' Garnett noted. But Garnett too was soon overcome. He left the room, and went to sit silently with Lord Clare next door, leaving Lady Louisa and Henry to say goodbye as best they could. After an hour Lady Louisa and Lord Henry emerged, and saying they would come back in the morning, made their way out past the ranks of prisoners massed in silent witness in the corridors and on the stairs. At two in the morning Dr Garnett made the last entry in his diary, which ran simply, 'After a violent struggle that commenced soon after twelve o'clock, this ill fated young man has just drawn his last breath. – June 4 1798.'

Too shocked to sleep, Lady Louisa and Lord Henry sat out the night at Leinster House. At six a messenger arrived from Newgate with a paper from Dr Garnett on which he had written, 'Mr Garnett presents his respectful compliments to Lady Louisa Conolly, and begs leave to communicate to her the melancholy intelligence of Lord Edward Fitzgerald's death. He drew his last breath at two o'clock this morning after a struggle that began soon after his friends left him last night.'

Lady Louisa immediately set about arranging the burial of Lord Edward's body in the damp crypt of St Werburgh's church, not far from the gaol. Lord Henry was too distraught and angry to stay on in the country and was now overcome for his mother as well as for himself. The same evening he was on the boat to Holyhead composing a furious letter to Lord Camden, writing out his grief in a torrent of accurate accusations. He declared unhesitatingly that by its refusal to operate on Lord Edward, the government had 'murdered my brother as much as if you had put a pistol to his head,' and he called Camden to account for his cruelty, saying, 'I implored, I entreated of you to let me see him. I never begged hard before. All, all in vain. You talked of lawyers' opinions, of what had been refused to others and could not be granted for me in the same situation. His was not a common case – he was *not* in the same situation. He was wounded and in a manner dying, and his bitterest enemy could not have murmured, had your heart softened, or had you swerved a little from duty (if it can be called one) in the cause of humanity.'

Lady Louisa tried to concentrate not on recriminations but on presenting a picture of Lord Edward as she thought her sister would like to remember him. She gave Lord Henry an account of their visit which a messenger would take to meet William Ogilvie and Lady Lucy Fitzgerald on the road from London and which they could carry to the Duchess, who was several hours ahead of them. 'Thanks to the great God our visit was timed to the moment that the wretched situation allowed of,' she wrote to Mr Ogilvie, and went on, 'I first approached his bed; he looked at me, knew me, kissed me, and said (what will never depart my ears), "it is heaven to see you!" and shortly after, turning to the other side of his bed, he said, "I can't see you!" I went round and he soon after kissed my face, and smiled at me, which I shall never forget, though I saw death in his dear face at the time. I then told him that Henry was come. He said nothing that marked surprise at his being in Ireland, but expressed joy at hearing it and said, "where is he, dear fellow?". Henry then took my place, and the two dear brothers frequently embraced each other, to the melting of a heart of stone, and yet God enabled both Henry and myself to remain quite composed. As everyone left the room, we told him we only were with him. He said, "that is very pleasant." However, he remained silent, and then I brought up the subject of Lady Edward, and told him that I had not left her until I saw her on board, and Henry told him of having met her on the road well. He said, "And the children too? – She is a charming woman," and then became silent again. That expression about Lady Edward proved to me that his senses were much lulled, and that he did not feel his situation to be what it was; but thank God they were enough alive to receive pleasure from his brother and me. Dear Henry, in particular, he looked at continually with expressions of pleasure . . . When we left him, we told him that, as he appeared inclined to sleep, we would wish him a good night and return in the morning. He said, "Do, do," but did not express any uneasiness at our leaving him. We accordingly tore ourselves away, and very shortly after Mr Garnett . . . sent me word that the last convulsions soon came on and ended at two o'clock so that we were within two hours and a half of the sad close to a life we prized so dearly.'

This letter was given to the Duchess at Coleshill in Warwickshire. Lady Louisa had carefully presented a picture of Lord Edward in his last hours that bore little relationship to the horror and pain of his death. But the Duchess of Leinster did not need any hints about the ways in which Lord Edward might be remembered. She had already accepted that he was a traitor and would in time come to see his treachery as justified. Others might call him a martyr and a fighter for his country's freedom. But to her he would always be as well her favourite and her beloved son.

Epilogue

Tony and Pamela, waiting at Harley Street, got the bad news at the same time. Tony stayed with Pamela partly because misery joined them, partly because, like her, he and Julie had nowhere to go. Before Lord Henry, Mr Ogilvie, the Duchess and Lady Lucy arrived back in London in the middle of June, Pamela, her daughters, Tony and Julie had been unceremoniously bundled off to the care of the Duke of Richmond at Goodwood House in Sussex. Mr Ogilvie afterwards claimed that in his absence, Pamela had begun a flirtation with Richard Brinsley Sheridan. But it was just as likely that the Duchess was worried that Pamela might lay claim to little Eddy and that the whole family found her grief, on top of their own, too much to bear.

At Goodwood, with her customary uncalculating generosity and outpouring of feeling, Pamela surrendered her trump card, the one object through whom she had emotional claims on the Fitzgerald family. 'My ever dearest Mother,' she wrote to the Duchess on 19 June, 'I don't need to tell you how impatient I am to press you to my sad heart and to see my son, the son whom I adore, and the only son I have. Maman, he's yours. I put him into your hands in the days of my happiness and I give him to you now as my greatest treasure. Let him be like his father. Oh, but let him be happier; that's the wish of his unhappy mother.' The Duchess ruthlessly traded on Pamela's emotional tenderness, holding on fast to little Eddy and noting without guilt some years later on the back of the letter, 'Dear Lady Edward giving me her treasure.'

Little good news reached Pamela and Tony at Goodwood. They did have the satisfaction of hearing that the United Irishmen in Kildare had taken revenge on Thomas Reynolds, whom many believed to have betrayed Lord Edward, informing against him so that he was arrested and taken to Dublin for trial. Kilkea Castle, gleaming after its renovation, was ransacked even before Lord Edward was detained, ironically by government troops quartered there. A gang of militia-men and dragoons ripped up Reynolds's newly pol-ished floors, shredded his curtains and smashed the fat upholstery of his drawing-room chairs in a fruitless search for arms. Francis Magan, though, remained unsuspected, and was left alone on Usher's Island, where he hoarded the fruits of his treacherous labour with ever-increasing reclusiveness until he died in 1843.

The rebellion made Pamela a pauper as well as a widow. An Act of Attainder was rushed through the Irish parlia-ment which posthumously condemned Lord Edward for high treason. His estate was declared forfeit and seized; with it went Pamela's small annuity. She now had no money and no home. Although the Fitzgeralds agreed to pay her a small allowance, principally for the education of little Pam, they showed no inclination to give her a home. In desperation she turned to the Mattiesons in Hamburg, and at the beginning of August 1798, less than two months after Lord Edward's death, she left England. Little Pam, Tony, Moirico and Julie went with her; tiny Lucy was left behind with Sophia Fitzgerald, who was unmarried and had always wanted a child of her own.

Eighteen months after arriving in Hamburg Pamela mar-ried again. Her second husband was Mr Pitcairn, the

American consul there. The marriage did not last, but it provided the excuse for the Fitzgerald family gradually to loosen their ties with Pamela, even as they hung on adoringly to her children. When Pamela remarried, Tony decided that he and his family should leave. With the money he and Julie had saved from their wages, and her skill as a seamstress, they decided to set themselves up in London. But Tony had never held his head high since his master's death. A few years later he fell ill, and died, it was said, of a broken heart. He left his children, and his children's children to walk unknown through the streets of London, part of the crowd, brushing shoulders with Lord Edward's descendants perhaps, but lost forever to history.

Historiographical Note
Sources
Index

Historiographical Note

The idea of Lord Edward as an incurable and innocent romantic – which may conceal the belief that because he was an aristocrat it was impossible for him to have been a committed revolutionary – was promulgated and advertised immediately after his death. Lady Louisa Conolly, shocked at learning the extent of her nephew's involvement in the rebellion, insisted – partly to save the feelings of the Duchess of Leinster, partly to save the honour of the extended family – that 'the friends he was entangled with pushed his destruction forward, screening themselves behind his valuable character.' The intimation that Lord Edward did not know what he was getting himself into was repeated by Lady Louisa often in the years to come, and reiterated by Lord and Lady Holland, who were intimate with Lord Edward's first biographer, Tom Moore. Writing in 1801, Lady Holland approvingly quoted Lady Louisa's analysis that 'when once inclined [Lord Edward] found numbers themselves ready either from the discontent of obscurity, poverty or ambition, to foment his disloyalty and avail themselves of so great and popular a name as his.' In fact, it was Lord Edward, back from Paris in 1793, who attempted to lead his more moderate colleagues on, not the other way round.

Neither the Duchess of Leinster nor William Ogilvie seems to have attempted to play down Lord Edward's politics or the fact that they infused his whole life. Indeed, the Duchess quoted Priestley to the effect that rebellion can be justified by the presence of an oppressive regime, and was determined to remember her son as a martyr to Ireland's freedom. But at some time in the nineteenth century the Duchess's huge archive of letters was selectively culled and all the political letters were removed. The whole of the archive stops in 1794, and although a few letters from Lord Edward do survive for dates later than this, detached from the main archive in the National Library in Dublin, most are only found in Moore's biography. The political beliefs that Lord Edward felt able to express to his mother after 1794 are thus almost entirely filtered through the pen of Moore, who had his own version of Lord Edward's life to tell.

Despite the vilification heaped on it by Lady Lucy Fitzgerald when it appeared in 1831, Moore's biography has manifold virtues, not the least being that he printed many letters that were subsequently destroyed. But Moore, like every biographer, had his own agenda, and his own relationship with his subject. Moore was an habitué of Holland House, a diner-out somewhat starstruck by the stylish and confident Foxite Whigs. 'Tom Moore loves a Lord,' Byron noted. He was also a romantic nationalist and a romantic poet, inclined to play up chivalry and neglect politics, especially where the aristocracy was concerned. He admits in his biography that as a young man he associated Lord Edward with 'all that was noble, patriotic and chivalrous', and this association lasted long enough to colour the depiction of a life which, after Scott and Byron (who himself noted what a marvellous novel it would make), lent and lends itself to romance.

Moore's natural inclinations were encouraged by members of the extended family who were happy for him to produce a romantic rather than a militant version of Lord Edward's life. His task was complicated when the Whigs finally came into office in 1830, and a noisy band of Irish MPs came with them. Lord Holland, now in government, became anxious that Moore's biography might fan the flames of discontent in Ireland, and hinted that he should postpone its publication. Moore refused, writing in his diary, 'I owned it was rather an unlucky moment for such a book, but that it was not of *my* choosing, as I had begun the work before any of this excitement occurred, and it must take its chance – I must only endeavour to keep the tone of the book as cool and moderate as the nature of its subject would admit of.' The result was that Moore omitted details of Lord Edward's military beliefs and of his associates which, even on the evidence of his own diary, he might have used. He mentions, for instance, having gone to Kildare and visited a man by the name of Garry, a farmer, 'who was one of Lord Edward's Captains in 1798', and talks with the maverick Judge Johnson of Leitrim about Lord Edward's military strategy. This caution, allied with Moore's own romanticism, had the effect of playing down Lord Edward's military importance and militancy, and of emphasising the image of him as a disorganised and ineffectual romantic. Neither Moore nor Lord Edward's relatives seem to have thought military enthusiasm and capacity consistent with romance:, in other words, a romantic *and* revolutionary life.

Moore's reliance on Lord Edward's daughter Pamela, Lady Campbell, as 'little Pam' became, and on Sir Francis Burdett, also coloured his interpretation. Lady Campbell's influence extended to later biographers, too. Less than two years old when her father died, Pamela grew up with her mother and repeated to Moore and others a clutch of stories which, where we can crosscheck them, seem to have been embroidered, if they are not entirely fanciful. The two most damaging are these: first, that, before they set out for Hamburg in 1796, Lord and Lady Edward dined at Devonshire House, where the Duke of York took Pamela aside and whispered, 'More is known of the plans of those [Lord Edward] thinks his friends than you can imagine; in short, everything is known.' The second is to the effect that on the way back from Basle to Hamburg Lord Edward confided the purpose and details of his trip to Switzerland to a woman who travelled with him. She happened to be an intimate of William Pitt and was thus able to pass on to the British government timely information about the negotiations between the French and the United Irishmen.

The first story sounds apocryphal because the British government could have known nothing more about United Irish plans in the spring of 1796 than it had known from Tone's paper to the French government of two years earlier. The reason is simple: there were no plans, only proposals, and it was about those proposals that Lord Edward and O'Connor were going to talk. The second of Lady Pamela's stories is also suspect, partly because it is unlikely that any intimate of Pitt would travel, as Lord Edward told his mother he did, as an outside passenger on a coach for hundreds of miles across Europe, and partly because there was, again, no plan: Lord Edward had left O'Connor behind to make one. Had the British government really known where the French fleet was headed when it left Brest four months later, it would not have sent its own navy in the direction of Lisbon.

Where we can check Lady Campbell's retelling of her father's story with any certainty, we can see that its primary purpose is to stress her parents' heroism. Describing the search of Leinster House after the arrests at Bond's, Lady Campbell said, according to Moore's diary (and his subsequent biography), 'The officer who came to make the search . . . saying, when he required her keys to look for papers, "It is a very disagreeable task for a gentleman to be employed in," and Lady Edward answering, with much dignity, "It is a task no gentleman would perform."' The sheriff's own account, however, in the Rebellion Papers in the Irish National Archive, has no such conversation. Carleton claimed, 'He went up and found [Lady Edward] in her dressing room, sitting near a drawer, open, with the key in it,' and describes, not Pamela's calm in the face of ungentlemanly behaviour, but her panic at the realisation that he had found compromising papers. The point is not that Lady Campbell or her mother were making things up, but that of the two different versions the one that was available and congenial to Moore became part of Lord Edward's life. Once the Fitzgerald archive was doctored subsequent biographers followed Moore, partly in the absence of other information.

Moore also relied on the histrionic and unstable Sir Francis Burdett, who had been infatuated with Arthur O'Connor in 1796 and 1797, and who liked to think of himself as privy to the drama that followed. 'Went to dine with Burdett,' Moore noted in his diary for 27 April 1831. 'Got him on the subject of Lord Edward Fitzgerald whom he knew intimately, and saw plainly, what I had long thought from what he said that both himself and Fox and the rest of their party were all along privy to the proceedings of Lord Edward and O'Connor on the rebellion – and I said to him, "Mr Fox surely must have known of Lord Edward's negotiations with France for an invasion?" "Oh certainly," he answered, "Fox himself was quite as incensed against the government as Edward."' This dinner was translated – perhaps with the addition of some of

Pamela Campbell's version – into the dinner at Devonshire House in Moore's biography, thus: 'Lord Edward set out from Dublin on his perilous embassy, – passing a day or two in London on his way, and, as I have been informed by a gentleman who was of the party, dining, on one of those days, at the house of Lord ****, where the company consisted of Mr Fox, Mr Sheridan, and several other distinguished Whigs, – all of whom had been known to concur warmly in every step of the popular cause in Ireland, and to whom, if Lord Edward did not give some intimation of the object of his present journey, such an effort of reserve and secrecy was, I must say, very unusual in his character.'

Bolstered by the stories of Sir Francis Burdett and Lady Campbell, and filtered through the romantic nationalism of Moore, the notion of Lord Edward's innocent romanticism became firmly entrenched in the story of his life, and was reproduced in one form or another in all the subsequent biographies of him. In more academic studies, however, another version of Lord Edward was growing – one that could be run side-by-side with a belief in his innocent incompetence, or that might even replace it. This was the view of Lord Edward as militant regicide; as, with Arthur O'Connor, the most consistently militant of the United Irishmen. Such a portrayal was made possible by readings of spies' reports in the nineteenth century and subsequent brilliant research by Marianne Elliott and others in French, Irish and British archives. It has four connected strands: Lord Edward's support for first a French-led, and then a purely domestic, uprising; his regicidal beliefs; a plan to provoke a domestic rising by spreading rumours of an attack on Catholic chapels; and a plan to start the rebellion with the assassination of the cream of Anglo-Ireland at the Kingston trial.

There seems little reason to doubt McNally's assertion that Lord Edward was a regicide. When the whole of the Irish parliament went into mourning after the death of Louis XVI, he defiantly wore ordinary clothes to the House. His increasing hatred of aristocracy as inhuman and corrupt is well documented, as is his belief in the 'levelling principle'. He lived out this increasing alienation from his own class with typical thoroughness, although he continued to see members of his immediate family until a few months before his death. Although his closest confidant in the

United movement was, after 1793, Arthur O'Connor, who was a well-connected member of the gentry, Lord Edward made a point of spending time with people of all social ranks and was always one of the most thoroughgoing populists in the movement, not only in terms of politics, but also in the way he translated his belief in the virtue of the people into his daily life.

But to stress Lord Edward's regicidal tendencies is to miss the point of his radicalism. His aim was to sever the British connection with Ireland, and to found a pristine new republic in which man could renew himself. The balance of these two objectives is difficult to assess, since we have so little writing after 1794 and our knowledge is thus weighted towards Lord Edward's idealistic, rather than his activist, years. The need for secrecy after 1794 also clouds everything and makes it impossible to say with any accuracy how his political beliefs developed. It does, however, seem fairly clear that getting rid of the King was the means and not the end. McNally's statement is thus more a stirring of Castle fears than a guide to priorities.

The origin of the idea to provoke rebellion by putting out rumours of an attack on Catholic chapels is obscure. The plan, formulated at the end of 1797, involved disseminating a rumour of an attack that would bring the people out on to the streets and allow an assault on Dublin Castle under the cover of the ensuing chaos. It is possible that this idea came from O'Connor, and that it was supported by Lord Edward as a way of provoking a rebellion. Yet it seems entirely out of character for him to have been prepared to use sectarianism in order to promote a republic that would be ecumenical. That the plan was something more than a late-night fantasy is clear from the postponement of Mass at the urging of moderate members of the United Irish executive; but it may possibly have been fuelled by rumour rather than anything that happened at a United Irish meeting, and the degree to which Lord Edward supported it is not clear.

The evidence for Lord Edward's involvement in the plan to attack the Kingston trial is also difficult to assess. This time it was Higgins rather than McNally who was the informer. If McNally seems to have sprinkled exaggerations and inventions among his reports, Higgins had a tendency to embroider after the event, particularly to make things look more horrific than his initial reporting suggested, and to exaggerate his own knowledge in the interest of larger rewards. In the case of the Kingston trial, he first writes to Cooke on 18 May 1798, 'last night it was proposed to make a decided attack on the Lord Chancellor and Peers assembled this day on the trial of the earl of Kingston, and there appeared two majority [*sic*] against it on the ground that they could not be properly armed or assemble in the daylight without the certain loss of thousands of lives, but they have decided on an attack of [*sic*] the Castle.' This report makes no mention of either Magan or Lord Edward, although the absence of their names is not conclusive proof that neither was involved.

After Lord Edward's death, Higgins tells a different story, suggesting that the majority of two against the plan to attack the trial was in fact only a veto of Magan's and that Lord Edward was at the meeting. This letter, dated 30 June 1798, reads, 'When I waited on you early in the last month and told you of the intention of the rebels to rise on the 14th Ult. you could hardly be brought to credit such. However, it turned out a most happy circumstance that Lord Edward was then with M. who found means to prevail on him to postpone his bloody purpose in the city, else on the day of Earl Kingston's [*sic*] trial you would have a shocking scene of blood and havoc in the city. I should not have used the word *prevail* because Lord Edward's purpose was put to a vote and carried by M.'s negative only.' The same letter, however, had Lord Edward insisting that the original plan for the rebellion should follow the long-agreed proposal for a rising in the city supported by the advance of armies from Kildare: 'You will please to remember that in some few days after, I again waited on you, acquainted you of the plan of rising from Garretstown, Naul and Dunboyne and circuitously round the metropolis to Dunleary etc. This plan to fall at once on the city was deranged the ensuing day by Lord Edward who insisted on his Kildare men and those of Carlow being brought in and he would take the field at Finglas, on the Tuesday following, and march into the city which was his great object to carry on account not only of the plunder for the rebels but the "tens of thousands that would instantly flock to the standard and the example it would be to the kingdom to follow": this was the language he used.'

Again, on 12 July, Higgins reiterates Lord Edward's involvement in the Kingston trial plan, and uses it as evidence that he himself should be amply rewarded for his services: 'For want of some knowledge how I was to be dealt by from Lord Camden's promise of reward, even from the act of service performed on his first landing without the uniform zeal and exertions which I hope you will allow I shewn [*sic*] during his administration and the variety of services rendered, obtaining for you papers, proceedings and insignias etc. preparatory to the Rebellion, and bringing forward to you also a person by whose advice and vote for delaying the attack upon both Houses of Parliament, Lord Camden etc. intended on the morning and at the time of the trial of the earl of Kingston, that a massacre should take place, defeated the infernal business and also delivered the country from a monster who could agree to and undertake to head such a murderous and diabolical plan! with this I obtained information for you which no other person could "of the time the rebels were to commence their attack etc. etc." [punctuation unclear]. I certainly am happy as a citizen and as a loyal subject warmly attached to my King and his government, that I have been able to do so, but being long promised situation or place, and having also long earned it, I beg to know whether such will be granted. The honour and justice of government is called upon and I rely on your candour and goodness to report my services. The pecuniary compensation talked of could not, I am sure, be thought any remuneration for the expense I have gone to and the services performed. FH.'

One of the difficulties in assessing this information is to gauge the degree of Magan's inside knowledge of the United Irishmen. Although Higgins made it clear that Magan sought elected office in the United Irishmen at his instigation, it is not clear how high Magan rose in the organisation. On 19 May (perhaps at a hastily convened meeting after the arrest of Lord Edward), Higgins reports that Magan was 'elected of the Committee', thus at least suggesting that he could not earlier have been a member of the national executive, as has been assumed by some: Higgins does not say to which committee Magan was elected. It also seems probable, from the evidence, that Lord Edward fell into Magan's hands by mistake rather than design, and that Magan might have claimed foresight in order to make sure of the reward. If Miss Moore had not asked Magan whether Lord Edward could hide at his house, and if he had not subsequently found out where Lord Edward was to stay on the night of the 19th, Magan would not, on the evidence of Higgins's letters, have been able to deliver him to the Castle. The lack of mention of Magan by other United Irishmen, and the fact that the government did not feel the need to arrest him in order to preserve his cover, also suggests that he was not at the top of the organisation. But, like the Castle officials themselves, we have few ways of assessing the validity of the spies' information. It is probable that as the rebellion drew near all sorts of ideas were floated as to how and when it should start, most of them quickly dismissed; schemes like the planned attack on the Kingston trial, calculated to send shivers through administrative officials whose families and friends might have been assassinated, were especially useful for getting the Castle to pay good money to informers, and may have been given prominence by them for that reason.

The question of the degree of Lord Edward's militancy, highlighted by these problems of evidence, may also always be unsolved. Up to the time of the French expedition, to be militant was to argue and plot for French assistance. Thereafter militancy seems to have centred on the demand for a domestic rebellion without French help. There is no doubt that Lord Edward was a militant through and through in the first phase. The nature of his support for a purely domestic rising is more difficult to gauge, however. It appears that from the end of 1797 he actively planned a domestic rising, while all the time hoping and working for French involvement. Only when the French unequivocally signalled that they would not be coming in the spring of 1798 did he give up hope in them. For a few months before O'Connor left the country at the end of December 1797, Lord Edward was perhaps caught up in the former's strident and ambitious demands for a purely domestic rising (although this is thrown into doubt by O'Connor's departure for France with money and memoranda from the United Irishmen). Thereafter he seems to have been more effective than O'Connor in preventing the movement from being split internally by the issue, adopting a wait-and-see policy while continuing to hope for French assistance, and to plan for a domestic rebellion. The incoherence of policy in the first few months of 1798 probably owes something to this attempt to keep the warring factions in the movement together, something to Lord Edward's own sense of isolation and despondency, and something to the fact that none of the leaders came up with a clear policy that all the others could endorse. Although O'Connor was disliked and mistrusted by many members of the movement, he, MacNeven and Emmet had time enough in gaol to agree on a common front to present to the government when they offered to give it information in return for an amnesty in the summer of 1798. Their statements throw no light on the movement's internal rifts or on plans for insurrection before March 1798, when Emmet and MacNeven were picked up.

What the cumulative evidence from spies and later researches does do, however, is dispel once and for all the idea of Lord Edward as a romantic who was used or led by men more ruthless than himself. That he was reckless, sometimes suicidally so, is not in doubt. But it must be remembered that he stayed at large longer than any other United leader except the Sheares brothers, that he was betrayed more by chance than by foresight, that he was trusted by his colleagues (albeit in the absence, after the arrest of Thomas Russell in the autumn of 1797, of any others with military training) with the responsibility for actually carrying out the rebellion, and that unlike some others he never took the proffered chance of escape from the country. His commitment to the cause was complete, and his opposition to the English connection and to Castle rule implacable.

Finally, a word about what was almost the last cheerful moment in Lord Edward's life, his gardening at Porto Bello. I have spent much time wondering whether Lord Edward's digging up of a bed of orange lilies was a gesture of anger directed at the Orange Order – or even at Protestants more generally for fomenting sectarian violence and compromising his hopes of an ecumenical republic. Certainly by the 1840s, orange lilies were used and regarded as a symbol of Protestant loyalism. But I have found no such identification as early as 1798, and in its absence have preferred to leave Lord Edward a contented rather than an angry gardener.

Sources

MANUSCRIPT SOURCES

British Library
Add. MS. 30990
A bundle of miscellaneous letters to Emily, Duchess of Leinster, mostly concerning the events of 1798, with a series of letters from Lord Edward Fitzgerald, 1796–7.
Add. MS. 59020
Letters of Lord Robert Fitzgerald to Lord Grenville.
Add. MS. 28065/6
Letters of Lord Robert Fitzgerald to the Duke of Leeds.

National Archives of Ireland
Rebellion Papers
Papers of Arthur O'Connor, including letters from Sir Francis Burdett, 1796–7; copy of cipher found in O'Connor's razor case in Margate; letter from Charles James Fox offering O'Connor a seat at Westminster.
Papers relating to Lord Edward Fitzgerald, including copy of a letter from Jagerhorn intercepted by Turner.
Copy of the testimony of Thomas Reynolds.
Report of the examination of George Cummins after the arrests at Bond's.
Account of the examination of Lady Edward Fitzgerald at Leinster House after the arrests at Bond's.
Letters of Francis Higgins to Edward Cooke.
Letters of Samuel Sproule to Edward Cooke.

Kent County Record Office

Pratt MSS
Letters of Lord Downshire to Lord Camden.
Letters of Turner to Downshire.
Diary of Dr Armstrong Garnett.
Various papers *re* the death and funeral of Lord Edward Fitzgerald.

Irish Georgian Society

Correspondence between Lady Louisa Conolly and Lady Sarah Lennox, 1759–1820.

National Library of Ireland

Leinster Papers
Correspondence of Emily, first Duchess of Leinster, especially:
Letters between Emily, Duchess of Leinster, and William Ogilvie, 1771–1813.
Letters from Lady Caroline Fox to Emily, Duchess of Leinster, 1756–74.
Letters from Lady Louisa Conolly to Emily, Duchess of Leinster, 1759–94.
Letters from Lady Sarah Lennox to Emily, Duchess of Leinster, 1759–94.
Letters from Lord Edward Fitzgerald to Emily, Duchess of Leinster, 1771–92.

Letters from William, Lord Offaly, to his mother, Emily, Duchess of Leinster, 1765–94.
Letters from other Fitzgerald children, Charles, Henry, Robert, Charlotte, Sophia and Lucy to their mother, Emily, Duchess of Leinster, 1768–94.
NOTE: This collection of 1,770 letters contains few letters sent after 1794, with the exception of the correspondence between Emily and William Ogilvie. Apart from letters sent by Emily to her husbands, it consists entirely of correspondence received.
Part of the collection was edited by Brian Fitzgerald and published as *Correspondence of Emily, Duchess of Leinster*, as follows:
Vol. 1, 1949: Letters of Emily, Duchess of Leinster; James, First Duke of Leinster; Caroline Fox, Lady Holland.
Vol. 2, 1953: Letters of Lord Edward Fitzgerald and Lady Sarah Napier (née Lennox).
Vol. 3, 1957: Letters of Lady Louisa Conolly and William, Marquis of Kildare (Second Duke of Leinster).
Will of Lord Edward Fitzgerald.
Mortgage of the Estate of Kilrush to Anne, Lady Cloncurry.

Public Record Office of Northern Ireland

De Ros Papers
Uncatalogued letters from the de Ros family papers, mainly letters which came into the archive via Lord Henry Fitzgerald, who married Charlotte de Ros in 1791, all dated post-1789.

McPeake Papers
Photocopies of material mostly relating to the events of 1798 but covering the years 1783–1815. Includes take-outs from the letters of Lady Louisa Conolly to Lady Sarah Lennox now in the possession of the Irish Georgian Society.

Leinster Papers
Bundle of material *re* 1798. It includes Stewart's autopsy report on Lord Edward Fitzgerald, dated 4 June 1798, which concludes that he died of a fever unrelated to the wounds he received at his arrest, and which was produced by 'the agitation of his mind'; details of an annuity intended for Pamela but rarely paid in full by the family.

Foster/Masserene Papers
Letter of Lady Roden to her daughter Harriet Skeffington *re* Lord Edward at the play, 20 February 1793.

Terling, Essex

Strutt Papers
Letters from Emily, Duchess of Leinster, to her daughter Lady Lucy Foley (née Fitzgerald), 1791–1810. General correspondence of Lady Lucy Foley, including letters from her Fitzgerald siblings, William Ogilvie and Lady Louisa Conolly. Letters from Emily, Duchess of Leinster, to her daughter Lady Charlotte Strutt (née Fitzgerald), 1793–1804.

SECONDARY SOURCES

Biographies of Lord Edward and His Family

Thomas Moore, *The Life and Death of Lord Edward Fitzgerald*, 2 vols, London, 1831; another ed., with additional material by Martin MacDermott, London, 1897. Ida A. Taylor, *The Life of Lord Edward Fitzgerald 1763–1798*, London, 1903. John Lindsay (pseud.), *The Shining Life and Death of Lord Edward Fitzgerald*, London, 1949. Patrick Byrne, *Lord Edward Fitzgerald*, Dublin, 1955. Gerald Campbell, *Edward and Pamela Fitzgerald. Being some Account of their Lives compiled from the letters of those who knew them,*

London, 1904.
La Belle Pamela (Lady Edward Fitzgerald), by her great-grand-daughter Lucy Ellis and Joseph Turquan, London, 1924.
Brian Fitzgerald, *Emily, Duchess of Leinster 1731–1814*, Dublin, 1949; *Lady Louisa Conolly 1743–1821*, Dublin, 1950.
Flann Campbell, 'The Elusive Mr Ogilvie 1740–1832', *Familia, Ulster Genealogical Review*, Vol. 2, no. 9, 1993.

Chapter One
Good accounts of the Battle of Eutaw Springs are found in 'Battles of the Revolution', *American Heritage*, Vol. XXV, 1/5, August 1975, and Major M. C. Ferrar, late 19th Foot, *A History of the Services of the 19th Regiment from its Foundation in 1688 to 1911*, London, 1911. General Greene's dispatch is reprinted in the *Magazine of History*, Vol. XXXV, 1928. Benjamin Quarles, *The Negro in the American Revolution*, Chapel Hill, 1961, gives a good account of the fates of freed slaves after the war.

The attitude of the Duke of Richmond to the American War is detailed in Alison Olson, *The Radical Duke. Career and Correspondence of Charles Lennox, third Duke of Richmond*, Oxford, 1961. Day-to-day life in the army is described in Colonel H. C. B. Rogers, OBE, *The British Army of the Eighteenth Century*, London, 1977. On Fox and his circle, the expansive Walter Sichel's *Sheridan*, 2 vols., London, 1907, provided a vast fund of anecdotal material. John Derry and Leslie Mitchell in their biographies of Fox and John Cannon in *The Fox/North Coalition; Crisis of the Constitution, 1782–4*, Oxford, 1969, give accounts of Fox's disastrous foray into office. Information on black people in Britain, on attitudes towards them, on noble savagery, on paintings of blacks and on Omai came from: Anthony J. Barber, *The African Link, Attitudes to the Negro in the Era of the Atlantic Slave Trade 1550–1807*, London, 1978; David Dabydeen, *Hogarth's Blacks. Images of Blacks in Eighteenth Century English Art*, Manchester, 1987; Gail McGregor, *The Noble Savage in the New World Garden. Notes Towards a Syntactics of Place*, Toronto, 1988; Lois Whitney, *Primitivism and the Idea of Progress in English Popular Literature of the Eighteenth Century*, Baltimore, 1934; and David Alexander, *Omai, 'Noble*

Savage', London, 1977.

Constantia Maxwell's *Dublin under the Georges 1714–1830*, London, 1936, is still useful on Dublin life under the Ascendancy. Peter Somerville-Large, *The Irish Country House. A Social History*, London, 1995, gives details of Carton life in the late 1770s and 1780s. Hely Dutton, *Observations on Mr Archer's Statistical Survey of the County of Dublin*, Dublin, 1802, gives a description of the soils in County Dublin and the efforts made to improve them.

Chapter Two

Excellent information on Canada in the eighteenth century, together with a map of Halifax, can be found in *The Historical Atlas of Canada*, Vol. 1, *From the beginning to 1800*, Toronto, 1987. J. M. Bumstead, 'The Cultural Landscape of Early Canada', in Bernard Bailyn and Philip D. Morgan (eds.), *Strangers Within the Realm. Cultural Margins of the First British Empire*, Chapel Hill, 1981, gives details of American immigration into Canada at the end of the Revolutionary War. Gustave Carnetot, in *Canada and the American Revolution*, London, 1967, explains the

way in which the Iroquois were used by the British during and after the Revolution. A good account of Iroquois village life can be found in Gary A. Warwick, *Reconstructing Ontario Iroquoian Village Organisation*, Toronto, 1984, and there are two accounts of Joseph Brant's life which give an excellent picture of the strains under which the Iroquois were operating: Robert A. Hecht, *Joseph Brant, Iroquois Ally of the British*, Charlottesville, 1975, and, more substantially, Isabel Thompson Kelsay, *Joseph Brant 1743–1807; Man of Two Worlds*, Syracuse, 1984. Boswell's interview with Brant appeared in the *London Magazine* of July 1776.

Elizabeth Linley's life has been well documented in Margot Bor and Lamond Clelland, *Still the Lark. A Biography of Elizabeth Linley*, London, 1962; portraits of the extended family are discussed in the exhibition catalogue *A Nest of Nightingales, the Linleys of Bath*, Dulwich Picture Gallery, 1988. The account of the deaths of Elizabeth and Lord Edward's daughter is in William Smyth, *Memoir of Mr Sheridan*, London, 1840.

The information about Lord Edward's visits to Paine

is from John Keane's excellent life, *Tom Paine, a Political Life*, London, 1995. *The Rights of Man* itself is still a breathtaking read, and there is a good account of Paine's beliefs in Gregory Claeys, *Thomas Paine: Social and Political Thought*, Boston, 1989. The White's Hotel Group that clustered around Paine in Paris is discussed in J. G. Alger, *Englishmen in the French Revolution*, London, 1889, and sketched with characteristic brilliance by Richard Holmes in *Footsteps, Adventures of a Romantic Biographer*, London, 1985. Alger also wrote the *Dictionary of National Biography (DNB)* entry on Pamela, which inclines to Madame de Genlis's story of her origins. Revolutionary fashions form the subject of Aileen Ribeiro's *Fashion and the French Revolution*, London, 1988, while David's costumes are illustrated in *Modes et Révolutions 1780–1804*, Musée de la Mode et du Costume, Paris, 1995.

There is a good deal of writing about Madame de Genlis, none of which finally resolves the mystery of Pamela's origins. Alger's *DNB* entry suggests that Madame de Genlis was substantially telling the truth. Jean Hammond, in *A Keeper of Royal Secrets. Being the Private and Political Life of Madame de Genlis*, London, 1913, leaves the matter open, but leans towards the illegitimacy theory. So does Violet Wyndham in her *Madame de Genlis. A Biography*, London 1958. Her latest biographer, Gabriel de Broglie, in *Madame de Genlis*, Paris, 1985, is similarly uncertain. Austin Dobson in *Four French Women*, London, 1890, and Linda Kelly, *Women of the French Revolution*, 1987, concentrate more on Madame de Genlis's importance as an educationalist, tutor of the future monarch and revolutionary woman than on her well-documented capacity for mystification. Marion Ward's *Forth*, London, 1982, a biography of the duc d'Orléans's agent Nathaniel Parker Forth, uses letters from Orléans to Forth to demonstrate the accuracy of Madame de Genlis's version. These same letters are used in other works as instances of the depth of fabrication necessary to conceal Pamela's origins. All letters coming out of the Palais-Royal were apparently read by government agents, and thus the postbag was an excellent way in which to establish a story as a truth, suggesting as it did the discovery of a private, and therefore unmediated and honest, communication. It is possible that both versions merge into a 'true' one; in other words, that there was a child called Nancy Sims, with the origins given by Madame de Genlis, and that Forth, looking for a wet-nurse in England for the young illegitimate Orléans baby, found Mrs Sims, who had recently lost her child and put Pamela, as she became, into her care. Later, when the duc d'Orléans and Madame de Genlis wanted Pamela back, her ancestry was simply grafted on to that of her wet-nurse's dead child. The £24 given to Mrs Sims when Pamela left for France then assumes the character of wages rather than a payment for a baby. Given the strategies for concealing the origins of other illegitimate aristocratic children – Henriette le Clerc, for one – it still seems counter-intuitive to think that Pamela was anybody but the duc d'Orléans's daughter, but the matter is irresolvable.

On the matter of Lord Edward's proposal which he asked Paine to take to the Convention in 1792, I have followed Lecky's figure of 4,000 Volunteers rather than Marianne Elliott's of 40,000. The latter seems excessively large given that, according to Thomas Bartlett, there were only 9,600 troops in Ireland in January 1793. An army of 40,000 in the days before Napoleon's *grandes armées* would have been among the biggest in Europe. Four thousand determined rebels might indeed have been enough to sweep up the country and take control of the capital, especially as the defending troops were scattered and the insurgents would optimistically have counted on gathering support from among the local population. With this figure in mind, Paris's offer, relayed by Oswald a few months later, of 20,000 troops seems extremely generous.

Chapters Three and Four
My information about the ownership of Lord Edward's house in Kildare comes from J. H. Andrews and Anngret Simms (eds), *Irish Historic Towns Atlas*, Dublin, 1996, which reproduces the map of Kildare Town in 1798 by Thomas Sherrard. The reference table for Sherrard's map makes it clear that the Duke of Leinster, as landlord, was paid ground rent by a Mr Hetherington for the house in

which Lord Edward lived. Presumably Hetherington had some form of long leasehold and sublet the property to Lord Edward. This contradicts the information of other biographies which followed Moore in believing that Lord Edward lived in Thomas Conolly's lodge in Kildare. Moore visited Kildare in 1830 and wrote in his diary, 'Stopped at Kildare to look at the spot where Lord Edward's cottage [Conolly's lodge] once stood – no trace of it now – it adjoined the Castle.' Moore may have been pointed towards the right site but have got its ownership wrong. Had Lord Edward moved into Conolly's lodge he would presumably not have needed to describe it in minute detail to his mother, since she would have known it well from her long residence in Ireland, and must have visited it when she, like the Conollys, attended the Curragh races. It also seems likely that Lord Edward would have wanted to avoid taking Conolly's house if he could since he knew that he would be carrying on treasonable activities there.

From 1798 onwards material about the United Irishmen and the rebellion poured out of Ireland and London. Amongst this mass I have picked out indispensable secondary sources and the particular contemporary and nineteenth-century works that have relevance to Lord Edward's life. I have not attempted to describe or interpret the rebellion itself in my text, partly because it lies beyond Lord Edward's life, and partly because it has been brilliantly researched and written about by the latest generation of Irish historians, both 'revisionist' and 'nationalist', who have put forward a convincing portrait of a political struggle aggravated by economic and sectarian grievances rather than the other way round, as had been promulgated until the mid-1960s.

My list of indispensable secondary works must start with Marianne Elliott's two books, *Partners in Revolution. The United Irishmen and France*, London, 1982, and *Wolfe Tone, Prophet of Irish Independence*, London, 1989. Without them my task would have been impossible, and I have usually followed Elliott's leads and interpretations, only differing perhaps in the degree of militancy which I ascribe to Lord Edward in 1797–8. I have also used Roy Foster's *Modern Ireland 1600–1972*, London, 1989, throughout. Of particular use in making sense of the United Irishmen and the political, social and military context in which they operated have been: David Dickson, Daire Keogh and Kevin Whelan (eds.), *The United Irishmen. Republicanism, Radicalism and Rebellion*, Dublin, 1993; Nancy J. Curtin, *The United Irishmen, Popular Politics in Ulster and Dublin*, 1994; Thomas Bartlett and Keith Jeffrey (eds.), *A Military History of Ireland*, Cambridge, 1996; Daire Keogh and Nicholas Furlong (eds.), *The Mighty Wave: The 1798 Rebellion in Wexford*, Dublin, 1996; and George Boyce and Alan O'Day (eds.), *The Making of Modern Irish History: Revisionism and the Revisionist Controversy*, London, 1996. E. P. Thompson's *The Making of the English Working Class*, London, 1963, and Roger Wells's *Insurrection. The British Experience 1795–1803*, Gloucester, 1983, helped me to think about the evidence of spies.

Nineteenth-century histories have obvious attractions for biographers; they tend towards narrative and rely heavily on anecdote. For this reason – and because when the Four Courts went up in flames in 1922 so did much of Irish history – W. E. H. Lecky's five-volume *History of Ireland in the Eighteenth Century*, London, 1892, is a fund of fascinating information despite its underlying Unionist bias and its penchant for interpreting the United Irishmen in *ad hominem* terms. I also relied on W. H. Maxwell, *A History of the Irish Rebellion in 1798*, London, 1845, and R. R. Madden's pioneering *The United Irishmen, their Lives and Times*, 3 series, 7 vols., London, 1842–5. Madden's *Literary Remains of the United Irishmen of 1798*, London, 1887, contains two sentimental ballads – presumably composed in the early nineteenth century – about Lord Edward that perfectly capture his romantic legend and which I (only just) resisted the temptation to use.

Good material about spies was also written in the nineteenth century. The doyen of this patient undercover work was W. J. Fitzpatrick, who did much to expose the activities of Higgins and was the first to identify Magan as the betrayer of Lord Edward. His three books, *A Note to the Cornwallis Papers*, London, 1859, *The Sham Squire*, London, 1866, and *Secret Service under Pitt*, London, 1892, show him to have had a nose for subterfuge and double-dealing worthy of his subjects. *The Life of Thomas Reynolds Esquire, formerly of Kilkea Castle, in the County of Kildare, by his son Thomas Reynolds*, 2 vols., London and Dublin, 1839, was a pre-emptive whitewash that failed entirely to dispel the aura of betrayal that hung around his father.

Much good material about 1798 was furnished by the United Irishmen themselves, who in exile put their journalistic and lawyerly skills to good use. Tone's marvellous *Life*, which paid such rich dividends to his posthumous reputation, owes much to his love of 'journalising', while lawyerly skills are to the fore in Valentine Lawless's account of his life, *Personal Recollections of the Life and Times, with extracts from the Correspondence of Valentine, Lord Cloncurry*, London, 1849, which frustratingly manages to leave out almost all of his activities in Ireland before he fled the country in 1797 and mentions Lord Edward in only the vaguest of friendly terms. Charles Teeling in his *History of the Irish Rebellion of 1798: A Personal Narrative*, Gloucester and London, 1876 (reprinted Shannon, 1972), was less discreet and did not

scruple to admit his politics. William MacNeven's *Pieces of Irish History*, New York, 1807, is careful, like its author. *The Drennan Letters, 1776–1819*, ed. D. A. Chart, Belfast, 1931, are full of good thumbnail sketches. In the absence of a full-length biography of Arthur O'Connor I used F. MacDermot, 'Arthur O'Connor', *Irish Historical Studies*, XV, 1966. O'Connor's *A Letter to the Electors of Antrim* was published in Dublin in 1797. The government published the reports of its Secret Committees to which various United Irishmen gave carefully annotated accounts of their activities, and these reports also included a good deal of propaganda material; both the Report of the Irish House of Lords and of the Irish House of Commons appeared immediately after the end of the rebellion in 1798, as did *An Account of the Late Insurrection in Ireland*, which gives a government account of the uprising. James Alexander's brush with Lord Edward is described in *Some Accounts of the first apparent symptoms of the late rebellion in the County of Kildare, and an adjoining part of King's County*, Dublin, 1800. The Shakespeare Gallery in

Exchequer Street is discussed in Robin Hamlyn, 'An Irish Shakespeare gallery', *Burlington Magazine*, Vol. 120, 1978. Finally, much good material was published in *Memoirs and Correspondence of Viscount Castlereagh, Second Marquess of Londonderry, edited by his brother Charles Vane, Marquess of Londonderry*, 2 vols., London, 1848.

NOTE ON TRANSLATIONS: Where a letter is quoted in French in a secondary source or is taken from the original manuscript, the translation is mine. If the letter is already translated and the original lost I have followed the published translations, although I have sometimes modified the punctuation for sense, on the grounds that the original probably erratically punctuated, if at all. I have followed the same line on punctuation with letters in English, updating spelling, punctuation and, sometimes, the use of upper-case initial letters in the middle of sentences. Where there is a scholarly edition already published or in preparation – as in the case of the Higgins letters – I have obviously followed that.

Index